A-Z
COMPUTER SCIENCE

A-Z COMPUTER SCIENCE

Prof. Pawan Vashisht

CENTRUM PRESS
NEW DELHI-110002 (INDIA)

CENTRUM PRESS
H.O.: 4360/4, Ansari Road, Daryaganj,
New Delhi-110 002 (India)
Ph.: 23278000, 23261597

B.O.: No. 1015, Ist Main Road, BSK IIIrd Stage
IIIrd Phase, IIIrd Block,
Bangalore - 560 085 (India)
Tel.: 080-41723429
Visit us at: www.centrumpress.com

A-Z Computer Science

First Edition, 2009

ISBN 978-93-80106-12-0

PRINTED IN INDIA

Printed at Salasar Imaging Systems, Delhi-110035 (India)

Contents

Preface

Computer Science study involves development of the ability to abstract the essential features of a problem and its solution, to reason effectively in the abstract plane, without confusion by a mass of highly relevant detail. The abstraction must then be related to the detailed characteristics of computers as the design of the solution progresses; and it must culminate in a program in which all the detail has been made explicit; and at this stage, the utmost care must be exercised to ensure a very high degree of accuracy.

At all stages the programmer must be articulate about his activity. The need for abstract thought together with meticulous accuracy, the need for imaginative speculation in the search for a solution, together with a sound knowledge of the practical limitations of the tools available for its implementation, the combination of formal rigour with a clear style for its explanation to others these are the combinations of attributes which should be inculcated and developed in a student by any university academic discipline; and which must be developed in high degree in students of computer science.

This book is designed to provide a comprehensive introduction to the design and analysis of computer algorithms and data structures. In terms of the computer science and computer engineering curricula, this book is written to be primarily focused on the Junior-Senior level Algorithms course, which is taught as a first-year graduate course in some schools.

Author

Chapter 1

Introduction to Computers

A computer is a tool and partner in every sphere of human life and activity. Computers are bringing many changes in industry, government, education, medicine, scientific research, law, social service and even arts like music, movies and paintings. The areas of application of computers are confined only by the limitation on creativity and imagination.

What is a computer? A child might define a computer to be an instrument capable of producing a combined effect of radio, movie and television. This definit ion is close but still does not visualize the power and capabilities of a computer.

Fig. Computer

A computer is an electronic machine, capable of performing basic operations like addition, subtraction, multiplication, division, etc. The computer is also capable of storing information, which can be used later. It can process millions of instructions in a few seconds and at the same time with high accuracy. Hence a computer can be defined as an automatic electronic machine for performing calculations or controlling operations that are expressible in numerical or logical terms. Computers are very accurate and save time by performing the assigned task very fast. They don't get bored. Humans have always needed to perform arithmetic like counting and adding. During the pre-historic period, they counted either on their fingers or by scratching marks on the bones and then with the help of stone, pebble and beads.

The early civilization had witnessed men develop number systems to keep track of the astronomical cycles, businesses, etc. The word 'computing' means 'an act of calculating'. After the invention of the manual calculating tools, the concept of using 'electronic gadgets' for computations were introduced which gave birth to the computers. The evolution of computers has passed through a number of stages before reaching the present state of development. During the early development period, certain machines had been developed and a brief note of them is given below.

HISTORY OF COMPUTERS

2500 BC – THE ABACUS

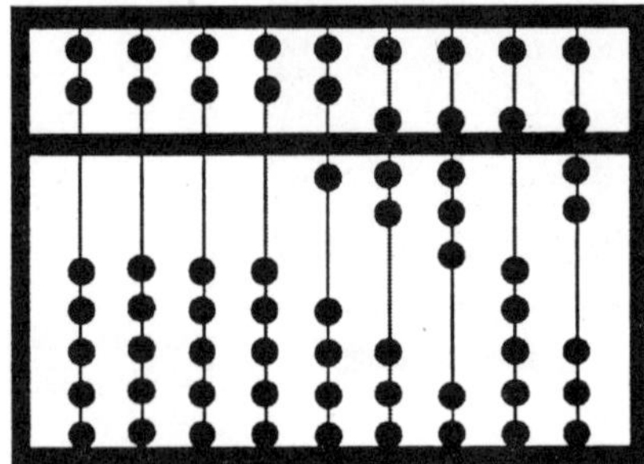

Fig. Abacus

Abacus is the first known calculating machine used for counting. It is made of beads strung on cords and is used for simple arithmetic calculations. The cords correspond to positions of decimal digits. The beads represent digits.

Numbers are represented by beads close to the crossbar. Abacus was mainly used for addition and subtraction and later for division and multiplication.

1614 AD – NAPIER'S BONES

0	1	2	3	4	5	6	7	8	9
0/0	0/1	0/2	0/3	0/4	0/5	0/6	0/7	0/8	0/9
0/0	0/2	0/4	0/6	0/8	1/0	1/2	1/4	1/6	1/8
0/0	0/3	0/6	0/9	1/2	1/5	1/8	2/1	2/4	2/7
0/0	0/4	0/8	1/2	1/6	2/0	2/4	2/8	3/2	3/6
0/0	0/5	1/0	1/5	2/0	2/5	3/0	3/5	4/0	4/5
0/0	0/6	1/2	1/8	2/4	3/0	3/6	4/2	4/8	5/4
0/0	0/7	1/4	2/1	2/8	3/5	4/2	4/9	5/6	6/3
0/0	0/8	1/6	2/4	3/2	4/0	4/8	5/6	6/4	7/2
0/0	0/9	1/8	2/7	3/6	4/5	5/4	6/3	7/2	8/1

Fig. Napier's Bones

The Napier's Bones was invented by John Napier, a Scottish mathematician as an aid to multiplication. A set of bones consisted of nine rods, one for each digit 1 through 9 and a constant rod for the digit '0'. A rod is similar to one column of a multiplication table.

1633 AD – THE SLIDSE RULE

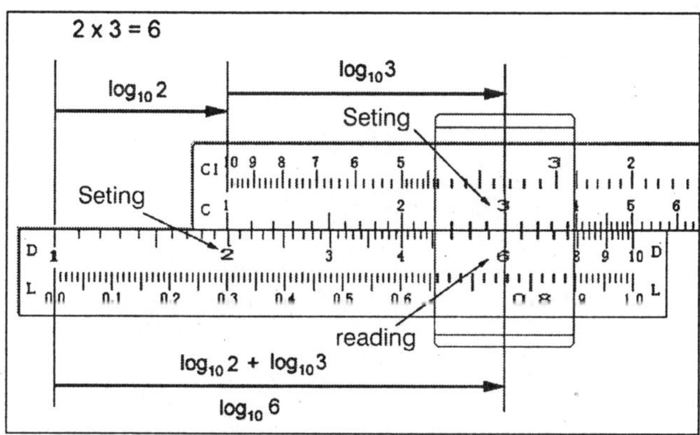

Fig. The Slide Rule

The Slide Rule was invented by William Oughtred. It is based on the principle that actual distance from the starting point of the rule is directly proportional to the logarithm of the numbers printed on the rule. The slide rule is embodied by the two sets of scales that are joined together, with a marginal space between them. The suitable alliance of two scales enabled the slide rule to perform multiplication and division by a method of addition and subtraction.

1642 AD – THE ROTATING WHEEL CALCULATOR

Fig. The Rotating Wheel Calculator

The Rotating Wheel Calculator was developed by a French philosopher, Blaise Pascal, using simple components such as gears and levers. This is a predecessor to today's electronic calculator. He was inspired by the computation work of his father's job and devised the model. He was only 19 years old, when he devised this model.

1890 AD - HOLLERITH TABULATING MACHINE

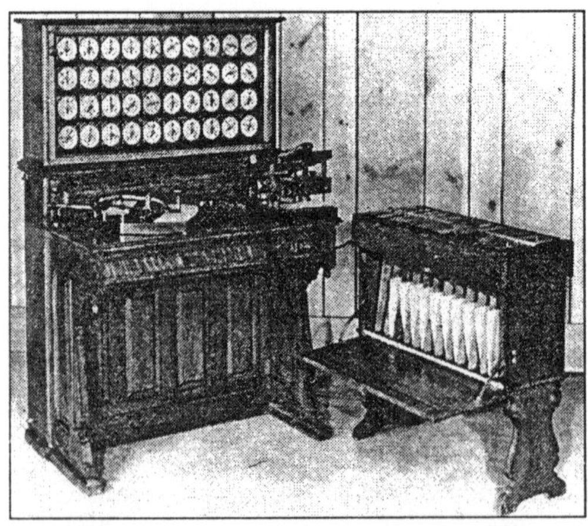

Fig. Hollerith Tabulating Machine

A tabulating machine using punched cards was designed by Herman Hollerith and was called as the Hollerith Tabulating Machine. This electronic machine is able to read the information on the punched cards and process it electronically.

1822 AD – THE DIFFERENCE ENGINE

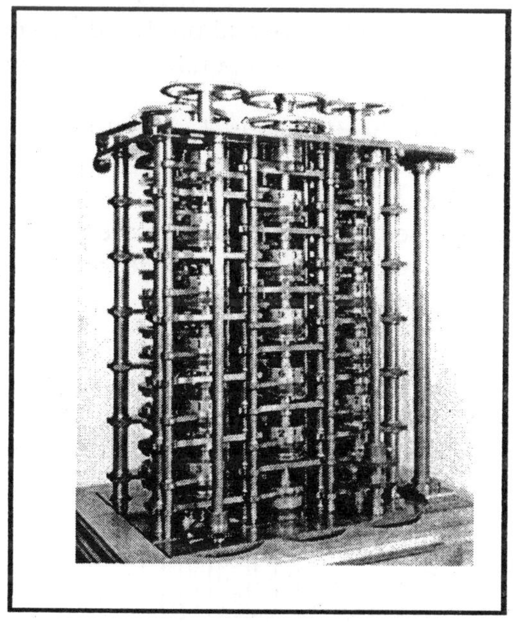

Fig. The Difference Engine

The Difference Engine was built by Charles Babbage, British mathematician and engineer which mechanically calculated mathematical tables. Babbage is called the father of today's computer.

GENERATION OF COMPUTERS

The evolution of electronic computers over a period of time can be traced effectively by dividing this period into various generations. Each generation is characterized by a major technological development that fundamentally changed the way computers operated.

These helped to develop smaller, cheaper, powerful, efficient and reliable devices. Now we could read about each generation and the developments that led to the current devices that we use today.

First Generation - 1940-1956: Vacuum Tubes

The first generation of computers used vacuum tubes for circuitry and magnetic drums for memory. They were large in size, occupied a lot of space and produced enormous heat. They were very expensive to operate and consumed large amount of electricity.

Sometimes the heat generated caused the computer to malfunction. First generation computers operated only on machine language.

Input was based on punched cards and paper tape, and output was displayed on printouts. First generation computers could solve only one problem at a time.

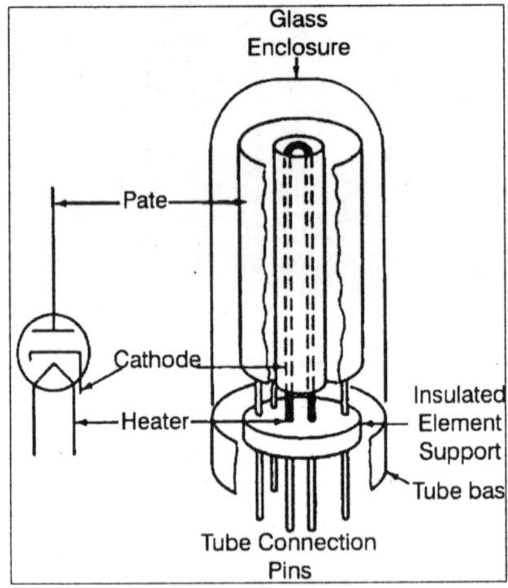

Fig. Vacuum Tube

The Universal Automatic Computer (UNIVAC) and the Electronic Numerical Integrator And Calculator (ENIAC) are classic examples of first-generation computing devices.

Second Generation - 1956-1963: Transistors

The second generation of computers witnessed the

vacuum tubes being replaced by transistors. The transistor was far superior to the vacuum tube, allowing computers to become smaller, faster, cheaper, energy-efficient and more reliable than their first-generation counter parts.

The transistors also generated considerable heat that sometimes caused the computer to malfunction. But it was a vast improvement over the vacuum tube. Second-generation computers used punched cards for input and printouts for output.

Fig. Transistor

Second-generation computers moved from the use of machine language to assembly languages, which allowed programmers to specify instructions in words.

High-level programming languages were also being developed at this time, such as early versions of COBOL and FORTRAN. The computers stored their instructions in their memory, which moved from a magnetic drum to magnetic core technology.

Third Generation - 1964-1971: Integrated Circuits

The development of the integrated circuit left its mark in the third generation of computers. Transistors were made smaller in size and placed on silicon chips, which dramatically increased the speed and efficiency of computers.

In this generation, keyboards and monitors were used

instead of punched cards and printouts. The computers were interfaced with an operating system which allowed to solve many problems at a time.

Fig. Integrated Circuit

Fourth Generation - 1971-Present: Microprocessors

The microprocessor brought forth the fourth generation of computers, as thousands of integrated circuits were built onto a single silicon chip.

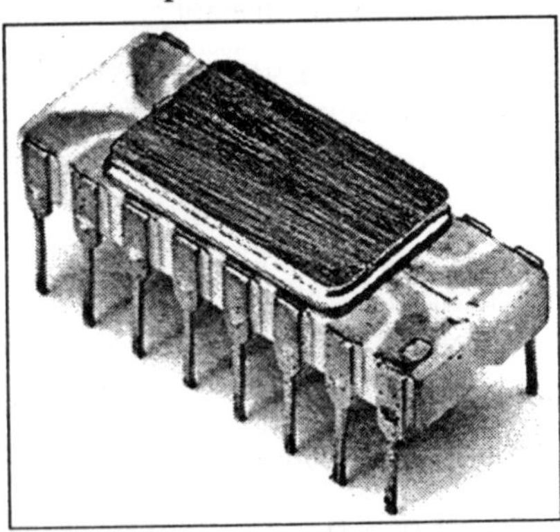

Fig. Microprocessor

As these small computers became more powerful, they could be linked together to form networks, which eventually led to the development of the Internet.

Fifth Generation - Present and Beyond: Artificial Intelligence

Fifth generation computing devices, based on artificial intelligence, are still in their developmental stage. Fifth generation computers will come close to bridging the gap between computing and thinking.

Data, Information and Programme

Computer is a tool for solving problems. Computers accept instructions and data, perform arithmetic and logical operations and produce information. Hence the instructions and data fed into the computer are converted into information through processing.

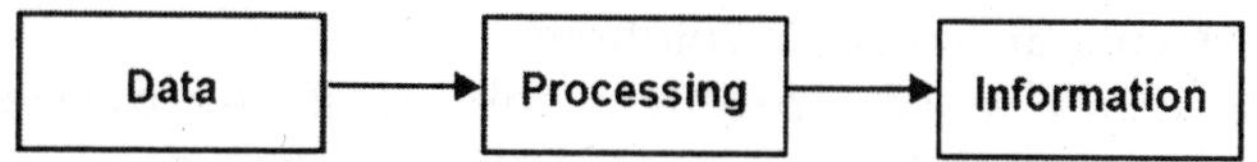

Fig. Data, Processing and Information

Basically data is a collection of facts from which information may be derived. Data is defined as an un-processed collection of raw facts in a manner suitable for communication, interpretation or processing.

Hence data are:

- Stored facts
- Inactive
- Technology based
- Gathered from various sources.

On the other hand information is a collection of facts from which conclusions may be drawn. Data that has been interpreted, translated, or transformed to reveal the underlying meaning. This information can be represented in textual, numerical, graphic, cartographic, narrative, or audiovisual forms.

Hence information is:

- Processed facts
- Active
- Business based
- Transformed from data.

Algorithm is defined as a step-by-step procedure or formula for solving a problem i.e. a set of instructions or procedures for solving a problem. It is also defined as a mathematical procedure that can usually be explicitly encoded in a set of computer language instructions that manipulate data. A computer programme (or set of programs) is designed to systematically solve a problem.

For example, a problem to calculate the length of a straight line joining any two given points.

The programmer must decide the programme requirements, develop logic and write instructions for the computer in a programming language that the computer can translate into machine language and execute. Hence, problem solving is an act of defining a problem, understanding the problem and arriving at workable solutions.

In other words, problem solving is the process of confronting a novel situation, formulating connection between the given facts, identifying the goal of the problem and exploring possible methods for reaching the goal. It requires the programmer to co-ordinate previous experience and intuition in order to solve the problem.

HARDWARE AND SOFTWARE

A computer system has two major components, hardware and software. In practice, the term hardware refers to all the physical items associated with a computer system. Software is a set of instructions, which enables the hardware to perform a specific task.

Computer Hardware

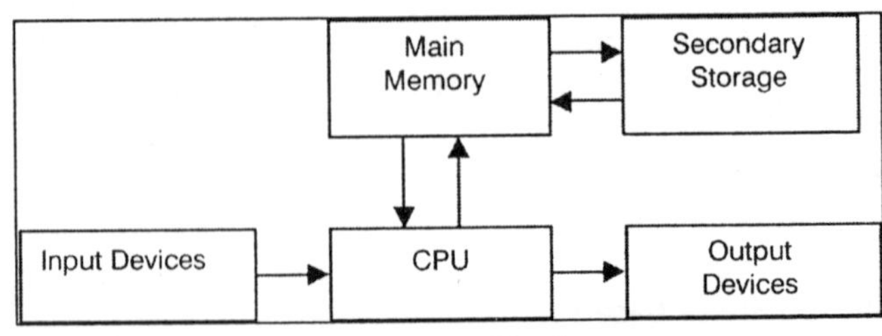

Fig. Computer Hardware

A computer is a machine that can be programmed to accept data (*input*), and process it into useful information (*output*). It also stores data for later reuse (*storage*). The *processing* is performed by the hardware. The computer hardware responsible for computing are mainly classified as follows:

- *Input devices* allows the user to enter the programme and data and send it to the processing unit. The common input devices are keyboard, mouse and scanners.
- The *Processor,* more formally known as the *central processing unit* (CPU), has the electronic circuitry that manipulates input data into the information as required. The central processing unit actually executes computer instructions.
- *Memory* from which the CPU fetches the instructions and data is called main memory. It is also called as primary memory and is volatile in nature.
- *Output devices* show the processed data – information – the result of processing. The devices are normally a monitor and printers.
- *Storage* usually means secondary *storage,* which stores data and programs. Here the data and programs are permanently stored for future use.
- The hardware devices attached to the computer are called peripheral equipment. Peripheral equipment includes all input, output and secondary storage devices.

Computer Software

Software refers to a programme that makes the computer to do something meaningful. It is the planned, step-by-step instructions required to turn data into information. Software can be classified into two categories: System Software and Application Software.

System software consists of general programs written for a computer. These programs provide the environment to run the application programs. System software comprises programs, which interact with the hardware at a very basic level.

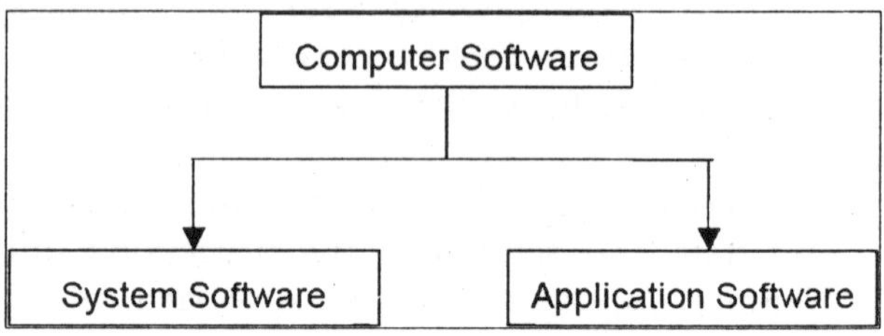

Fig. Software Categories

They are the basic necessity of a computer system for its proper functioning. System software serves as the interface between hardware and the user. The operating system, compilers and utility programs are examples of system software.

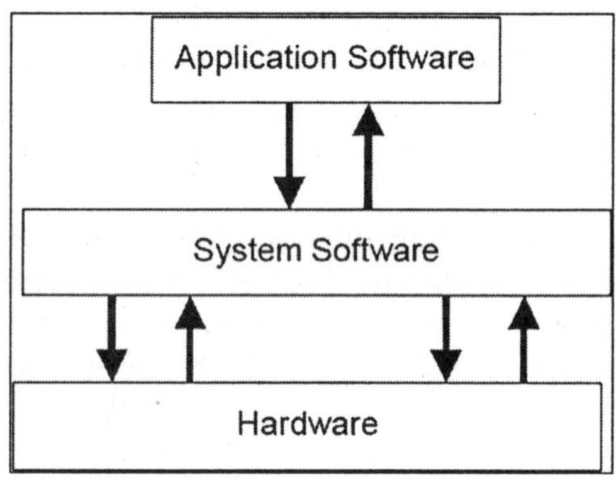

Fig. System Software

The most important type of system software is the operating system. An operating system is an integrated set of specialized programs that is used to manage the overall operations of a computer. It acts like an interface between the user, computer hardware and software. Every computer must have an operating system to run other programs.

DOS (Disk Operating System), Unix, Linux and Windows are some of the common operating systems. The compiler software translates the source programme (user written programme) into an object programme (binary form). Specific compilers are available for computer programming languages like FORTRAN, COBOL, C, C++ etc. The utility programs support the computer for specific tasks like file copying, sorting, linking a object programme, etc.

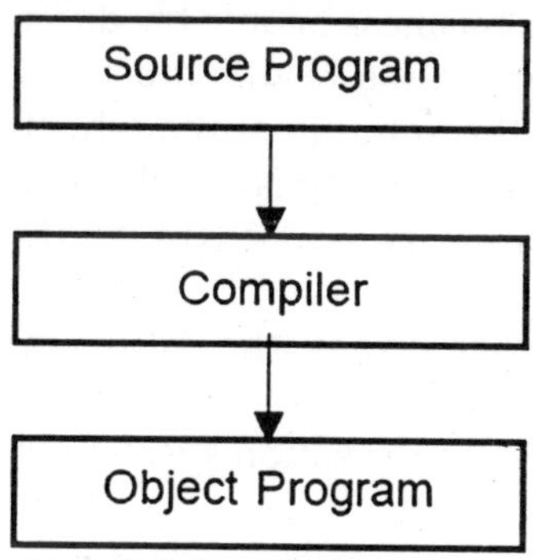

Fig. Compiler

An Application Software consists of programs designed to solve a user problem. It is used to accomplish specific tasks rather than just managing a computer system. Application software are inturn, controlled by system software which manages hardware devices.

Some typical examples are: railway reservation system, game programs, word processing software, weather forecasting programs. Among the application software some are packaged for specific tasks. The commonly used Application Software packages are word processor, spread sheet, database management system and graphics.

One of the most commonly used software package is word processing software. Anyone who has used a computer as a word processor knows that it is far more than a fancy typewriter.

The great advantage of word processing over a typewriter is that we can make changes without retyping the entire document. The entire writing process is transformed by this modern word processing software.

This software let us create, edit, format, store and print text and graphics. Some of the commonly used word processors are Microsoft Word, WordStar, WordPerfect, etc. Spreadsheet software packages allow the user to manipulate numbers.

Repetitive numeric calculations, use of related formulae and creation of graphics and charts are some of the basic tools. This capability lets business people try different combinations of numbers and obtain the results quickly. Lotus1-2-3, Excel, etc. are some of the famous spreadsheet applications. A database management system is a collection of programs that enable to store, modify and extract information from a database.

A database organizes the information internally. Computerized banking system, Automated Teller Machine, Airlines and Railway reservation system etc., are some of the database applications.

Type of Software	Functions	Examples
Word Processors	All personal computers are loaded with word processing software which has the same function as a typewriter for writing letters, preparing reports and printing.	Microsoft Word Word Perfect, Word Star.
Spreadsheet	A table containing text and figures, which is used to Calvulations and draw charts	Microsoft Excel, Lotus 1-2-3.
Database Management System	Used for storing, retrieval and Manipulation of Information	Microsoft Access, Oracle.

Types of Computers

Classification of the electronic computers may be based on either their principles of operation or their configuration. By configuration, we mean the size, speed of doing computation and storage capacity of a computer.

Classification based on Principles of Operation

Based on the principles of operation, computers are classified into three types, analog computers, digital computers and hybrid computers.

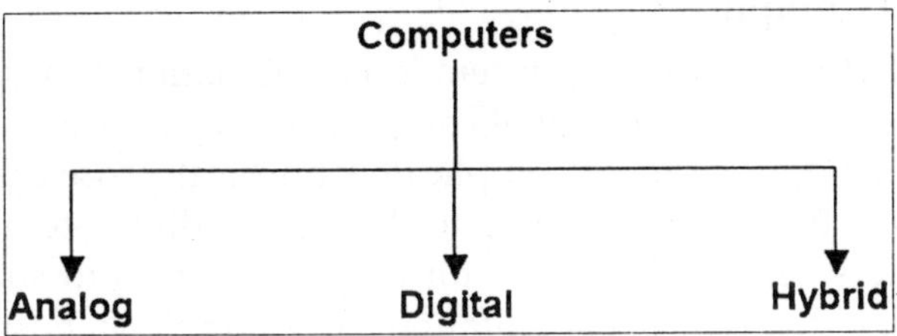

Fig. Classification of Computers

Analog Computers

Analog Computer is a computing device that works on continuous range of values. The analog computers give approximate results since they deal with quantities that vary continuously. It generally deals with physical variables such as voltage, pressure, temperature, speed, etc.

Digital Computers

On the other hand a digital computer operates on digital data such as numbers. It uses binary number system in which there are only two digits 0 and 1.

Each one is called a bit. The digital computer is designed using digital circuits in which there are two levels for an input or output signal. These two levels are known as logic 0 and logic 1.

Digital Computers can give the results with more accuracy and at a faster rate. Since many complex problems in engineering and technology are solved by the application of numerical methods, the electronic digital computer is very well suited for solving such problems.

Hence digital computers have an increasing use in the field of design, research and data processing. Digital computers are made for both general purpose and special purpose. Special purpose computer is one that is built for a specific application.

General purpose computers are used for any type of applications. It can store different programs and do the jobs as per the instructions specified on those programs. Most of the computers that we see fall in this category.

Hybrid Computers

A hybrid computing system is a combination of desirable features of analog and digital computers. It is mostly used for automatic operations of complicated physical processes and machines. Now-a-days analog-to-digital and digital-to-analog converters are used for transforming the data into suitable form for either type of computation. For example, in hospital's automated intensive care unit, analog devices might measure the patients temperature, blood pressure and other vital signs.

These measurements which are in analog might then be converted into numbers and supplied to digital components in the system. These components are used to monitor the patient's vital sign and send signals if any abnormal readings are detected. Hybrid computers are mainly used for specialized tasks.

CLASSIFICATION OF COMPUTERS BASED ON CONFIGURATION

Based on performance, size, cost and capacity, the digital computers are classified into four different types: Super computers, Mainframe computers, Mini computers and Micro computers.

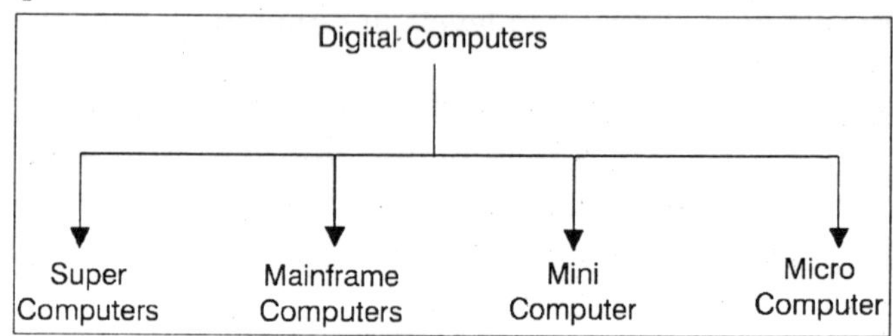

Fig. Classification of Digital Computers

Super Computers

The mightiest computers but at the same time, the most expensive ones are known as super computers. Super computers process billions of instructions per second. In other words, super computers are the computers normally used to solve intensive numerical computations. Examples of such applications are stock analysis, special effects for movies, weather forecasting and even sophisticated artworks.

Mainframe Computers

Mainframe computers are capable of processing data at very high speeds – hundreds of million instructions per second. They are large in size. These systems are also expensive. They are used to process large amount of data quickly. Some of the obvious customers are banks, airlines and railway reservation systems, aerospace companies doing complex aircraft design, etc.

Mini Computers

The mini computers were developed with the objective of bringing out low cost computers. They are lower to mainframe computers, in terms of speed and storage capacity. Some of the hardware features available in mainframes were not included in the mini computer hardware in order to reduce the cost.

Some features which were handled by hardware in mainframe computers were done by software in mini computers. Hence the performance of mini computer is less than that of the mainframe. However, the mini computer market has diminished somewhat as buyers have moved towards less expensive but increasingly powerful personal computers.

Micro Computers

The invention of microprocessor (single chip CPU) gave birth to the micro computers. They are several times cheaper than mini computers.

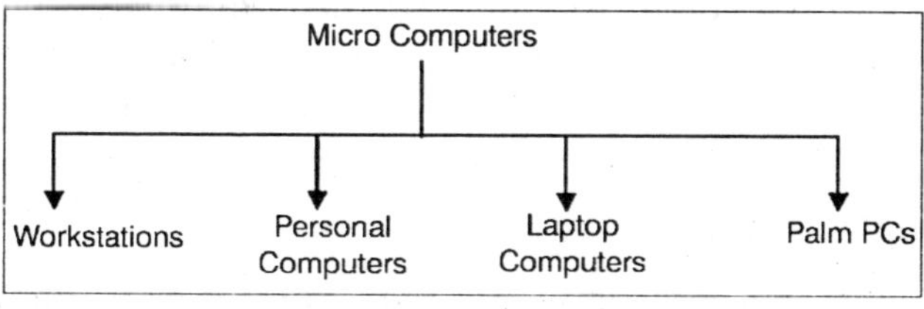

Fig. Classification of Micro Computers

The micro computers are further classified into workstation, personal computers, laptop computers and still smaller computers. Although the equipment may vary from the simplest computer to the most powerful, the major functional units of the computer system remain the same: input, processing, storage and output.

Workstations

Workstations are also desktop machines mainly used for intensive graphical applications. They have more processor speed than that of personal computers.

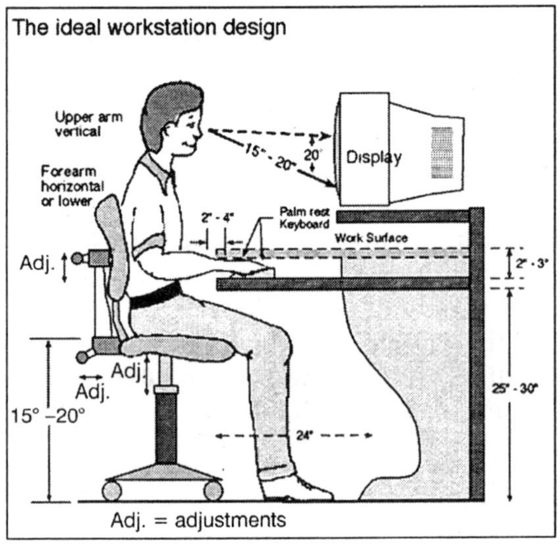

Fig. Workstation

Workstations use sophisticated display screens featuring highresolution colour graphics. Workstations are used for executing numeric and graphic intensive applications such as Computer Aided Design (CAD), simulation of complex systems and visualizing the results of simulation.

Personal Computers

Today the personal computers are the most popular computer systems simply called PCs. These desktop computers are also known as home computers. They are usually easier to use and more affordable than workstations.

Fig. Personal Computer

They are self-contained desktop computers intended for an individual user. Most often used for word processing and small database applications.

Laptop Computers

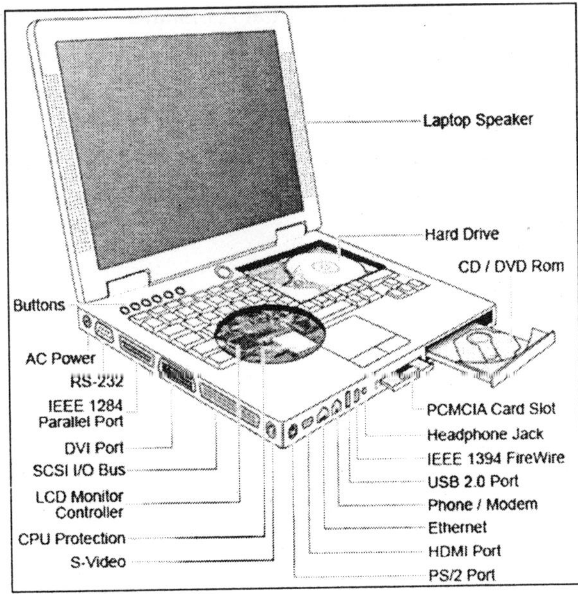

Fig. Laptop Computer

Laptop computers are portable computers that fit in a briefcase. Laptop computers, also called notebook computers, are wonderfully portable and functional, and popular with travelers who need a computer that can go with them.

Getting Smaller Still

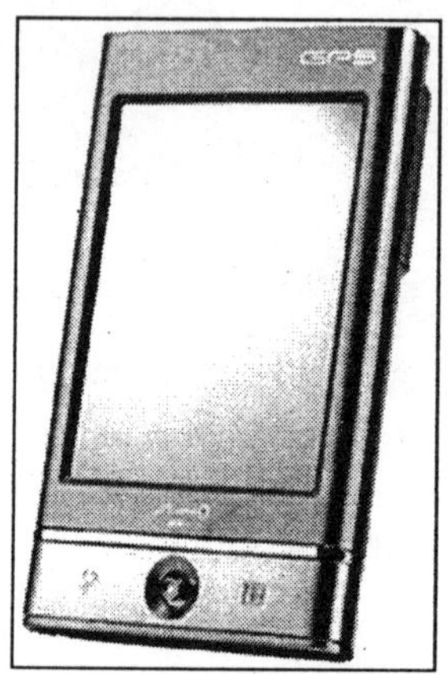

Fig. Personal Digital Assistants

Pen-based computers use a pen like stylus and accept handwritten input directly on a screen. Pen-based computers are also called Personal Digital Assistants (PDA). Special engineering and hardware design techniques are adopted to make the portable, smaller and light weight computers.

Chapter 2

Number Systems

There are several kinds of data such as, numeric, text, date, graphics, image, audio and video that need to be processed by a computer. The text data usually consist of standard alphabetic, numeric, and special characters. The graphics data consist of still pictures such as drawings and photographs. Any type of sound, including music and voice, is considered as audio data.

Video data consist of motion pictures. The data has to be converted into a format that the computer understands. Data can be classified into two forms, analog data and digital data. Analog data can have any value within a defined range and it is continuous.

Sound waves, telephone signals, temperatures and all other signals that are not broken into bits are examples of analog data. Digital data can be represented by a series of binary numbers and it is discrete. The Arithmetic and Logic Unit (ALU) of the computer performs arithmetic and logical operations on data.

Computer arithmetic is commonly performed on two different types of numbers, integer and floating point. As the hardware required for arithmetic is much simpler for integers than floating point numbers, these two types have entirely different representations. An integer is a whole number and the floating-point number has a fractional part.

To understand about how computers store data in the memory and how they handle them, one must know about bits and bytes and the number systems. Bits and bytes are common computer jargons. Both the main memory (Random

Access Memory or RAM) and the hard disk capacities are measured in terms of bytes. The hard disk and memory capacity of a computer and other specifications are described in terms of bits and bytes.

For instance, a computer may be described as having a 32-bit Pentium processor with 128 Megabytes of RAM and hard disk capacity of 40 Gigabytes.

BITS AND BYTES

A numbering system is a way of representing numbers. The most commonly used numbering system is the decimal system. Computer systems can perform computations and transmit data thousands of times faster in binary form than they can use decimal representations.

It is important for every one studying computers to know how the binary system and hexadecimal system work. A bit is small piece of data that is derived from the words "binary digit". Bits have only two possible values, 0 and 1. A binary number contains a sequence of 0s and 1s like 10111. A collection of 8 bits is called as a byte. With 8 bits in a byte, we can represent 256 values ranging from 0 to 255 as shown below:

0 = 0000 0000
1 = 0000 0001
2 = 0000 0010
3 = 0000 0011
....
....
....
254 = 1111 1110
255 = 1111 1111

Bytes are used to represent characters in a text. Different types of coding schemes are used to represent the character set and numbers. The most commonly used coding scheme is the American Standard Code for Information Interchange (ASCII). Each binary value between 0 and 127 is used to represent a specific character.

The ASCII value for a blank character (blank space) is 32 and the ASCII value of numeric 0 is 48. The range of ASCII values for lower case alphabets is from 97 to 122 and the range of ASCII values for the upper case alphabets is 65 to 90.

Computer memory is normally represented in terms of Kilobytes or Megabytes.

In metric system, one Kilo represents 1000, that is, 103. In binary system, one Kilobyte represents 1024 bytes, that is, 210. The following table shows the representation of various memory Sizes.

Name	Abbreviation	Size (Bytes)
Kilo	K	2^{10}
Mega	M	2^{20}
Giga	G	2^{30}
Tera	T	2^{40}
Peta	P	2^{50}
Exa	E	2^{60}
Zetta	Z	2^{70}
Yotta	Y	2^{80}

In a 2GB (Gigabytes) storage device (hard disk), totally 21,47,483,648 bytes can be stored. Nowadays, databases having size in Terabytes are reported; Zetta and Yotta size databases are yet to come.

DECIMAL NUMBER SYSTEM

In our daily life, we use a system based on digits to represent numbers. The system that uses the decimal numbers or digit symbols 0 to 9 is called as the decimal number system. This system is said to have a base, or radix, of ten. Sequence of digit symbols are used to represent numbers greater than 9. When a number is written as a sequence of decimal digits, its value can be interpreted using the positional value of each digit in the number.

The positional number system is a system of writing numbers where the value of a digit depends not only on the digit, but also on its placement within a number. In the positional number system, each decimal digit is weighted relative to its position in the number. This means that each digit in the number is multiplied by ten raised to a power corresponding to that digit's position. Thus the value of the decimal sequence 948 is:

$$948_{10} = 9 \times 10^2 + 4 \times 10^1 + 8 \times 10^0$$

Fractional values are represented in the same manner, but the exponents are negative for digits on the right side of the decimal point. Thus the value of the fractional decimal sequence 948.23 is:

$$948.23_{10} = 9 \times 10^2 + 4 \times 10^1 + 8 \times 10^0 + 2 \times 10^{-1} + 3 \times 10^{-2}$$

- In general, for the decimal representation of $x = \{.... x_2\, x_1\, x_0 .\, x_{-1}\, x_{-2}\, x_{-3} ....\}$, the value of $\times$ is $x = s_i\, x_i\, 10^i$ where i =.... 2, 1, 0, – 1, –2,....

BINARY NUMBER SYSTEM

Ten different digits 0 – 9 are used to represent numbers in the decimal system. There are only two digits in the binary system, namely, 0 and 1. The numbers in the binary system are represented to the base two and the positional multipliers are the powers of two.

The leftmost bit in the binary number is called as the most significant bit (MSB) and it has the largest positional weight. The rightmost bit is the least significant bit (LSB) and has the smallest positional weight. The binary sequence 10111_2 has the decimal equivalent:

$$\begin{aligned} 10111_2 &= 1 \times 2^4 + 0 \times 2^3 + 1 \times 2^2 + 1 \times 2^1 + 1 \times 2^0 \\ &= 16 + 0 + 4 + 2 + 1 \\ &= 23_{10} \end{aligned}$$

The decimal equivalent of the fractional binary sequence can be estimated in the same manner. The exponents are negative powers of two for digits on the right side of the binary point. The binary equivalent of the decimal point is the binary point. Thus the decimal value of the fractional binary sequence 0.1011_2 is:

$$\begin{aligned} 0.1011_2 &= 1 \times 2^{-1} + 0 \times 2^{-2} + 1 \times 2^{-3} + 1 \times 2^{-4} \\ &= 0.5 + 0 + 0.125 + 0.0625 \\ &= 0.6875_{10} \end{aligned}$$

HEXADECIMAL NUMBER SYSTEM

Hexadecimal representation of numbers is more efficient

in digital applications because it occupies less memory space for storing large numbers. A hexadecimal number is represented using base 16. Hexadecimal or Hex numbers are used as a shorthand form of binary sequence.

This system is used to represent data in a more compact manner. In the hexadecimal number system, the binary digits are grouped into sets of 4 and each possible combination of 4 binary digits is given a symbol as follows:

0000 = 0	1000 = 8
0001 = 1	1001 = 9
0010 = 2	1010 = A
0011 = 3	1011 = B
0100 = 4	1100 = C
0101 = 5	1101 = D
0110 = 6	1110 = E
0111 = 7	1111 = F

Since 16 symbols are used, 0 to F, the notation is called hexadecimal. The first ten symbols are the same as in the decimal system, 0 to 9 and the remaining six symbols are taken from the first six letters of the alphabet sequence, A to F. The hexadecimal sequence $2C_{16}$ has the decimal equivalent:

$$\begin{aligned} 2C_{16} &= 2 \times 16^1 + C \times 16^0 \\ &= 32 + 12 \\ &= 44_{10} \end{aligned}$$

The hexadecimal representation is more compact than binary representation. It is very easy to convert between binary and hexadecimal systems. Each hexadecimal digit will correspond to four binary digits because $2^4 = 16$. The hexadecimal equivalent of the binary sequence 110010011101_2 is:

1100 1001 1101

C 9 D $= C9D_{16}$

DECIMAL TO BINARY CONVERSION

To convert a binary number to a decimal number, it is required to multiply each binary digit by the appropriate power of 2 and add the results. There are two approaches for converting a decimal number into binary format.

Repeated Division by 2

Any decimal number divided by 2 will leave a remainder of 0 or 1.

Repeated division by 2 will leave a string of 0s and 1s that become the binary equivalent of the decimal number. Suppose it is required to convert the decimal number M into binary form, dividing M by 2 in the decimal system, we will obtain a quotient M_1 and a remainder r_1, where r_1 can have a value of either 0 or 1.

ie., $M = 2 * M_1 + r_1 \; r_1 = 0 \text{ or } 1$

Next divide the quotient M_1 by 2. The new quotient will be M_2 and the new remainder r_2.

ie., $M_1 = 2 * M_2 + r_2 \; r_2 = 0 \text{ or } 1$

so that

$$M = 2\,(2 * M_2 + r_2) + r_1$$
$$= 2^2 M_2 + r_2 * 2^1 + r_1 * 20$$

Next divide the quotient M_2 by 2. The new quotient will be M_3 and the new remainder r_3

i.e., $M_2 = 2 * M_3 + r_3$

so that

$$M = 2\,(2 * (2 * M_3 + r_3) + r_2) + r_1$$
$$= 2^2(2 * M_3 + r_3) + r_2 * 2^1 + r * 2^0$$
$$= 2^3 M_3 + r_3 * 2^2 + r_2 * 2^1 + r_1 * 2^0$$

The above process is repeated until the quotient becomes 0, then

$$M = 1 * 2^k + r_k * 2^{k-1} + \dots + r_3 * 2^2 + r_2 * 2^1 + r_1 * 2^0$$

Example: Convert 23_{10} into its equivalent binary number.

	Quotient	Remainder
23/2	11	1 (LSB) ↑
11/2	5	1
5/2	2	1
2/2	1	0
1/2	0	1 (MSB)

To write the binary equivalent of the decimal number, read the remainders from the bottom upward as:

$$23_{10} = 10111_2$$

The number of bits in the binary number is the exponent of the smallest power of 2 that is larger than the decimal number.

Consider a decimal number 23. Find the exponent of the smallest power of 2 that is larger than 23.

$$16 < 23 < 32$$
$$2^4 < 23 < 2^5$$

Hence, the number 23 has 5 bits as 10111. Consider another example.

Find the number of bits in the binary representation of the decimal number 36 without actually converting into its binary equivalent.

The next immediate large number than 36 that can be represented in powers of 2 is 64.

$$32 < 36 < 64$$
$$2^5 < 36 < 2^6$$

Hence, the number 36 should have 6 bits in its binary representation.

Sum of Powers of 2: A decimal number can be converted into a binary number by adding up the powers of 2 and then adding bits as needed to obtain the total value of the number. For example, to convert 36_{10} to binary:

a. Find the largest power of 2 that is smaller than or equal to 36

$$36_{10} > 32_{10}$$

b. Set the 32's bit to 1 and subtract 32 from the original number.

$$36 - 32 = 4$$

c. 16 is greater than the remaining total. Therefore, set the 16's bit to 0

d. 8 is greater than the remaining total. Hence, set the 8's bit to 0

e. As the remaining value is itself in powers of 2, set 4's bit to 1 and subtract 4

$$4 - 4 = 0$$

Conversion is complete when there is nothing left to subtract. Any remaining bits should be set to 0. Hence

$$36 = 100100_2$$

The conversion steps can be given as follows:

32 16 8 4 2 1
1   36 – 32 = 4
32 16 8 4 2 1
1 0 0 1   4 – 4 = 0
32 16 8 4 2 1
1 0 0 1 0 0 36_{10} = 1001002

Example: Convert 91_{10} to binary using the sum of powers of 2 method..

The largest power of 2 that is smaller than or equal to 91 is 64.

64 32 16 8 4 2 1
1   91–64 = 27   64 32 16 8 4 2 1
1 0 1   91–(64 + 16) = 11

(Since 32 > 27, set the 32's bit 0 and 16 < 27. set the 16's bit 1)

64 32 16 8 4 2 1
1 0 1 1   91–(64+16+8) = 3
64 32 16 8 4 2 1
1 0 1 1 0 1 1   91–(64+16+8+2) = 1
64 32 16 8 4 2 1
1 0 1 1 0 1 1 91–(64+16+8+2+1) = 0

Hence $91_{10} = 1011011_2$

Conversion of Fractional Decimal to Binary

The decimal fractions like 1/2, 1/4, 1/8 etc., can be converted into exact binary fractions. Sum of powers method can be applied to these fractions.

$$0.5_{10} = 1 * 2^{-1} = 0.1_2$$
$$0.25_{10} = 0 * 2^{-1} + 1 * 2^{-2} = 0.01_2$$
$$0.125_{10} = 0 * 2^{-1} + 0 * 2^{-2} + 1 * 2^{-3} = 0.001_2$$

The fraction 5/8 = 4/8 + 1/8 = 1/2 + 1/8 has the binary equivalent:

$$5/8 = 1 * 2^{-1} + 0 * 2^{-2} + 1 * 2^{-3}$$
$$= 0.101_2$$

Exact conversion is not possible for the decimal fractions that cannot be represented in powers of 2. For example, 0.210 cannot be exactly represented by a sum of negative powers of 2. A method of repeated multiplication by 2 has to be used to convert such kind of decimal fractions.

The steps involved in the method of repeated multiplication by 2:

- Multiply the decimal fraction by 2 and note the integer part. The integer part is either 0 or 1.
- Discard the integer part of the previous product. Multiply the fractional part of the previous product by 2. Repeat the first step until the fraction repeats or terminates.

The resulting integer part forms a string of 0s and 1s that become the binary equivalent of the decimal fraction.

Example: Integer part

	Integer part
0.2 * 2 = 0.4	0
0.4 * 2 = 0.8	0
0.8 * 2 = 1.6	1
0.6 * 2 = 1.2	1
0.2 * 2 = 0.4	0 ↓

(Fraction repeats, the product is the same as in the first step). Read the integer parts from top to bottom to obtain the equivalent fractional binary number.

Hence $0.2_{10} = 0.00110011_{...2}$

Conversion of Decimal to Hexadecimal

Decimal numbers' conversion to hexadecimal is similar to binary conversion. Decimal numbers can be converted into hexadecimal format by the sum of weighted hex digits method and by repeated division by 16.

The sum of weighted hex digits method is suitable for small decimal numbers of maximum 3 digits. The method of repeated division by 16 is preferable for the conversion of larger numbers.

The exponent of the smallest power of 16 that is greater than the given decimal number will indicate the number of hexadecimal digits that will be present in the converted hexadecimal number. For example, the decimal number 948, when converted into hexadecimal number has 3 hexadecimal digits.

$$(16^3 = 4096) > 948 > (16^2 = 256)$$

Hence, the hexadecimal representation of 948 has 3 hex digits. The conversion process is as follows:

16^2	16^1	16^0	
3			948 – (3 * 256) = 180
16^2	16^1	16^0	
3	B		948 – (3 * 256 + 11 * 16) = 4
16^2	16^1	16^0	
3	B	4	948 – (3 * 256 + 11 * 16 + 4) = 0

Hence, $948_{10} = 3B4_{16}$

The steps involved in the repeated division by 16 to obtain the hexadecimal equivalent are as follows:

- Divide the decimal number by 16 and note the remainder. Express the remainder as a hex digit.
- Repeat the process until the quotient is zero

Example:

Process	*Quotient*	*Remainder*
948/16 =	59	4 (LSB) ↑
59/16 =	3	11 (B)
3/16 =	0	3 (MSB)

$948_{10} = 3B_{416}$

Octal Representation

An octal number is represented using base 8. Octal representation is just a simple extension of binary and decimal representations but using only the digits 0 to7. To convert an octal number to a decimal number, it is required to multiply each octal digit by the appropriate power of 8 and add the results.

Example: What is the decimal value of the octal number 711_8?

$$7 * 8^2 + 1 * 8^1 + 1 * 8^0 = 457_{10}$$

The steps involved in the repeated division by 8 to obtain the octal equivalent are as follows:

- Divide the decimal number by 8 and note the remainder. Express the remainder as an octal digit.
- Repeat the process until the quotient is zero.

What is the octal representation of the decimal number 64_{10}?

	Quotient	Remainder
64/8	8	0 (LSB)
8/8	1	0
1/8	0	1 (MSB)

Hence $64_{10} = 100_8$

REPRESENTATION OF SIGNED NUMBERS

If computers represent non-negative integers (unsigned) only, the binary representation is straightforward, as we had seen earlier. Computers have also to handle negative integers (signed).

The normal convention that is followed to distinguish between a signed and unsigned number is to treat the most significant (leftmost) bit in the binary sequence as a sign bit. If the leftmost bit is 0, the number is positive, and if the leftmost bit is 1, the number is negative.

Sign+magnitude Representation

The simplest form of representing a negative integer is the sign+magnitude representation. In a sequence of n bits, the leftmost bit is used for sign and the remaining n-1 bits are used to hold the magnitude of the integer. Thus in a sequence of 4 bits,

$$0100 = +4$$
$$1100 = -4$$

As there are several drawbacks in this representation, this method has not been adopted to represent signed integers. There are two representations for 0 in this approach.

$$0000 = +0_{10}$$
$$1000 = -0_{10}$$

Hence it is difficult to test for 0, which is an operation, performed frequently in computers. Another drawback is that, the addition and subtraction require a consideration of both the sign of the numbers and their relative magnitude, in order to carry out the required operation.

This would actually complicate the hardware design of

the arithmetic unit of the computer. The most efficient way of representing a signed integer is a 2's-complement representation. In 2's complement method, there is only one representation of 0.

2'S-complement Representation

This method does not change the sign of the number by simply changing a single bit (MSB) in its representation. The 2's-complement method used with -ve numbers only is as follows:

- Invert all the bits in the binary sequence (ie., change every 0 to1 and every 1 to 0 ie.,1's complement)
- Add 1 to the result

This method works well only when the number of bits used by the system is known in the representation of the number. Care should be taken to pad (fill with zeros) the original value out to the full representation width before applying this algorithm.

Example: In a computer that uses 8-bit representation to store a number, the wrong and right approaches to represent –23 are as follows:

Wrong Approach

The binary equivalent of 23 is 10111.
Invert all the bits ⇒ 01000
Add 1 to the result ⇒ 01001
Pad with zeros to make 8-bit pattern ⇒ 00001001 ⇒ + 9

Right Approach

The binary equivalent of 23 is 10111
Pad with zeros to make 8-bit pattern ⇒ 00010111
Invert all the bits ⇒ 11101000
Add 1 to the result ⇒ 11101001 ⇒ –23

Manual Method to Represent Signed Integers in 2's Complement Form

This is an easier approach to represent signed integers. This is for -ve numbers only.

Step 1: Copy the bits from right to left, through and including the first 1.

Step 2: Copy the inverse of the remaining bits.

Example: To represent –4 in a 4-bit representation: The binary equivalent of the integer 4 is 0100. As per step1, copy the bits from right to left, through and including the first 1 ⇒ 100

As per step2, copy the inverse of the remaining bits ⇒ 1 100 ⇒ –4

Example: To represent –23 in a 8-bit representation: The binary equivalent of 23 is 00010111

As per step 1: 1

As per step 2: 11101001 ⇒ –23

Interpretation of Unsigned and Signed Integers

Signed number versus unsigned number is a matter of interpretation. A single binary sequence can represent two different values. For example, consider a binary sequence 11100110_2. The decimal equivalent of the above sequence when considered as an unsigned integer is:

$$111001102 = 230_{10}$$

The decimal equivalent of the sequence when considered as a signed integer in 2's complement form is:

111001102 = -26_{10} (after 2's complement and add negative sign).

When comparing two binary numbers for finding which number is greater, the comparison depends on whether the numbers are considered as signed or unsigned numbers.

Example:

X = 1001

Y = 0011

Is (X > Y)/* Is this true or false? */

It depends on whether X and Y are considered as signed or unsigned.

If X and Y are unsigned:

X is greater than Y

If X and Y are signed:

X is less than Y.

Range of Unsigned and Signed Integers

In a 4-bit system, the range of unsigned integers is from 0 to 15, that is, 0000 to 1111 in binary form. Each bit can have one of two values 0 or 1. Therefore, the total number of patterns of 4 bits will be 2 × 2 × 2 × 2 = 16. In an n-bit system, the total number of patterns will be 2^n.. Hence, if n bits are used to represent an unsigned integer value, the range is from 0 to 2^n-1, that is, there are 2^n different values.

In case of a signed integer, the most significant (left most) bit is used to represent a sign. Hence, half of the 2^n patterns are used for positive values and the other half for negative values. The range of positive values is from 0 to $2^{n-1}-1$ and the range of negative values is from –1 to -2^{n-1}. In a 4-bit system, the range of signed integers is from –8 to +7.

BINARY ARITHMETIC

Digital arithmetic usually means binary arithmetic. Binary arithmetic can be performed using both signed and unsigned binary numbers.

Binary Addition – Unsigned numbers

When two digits are added, if the result is larger than what can be contained in one digit, a carry digit is generated. For example, if we add 5 and 9, the result will be 14. Since the result cannot fit into a single digit, a carry is generated into a second digit place. When two bits are added it will produce a sum bit and a carry bit. The carry bit may be zero.

Example:

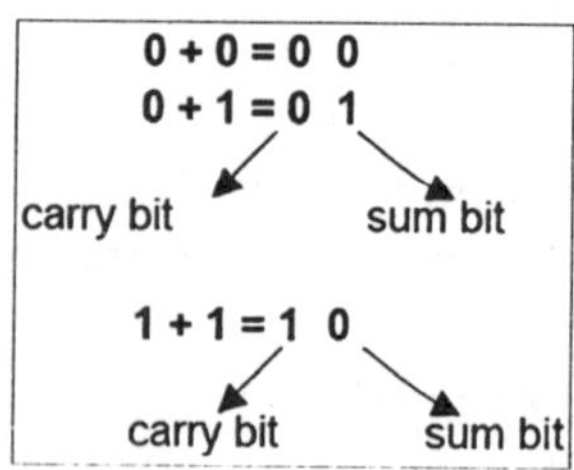

The sum bit is the least significant bit (LSB) of the sum of two 1-bit binary numbers and the carry bit holds the value of carry (0 or 1) resulting from the addition of two binary numbers.

Example: Calculate the sum of the numbers, 1100 and 1011:

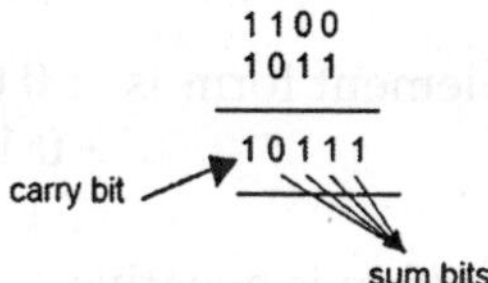

Example: Calculate 10111 + 10110

```
  111      Carry bits
 10111
 10110
------
101101
```

In unsigned binary addition, the two operands are called augend and addend. An augend is the number in an addition operation to which another number is added. An addend is the number in an addition operation that is added to another.

Binary Addition – Signed Numbers

Signed addition is done in the same way as unsigned addition. The only difference is that, both operands must have the same number of magnitude bits and each must have a sign bit. As we have already seen, in a signed number, the most significant bit (MSB) is a sign bit while the rest of the bits are magnitude bits. When the number is negative, the sign bit is 1 and when the number is positive, the sign bit is 0.

Example: Add $+2_{10}$ and $+5_{10}$. Write the operands and the sum as 4-bit signed binary numbers.

```
+2   0010
+5   0101
---  ----
+7   0111
```

(0 = sign bit; 111 = magnitude bits)

If the result of the operation is positive, we get a positive number in ordinary binary notation.

Example: (Use of 2's complement in signed binary addition)

Add $-7_{10} + 5_{10}$ using 4-bit system.

In 2'complement form, -7 is represented as follows:
In binary form, 7 is represented as: 0 1 1 1
Invert the bits (1 to 0 and 0 to 1) 1 0 0 0
Add 1 1
Hence, -7 in 2's complement form is 1 0 0 1 (–7)
+ 0 1 0 1 (5)
1 1 1 0 (–2)

If the result of the operation is negative, we get a negative number in 2's complement form. In some cases, there is a carry bit beyond the end of the word size and this is ignored.

Example: Add $-4_{10} + 4_{10}$. Use 4 -bit system.

1 1 0 0 (-4 in 2's complement form)
0 1 0 0 (+4)
1 0 0 0 0 = 0

In the above example, the carry bit goes beyond the end of the word and this can be ignored. In this case both operands are having different signs. There will be no error in the result. On any addition, the result may be larger than can be held in the word size being used and this would result in overflow.

The overflow condition is based on the rule: If two numbers are added and if they are either positive or negative, then overflow occurs if and only if the result has the opposite sign.

Example: Add $(-7_{10}) + (-5_{10})$ using the word size 4.

1 0 0 1 (–7 in 2's complement form)
1 0 1 1 (–5 in 2's complement form)
1 0 1 0 0 (The result is wrong)

In the above example both operands are negative. But the MSB of the result is 0 that is the result is positive (opposite sign) and hence overflow occurs and the result is wrong.

Binary Subtraction

Subtrahend and minuend are the two operands in an unsigned binary subtraction. The minuend is the number in a subtraction operation from which another number is subtracted. The subtrahend is the number that is subtracted from another number. Simple binary subtraction operations are as follows:

0 – 0 = 0
1 – 0 = 1
1 – 1 = 0
10 – 1 = 1

When subtracting 1 from 0, borrow 1 from the next most significant bit (MSB). When borrowing from the next most significant bit, if it is 1, replace it with 0.

If the next most significant bit is 0, we must borrow from a more significant bit that contains 1 and replace it with 0 and all 0s up to that point become 1s.

Example: Subtract 1101 – 1010

```
         borrow
 0 1  ↙
 1 1 0 1    (minuend)
-1 0 1 0    (subtrahend)
--------
 0 0 1 1
--------
```

When subtracting the 2nd least significant bit (1 in the subtrahend) from 0 (in the minuend), a 1 is borrowed from the more significant bit (3rd bit from right in the minuend) and hence 10 – 1 = 1.

The 3rd least significant bit is made as 0.

Example: Subtract 1000 – 101 0 1 1after borrowing, the minuend will become 10000 1110 –101101 (subtrahend) 0011 difference as per the basic operations for subtraction

To subtract one number (subtrahend) from another (minuend), take the 2's complement of the subtrahend and add it to the minuend.

Example: Subtract (+2) – (+7) using 4-bit system

0 0 1 0 (+2)
0 1 1 1 (+7)
1 0 0 1 (–7 in 2's complement form)
0 0 1 0 (2)
+ 1 0 0 1 (–7)
1 0 1 1 (–5)

Example: Subtract (–6) – (+4) using 4 bit system

Minuend –6

2's complement of the Subtrahend –4

```
   1 0 1 0
   1 1 0 0
 1 0 1 1 0
```

Both numbers are represented as negative numbers. While adding them, the result will be: 10110. As the word size is 4, the carry bit goes beyond the end of the word and the result is positive as the MSB is 0. This case leads to overflow and hence the result is wrong. The overflow rule works in subtraction also.

BOOLEAN ALGEBRA

Boolean algebra is a mathematical discipline that is used for designing digital circuits in a digital computer. It describes the relation between inputs and outputs of a digital circuit. The name Boolean algebra has been given in honour of an English mathematician George Boole who proposed the basic principles of this algebra.

As with any algebra, Boolean algebra makes use of variables and operations (functions). A Boolean variable is a variable having only two possible values such as, true or false, or as, 1 or 0. The basic logical operations are and, or and not, which are symbolically represented by dot, plus sign, and by over bar/ single apostrophe.

Example:

A and B = A. B

A or B = A + B

not A = A′ (or $\overline{A}$)

A Boolean expression is a combination of Boolean variables, Boolean Constants and the above logical operators. All possible operations in Boolean algebra can be created from these basic logical operators. There are no negative or fractional numbers in Boolean algebra.

The operation and yields true (binary value 1) if and only if both of its operands are true. The operation or yields true if either or both of its operands are true. The unary operation not inverts the value of its operand. The basic logical operations can be defined in a form known as Truth Table, which is a list of all possible input values and the output response for each input combination.

Boolean Operators (Functions)

And Operator

The and operator is defined in Boolean algebra by the use of the dot (.) operator. It is similar to multiplication in ordinary algebra. The and operator combines two or more input variables so that the output is true only if all the inputs are true. The truth table for a 2-input and operator is shown as follows:

A	B	Y
0	0	0
0	1	0
1	0	0
1	1	1

The above 2-input and operation is expressed as:

$$Y = A. B$$

Or Operator

The plus sign is used to indicate the or operator. The or operator combines two or more input variables so that the output is true if at least one input is true. The truth table for a 2-input or operator is shown as follows:

A	B	Y
0	0	0
0	1	1
1	0	1
1	1	1

- The above 2-input or operation is expressed as:

$$Y = A + B$$

Not Operator

The not operator has one input and one output. The input is either true or false, and the output is always the opposite, that is, the not operator inverts the input.

The truth table for a not operator where A is the input variable and Y is the output is shown below:

A	Y
0	1
1	0

- The not operator is represented algebraically by the Boolean expression: $Y = \overline{A}$ Example: Consider the Boolean equation:

Example: Consider the Boolean equation:

$$D = A + (\overline{B} . C)$$

D is equal to 1 (true) if A is 1 or if ($\overline{B}$. C) is 1, that is, B = 0 and C = 1. Otherwise D is equal to 0 (false).

The basic logic functions and, or, and not can also be combined to make other logic operators.

Nand Operator

The Nand is the combination of not and and. The Nand is generated by inverting the output of an and operator. The algebraic expression of the Nand function is:

$$Y = \overline{A . B}$$

The Nand function truth table is shown below:

A	B	Y
0	0	1
0	1	1
1	0	1
1	1	0

A Nand B = Not (A and B)

Nor Operator

The Nor is the combination of not and or. The Nor is generated by inverting the output of an or operator. The algebraic expression of the Nor function is:

$$Y = \overline{A + B}$$

The Nor function truth table is shown below:

A	B	Y
0	0	1
0	1	0
1	0	0
1	1	0

A Nor B = Not (A or B)

Laws of Boolean Algebra

Boolean algebra helps to simplify Boolean expressions in order to minimize the number of logic gates in a digital circuit. This Chapter focuses on the theorems of Boolean algebra for manipulating the Boolean expressions in order to simplify them.

BOOLEAN IDENTITIES

Laws of Complementation

The term complement simply means to change 1s to 0s and 0s to 1s.

Basic properties of AND operator

Theorem: If A = 0, then $\overline{A} = 1$
Theorem: If A = 1, then $\overline{A} = 0$
Theorem: The complement to complement of A is A itself.

$$\overline{\overline{A}} = A$$

Theorem: A. 1 = A
If A equals 0 and the other input is 1, the output is 0.
If A equals 1 and the other input is 1, the output is 1.
Thus the output is always equal to the A input.
Theorem: A. 0 = 0
As one input is always 0, irrespective of A, the output is always 0.
Theorem: A. A = A
The output is always equal to the A input.
Theorem: A. A = 0
Regardless of the value of A, the output is 0.

Basic Properties of OR Operator

Theorem: A + 1 = 1

If A equals 0 and the other input is 1, the output is 1.

If A equals 1 and the other input is 1, the output is 1.

Thus the output is always equal to 1 regardless of what value A takes on.

Theorem: A + 0 = A

The output assumes the value of A.

Theorem: A + A = A

The output is always equal to the A input.

Theorem: A + A = 1

Regardless of the value of A, the output is 1.

Simplification of Boolean Expressions

Before seeing the important theorems used in the simplification of Boolean expressions, some Boolean mathematical concepts need to be understood.

Literal

A literal is the appearance of a variable or its complement in a Boolean expression.

Product Term

A product term in a Boolean expression is a term where one or more literals are connected by AND operators. A single literal is also a product term.

Example: $A\overline{B}$, AC , $\overline{AC}$, and $\overline{E}$ are the product terms.

Minterm

A minterm is a product term, which includes all possible variables either complemented or uncomplemented. In a Boolean expression of 3 variables, x, y, and z, the terms xyz, $\overline{x}$ yz, and $\overline{xyz}$ are minterms. But $\overline{xy}$ is not a minterm. Minterm is also called as a standard product term.

Sum Term

A sum term in a Boolean expression is a term where one or more literals are connected by OR operators.

Example: $A + \overline{B} + D$

Maxterm

A maxterm is a sum term in a Boolean expression, which includes all possible variables in true or complement form. In a Boolean expression of 3 variables, x, y, and z, the terms $x + y + z$, and $x + \overline{y} + \overline{z}$ are the maxterms. Maxterm is also called as standard sum term.

Sum-of-products (SOP)

A sum of products expression is a type of Boolean expression where one or more product terms are connected by OR operators.

Example: $\overline{A} + AB + \overline{ABC}$

In an expression of 3 variables, A, B, and C, the expression $ABC + AB\overline{C} + \overline{A}B\overline{C}$ is also called as a canonical sum or sum of standard product terms or sum of minterms.

Product-of-sums (POS)

Product of sums is a type of Boolean expression where several sum terms are connected by AND operators.

Example: $(A+B)(\overline{A}+\overline{B})(\overline{A}+B)$

A canonical product or product of standard sum terms is a product of sums expression where all the terms are maxterms. The above example is a canonical product in a Boolean expression of two variables A and B.

Theorem: Commutative Law

A mathematical operation is commutative if it can be applied to its operands in any order without affecting the result. Addition and multiplication operations are commutative.

Example:

$$A + B = B + A$$
$$AB = BA$$

Subtraction is not commutative:

$$A - B \neq B - A$$

There is no subtraction operation in Boolean algebra.

Theorem: Associative Law

A mathematical operation is associative if its operands can be grouped in any order without affecting the result. In other words, the order in which one does the OR operation does not affect the result.

$$(A + B) + C = A + (B+C) = (A + C) + B$$

Similarly, the order in which one does the AND operation does not affect the result.

$$(AB)C = A(BC) = (AC)B$$

Theorem: Distributive Law. The distributive property allows us to distribute an AND across several OR functions.

Example: $A(B+C) = AB + AC$

The following distributive law is worth noting because it differs from what we would find in ordinary algebra. $A + (B. C) = (A + B). (A + C)$.

The simplest way to prove the above theorem is to produce a truth table for both the right hand side (RHS) and the left hand side (LHS) expressions and show that they are equal.

A	B	C	BC	LHS	A+B	A+C	RHS
0	0	0	0	0	0	0	0
0	0	1	0	0	0	1	0
0	1	0	0	0	1	0	0
0	1	1	1	1	1	1	1
1	0	0	0	1	1	1	1
1	0	1	0	1	1	1	1
1	1	0	0	1	1	1	1
1	1	1	1	1	1	1	1

Minimum Sum of Products

A minimum sum of products expression is one of those Sum of Products expressions for a Boolean expression that has the fewest number of terms.

Consider the following Boolean Expression:

$$\overline{A}\,B\overline{C} + \overline{A}\,B\,C + A\overline{B}\,\overline{C} + A\overline{B}\,C + A\,B\,C$$

Using Associativity Law

$$= \overline{A}(B\overline{C} + \overline{A}\,B\,C) + (A\overline{B}\,\overline{C} + A\overline{B}\,C) + A\,B\,C$$

$$= \overline{A}\,B\overline{C}(+ C) + A\,\overline{B}(\overline{C} + C) + ABC$$

Using Theorem 11

$$= \bar{A}B(1) + A\bar{B}(1) + ABC$$

Using Theorem 4

$$= \bar{A}B + A\bar{B} + ABC$$

The above expression is in the minimum sum of products form. The given Boolean expression can be rewritten as follows using theorem 10.

$$\bar{A}B\bar{C} + \bar{A}BC + A\bar{B}\bar{C} + A\bar{B}C + ABC + A\bar{B}C \quad (A\bar{B}C + A\bar{B}C = A\bar{B}C)$$

$$= (\bar{A}B\bar{C} + \bar{A}BC) + (A\bar{B}\bar{C} + A\bar{B}C) + (A\bar{B}C + ABC)$$

$$= \bar{A}B\bar{C}(+C) + A\bar{B}(\bar{C} + C) + AC(B + \bar{B})$$

$$= \bar{A}B + A\bar{B} + AC$$

The same Boolean expression can be simplified into many minimum sum of products form.

Examples: Simplify the following Boolean Expression

$$\bar{A}B\bar{C} + \bar{A}BC$$

Let $x = \bar{A}B$ and $y = \bar{C}$

The above Boolean expression becomes

$$xy + x\bar{y}$$

$$= x(y + \bar{y})$$

$$= x = \bar{A}B$$

Prove that $A + \bar{A}B = A + B$

According to Distributive Law

$$A + \bar{A}B = (A + \bar{A})(A + B) = 1 \cdot (A + B) = A + B$$

Simplify the following Boolean Expression

$$\bar{A}\bar{B}\bar{C} + \bar{A}B\bar{C} + \bar{A}BC + A\bar{B}\bar{C}$$

$$= \bar{A}\bar{C} + (\bar{B} + B) + \bar{A}BC + A\bar{B}\bar{C}$$

$$= \bar{A}\bar{C} + \bar{A} + BC + A\bar{B}\bar{C}$$

$$= \bar{A}(\bar{C} + BC) + A\bar{B}\bar{C}$$

$$= \bar{A}(\bar{C} + B)(\bar{C} + C) + A\bar{B}\bar{C}$$

$$= \bar{A}(\bar{C} + B) + A\bar{B}\bar{C}$$

$$= \bar{A}\bar{C} + \bar{A}B + A\bar{B}\bar{C} \quad \text{(one minimal form)}$$

In the given Boolean Expression, if the second and third terms are grouped, it will give.

$$\bar{A}\bar{B}\bar{C} + (\bar{A}B\bar{C} + \bar{A}BC) + A\bar{B}\bar{C}$$

$$= \bar{A}\bar{B}\bar{C} + \bar{A}B(\bar{C} + C) + A\bar{B}\bar{C}$$

$$= \bar{A}\bar{B}\bar{C} + \bar{A}B + A\bar{B}\bar{C}$$

$$= \bar{B}\bar{C}(\bar{A} + A)\bar{A}B$$

$$= \bar{B}\bar{C} + \bar{A}B \quad \text{(most minimal form)}$$

DeMorgan's Theorems

Theorem: $\overline{A + B} = \bar{A}\bar{B}$

Theorem: $\overline{AB} = \bar{A} + \bar{B}$

The above identities are the most powerful identities used in Boolean algebra. By constructing the truth tables, the above identities can be proved easily.

Example: Given Boolean function $f(A,B,C,D) = D\bar{A}B + \bar{A}B + D\,A\,C$, Find the complement of the Boolean function

$$\bar{f}\ (A,B,C,D) = \overline{D\bar{A}B + A\bar{B} + DAC}$$

Apply DeMorgan's Law

$$= \overline{(D\bar{A}B)}\ \overline{(\bar{B}A)}\ \overline{(DAC)}$$

Apply DeMorgan's Law

$$= (\bar{D} + A + \bar{B}) \qquad (\bar{A} + B)\ (\bar{D} + \bar{A} + \bar{C})$$

In the above problem, the given Boolean function is in the sum of products form and its complement is in the product of sums form. The DeMorgan's theorem says that any logical binary expression remains unchanged if we,

- Change all varibales to their complements
- Change all AND operations to OR operations
- Change all OR operations to AND operations
- Take the complement of the entire expression

A practical operational way to look at DeMorgan's theorem is that the inversion of an expression may be broken at anypoint and the operation at that point replaced by its oppostie (i.e., AND replaced by OR or vice versa).

Chapter 3

Components of Computer

Computers are often compared to human beings since both have the ability to accept data, store, work with it, retrieve and provide information. The main difference is that human beings have the ability to perform all of these actions independently. Human beings also think and control their own activities. The computer, however, requires a programme (a predefined set of instructions) to perform an assigned task. Human beings receive information in different forms, such as eyes, ears, nose, mouth, and even sensory nerves.

The brain receives or accepts this information, works with it in some manner, and then stores in the brain for future use. If information at the time requires immediate attention, brain directs to respond with actions. Likewise the Central Processing Unit (CPU) is called the brain of the computer. It reads and executes programme instructions, performs calculations and makes decisions.

COMPUTER SYSTEM

A computer system is the integration of physical entities called hardware and non-physical entities called software. The hardware components include input devices, processor, storage devices and output devices. The software items are programs and operating aids (systems) so that the computer can process data.

Functional Units of a Computer System

Computer system is a tool for solving problems. The hardware should be designed to operate as fast as possible.

The software (system software) should be designed to minimize the amount of idle computer time and yet provide flexibility by means of controlling the operations. Basically any computer is supposed to carry out the following functions.

- Accept the data and programme as input
- Store the data and programme and retrieve as and when required.
- Process the data as per instructions given by the programme and convert it into useful information
- Communicate the information as output

Based on the functionalities of the computer, the hardware components can be classified into four main units, namely

- Input Unit
- Output Unit
- Central Processing Unit
- Memory Unit

These units are interconnected by minute electrical wires to permit communication between them. This allows the computer to function as a system. The block diagram is shown below.

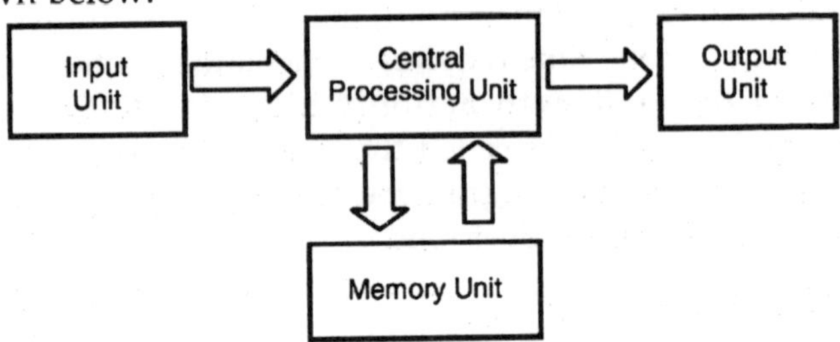

Fig. Functional Units of a Computer System

Input Unit

A computer uses input devices to accept the data and programme. Input devices allow communication between the user and the computer. In modern computers keyboard, mouse, light pen, touch screen etc, are some of the input devices.

Output Unit

Similar to input devices, output devices have an interface

between the computer and the user. These devices take machine coded output results from the processor and convert them into a form that can be used by human beings. In modern computers, monitors (display screens) and printers are the commonly used output devices.

Central Processing Unit

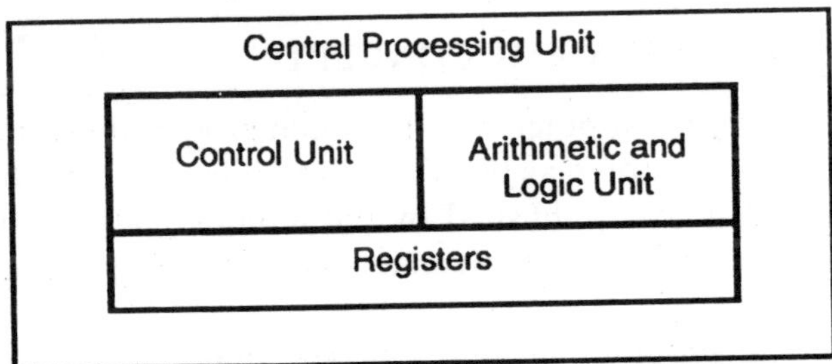

CPU is the brain of any computer system. It is just like the human brain that takes all major decisions, makes all sorts of calculations and directs different parts of the computer function by activating and controlling the operation. It consists of arithmetic and logic units, control unit and internal memory (registers).

The control unit of the CPU coordinates the action of the entire system. Programs (software) provide the CPU, a set of instruction to follow and perform a specific task. Between any two components of the computer system, there is a pathway called a bus which allows for the data transfer between them.

Control unit controls all the hardware operations, ie, those of input units, output units, memory unit and the processor. The arithmetic and logic units in computers are capable of performing addition, subtraction, division and multiplication as well as some logical operations. The instructions and data are stored in the main memory so that the processor can directly fetch and execute them.

Memory Unit

In the main memory, the computer stores the programme and data that are currently being used. In other words since the computers use the stored programme concept, it is necessary to store the programme and data in the main memory before processing. The main memory holds data and programme only temporarily. Hence there is a need for storage devices to provide backup storage. They are called secondary storage devices or auxiliary memory devices. Secondary storage devices can hold more storage than main memory and is much less expensive.

STORED PROGRAMME CONCEPT

All modern computers use the stored programme concept. This concept is known as the Von – Neumann concept due to the research paper published by the famous mathematician John Von Neuman. The essentials of the stored programme concept are:

- The programme and data are stored in a primary memory (main memory)
- Once a programme is in memory, the computer can execute it automatically without manual intervention.
- The control unit fetches and executes the instructions in sequence one by one.
- An instruction can modify the contents of any location in The stored programme concept is the basic operating principle for every computer.

CENTRAL PROCESSING UNIT

FUNCTIONS OF A CENTRAL PROCESSING UNIT

The CPU is the brain of the computer system. It performs arithmetic operations as well as controls the input, output and storage units. The functions of the CPU are mainly classified into two categories:

- Co – ordinate all computer operations
- Perform arithmetic and logical operations on data

The CPU has three major components.

- Arithmetic and Logic Unit
- Control Unit
- Registers (internal memory)

The arithmetic and logic unit (ALU) is the part of CPU where actual computations take place. It consists of circuits which perform arithmetic operations over data received from memory and are capable of comparing two numbers.

The control unit directs and controls the activities of the computer system. It interprets the instructions fetched from the main memory of the computer, sends the control signals to the devices involved in the execution of the instructions.

While performing these operations the ALU takes data from the temporary storage area inside the CPU named registers. They are high-speed memories which hold data for immediate processing and results of the processing.

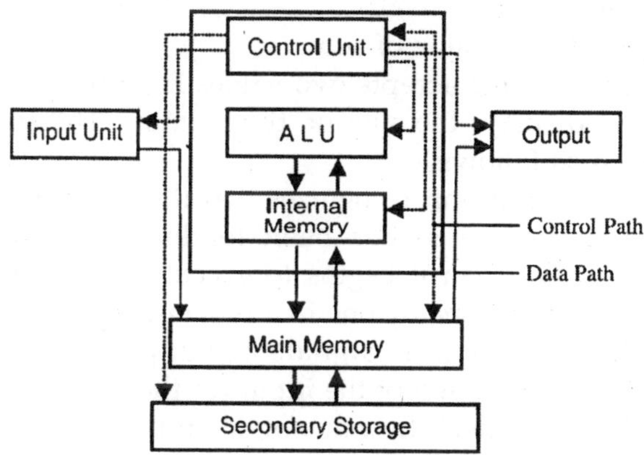

Fig. Functions of a CPU

Working with Central Processing Unit

The CPU is similar to a calculator, but much more powerful. The main function of the CPU is to perform arithmetic and logical operations on data taken from main memory. The CPU is controlled by a list of software instructions. Software instructions are initially stored in secondary memory storage device such as a hard disk, floppy disk, CD-ROM, or magnetic tape. These instructions are then loaded onto the computer's main memory.

When a programme is executed, instructions flow from the main memory to the CPU through the bus. The instructions are then decoded by a processing unit called the instruction decoder that interprets and implements the instructions. The ALU performs specific operations such as addition, multiplication, and conditional tests on the data in its registers, sending the resulting data back to the main memory or storing it in another register for further use.

To understand the working principles of CPU, let us go through the various tasks involved in executing a simple programme. This programme performs arithmetic addition on two numbers. The algorithm of this programme is given by

- Input the value of a
- Input the value of b
- Sum = a + b
- Output the value of sum

This programme accepts two values from the keyboard, sums it and displays the sum on the monitor. The steps are summarized as follows:

- The control unit recognizes that the programme (set of instructions) has been loaded into the main memory. Then it begins to execute the programme instructions one by one in a sequential manner.
- The control unit signals the input device (say keyboard) to accept the input for the variable 'a'.
- The user enters the value of 'a' on the keyboard.
- The control unit recognizes and enables to route the data (value of a) to the pre-defined memory location (address of 'a').
- The steps 2 to 4 will be repeated for the second input 'b'. The value of 'b' is stored in the memory location (address of 'b').
- The next instruction is an arithmetic instruction. Before executing the arithmetic instruction, the control unit enables to send a copy of the values stored in address of 'a' and address of 'b' to the internal registers of the ALU and signals the ALU to perform the sum operation.
- The ALU performs the addition. After the computation, the control unit enables to send the

copy of the result back to the memory (address of 'sum').

- Finally, the result is displayed on the monitor. The control unit enables to send the copy of the values of the address of 'sum' to the monitor (buffer) and signals it. The monitor displays the result.
- Now this programme execution is complete.

The data flow and the control flow of CPU during the execution of this programme is given as,

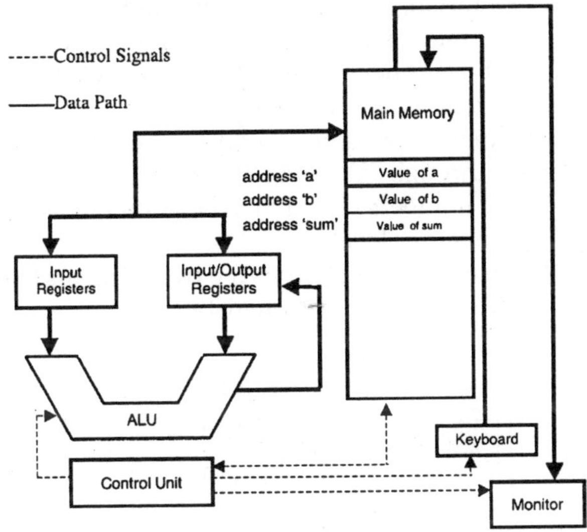

Fig. Working Principles of a CPU

Arithmetic and Logic Unit – ALU

The ALU is the computer's calculator. It executes arithmetic and logical operations. The arithmetic operations include addition, subtraction, multiplication and division. The logical operation compares numbers, letters and special characters. The ALU also performs logic functions such as and, or and not.

The ALU functions are directly controlled by the control unit. The control unit determines when the services of the ALU are needed, and it provides the data to be operated.

The control unit also determines what is to be done with the results.

Arithmetic Operations

Arithmetic operations include addition, subtraction, multiplication, and division. While performing these operations, the ALU makes use of the registers. Data to be arithmetically manipulated are copied from main memory and placed in registers for processing. Upon completion of the arithmetic operation, the result can be transferred from the register to the main memory. In addition to registers, the arithmetic unit uses one or more adders that actually perform arithmatic operations on the binary digits.

The arithmetic operation in adding two numbers can be demonstrated through following steps:

Step 1: The numbers (5 and 8) to be added up are put into two separate memory locations.

Step 2: The control unit fetches the two numbers from their memory locations into the data registers.

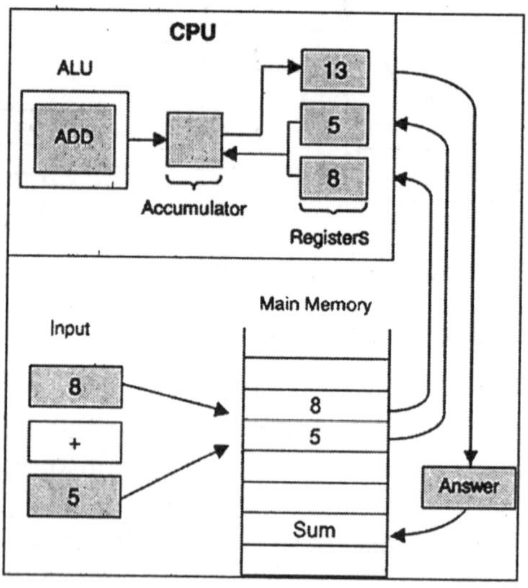

Fig. Arithmetic Logic Unit

Step 3: The arithmetic unit looking at the operator (+) uses the accumulator and adds the two numbers.

Step 4: The ALU stores the result in memory buffer register.

Step 5: Then the control unit stores the result into a user desired memory location, say 'sum'.

Logical Operations

The importance of the logic unit is to make logical operations. These operations include logically comparing two data items and take different actions based on the results of the comparison.

Functional Description

Some of the basic functions performed by the ALU are - add, subtract, logical AND, logical OR, shift left and shift right on two's complement binary numbers. The inputs to be calculated are stored in the input register (AREG) and the input/ output register (ACCUM) for add, AND and OR functions. The shift left and shift right functions operate on the value in the ACCUM.

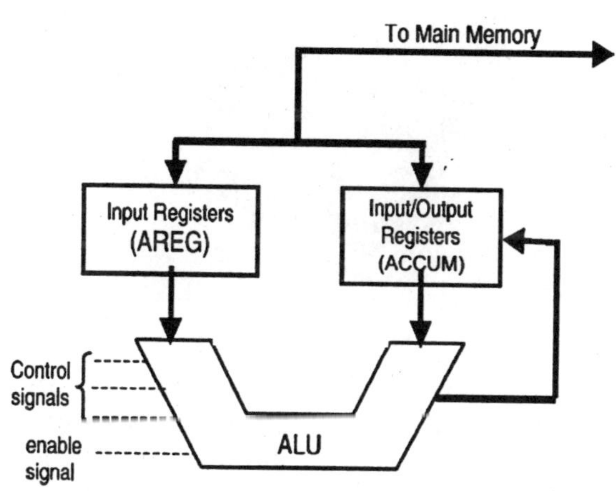

Fig. Functional Description of ALU

The above figure illustrates the functional level block diagram of the ALU. The control unit controls the operations of the ALU by giving appropriate control signals to select a specific function and then enable the operation after the data are fed into the registers. The enable bit is made 1 after the data to be operated are transferred from main memory.

MEMORY UNIT

Memory units are the storage areas in a computer. The term "memory" usually refers to the main memory of the computer, whereas, the word "storage" is used for the memory that exists on disks, CDs, floppies or tapes. The main memory is usually called a physical memory which refers to the 'chip' (Integrated Circuit) capable of holding data and instruction.

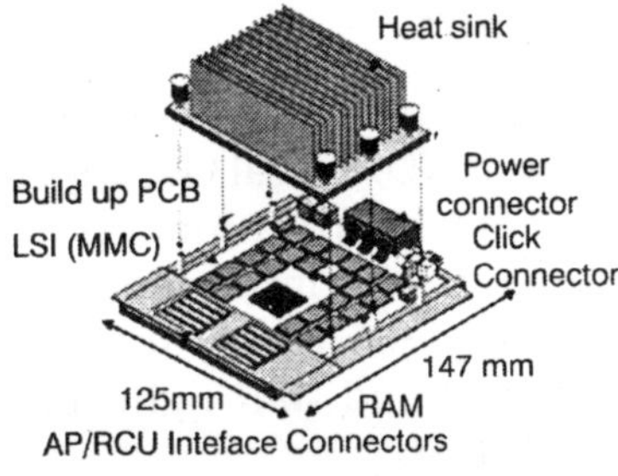

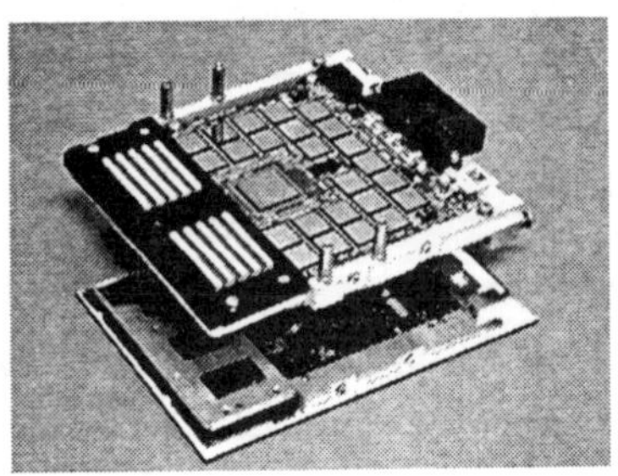

Fig. Memory Unit

There are different types of memory. They are Random Access Memory (RAM), Read Only Memory (ROM), Programmable Read- Only Memory (PROM), Erasable Programmable Read-Only Memory (EPROM), Electrically Erasable Programmable Read-Only Memory (EEPROM).

Random Access Memory - RAM

RAM is the most common type of memory found in the modern computers. This is really the main store and is the place where the programme gets stored. When the CPU runs a programme, it fetches the programme instructions from the RAM and carries them out. If the CPU needs to store the results of the calculations it can store them in RAM. When we switch off a computer, whatever is stored in the RAM gets erased. It is a volatile form of memory.

Read Only Memory - ROM

In ROM, the information is burnt (pre-recorded) into the ROM chip at manufacturing time. Once data has been written into a ROM chip, it cannot be erased but we can read it. When we switch off the computer, the contents of the ROM are not erased but remain stored permanently. ROM is a non-volatile memory. ROM stores critical programs such as the programme that boots the computer.

Programmable Read Only Memory - PROM

PROM is a memory on which data can be written only once. A variation of the PROM chip is that it is not burnt at the manufacturing time but can be programmed using PROM programmer or a PROM burner. PROM is also a non-volatile memory.

Erasable Programmable Read Only Memory - EPROM

In EPROM, the information can be erased and reprogrammed using a special PROM - programmer. EPROM is non-volatile memory. A EPROM differs from a PROM in that a PROM can be written to only once and cannot be erased. But an ultraviolet light is used to erase the contents of the EPROM.

Electrically Erasable Programmable Read Only Memory - EEPROM

EEPROM is a recently developed type of memory. This is equivalent to EPROM, but does not require ultraviolet light to erase its content. It can be erased by exposing it to an electrical charge. It is also non-volatile in nature. EEPROM is not as fast as RAM or other types of ROM. A flash memory is a special type of EEPROM that can be erased and reprogrammed. The main memory must store many data items and have some way of retriving them when they are needed.

The memory can be compared to the boxes at a post office. Each box-holder has a box with a unique number which is called its address. This address serves to identify the box. The memory has a number of locations in its store. Each location in a memory has a unique number called its memory address.

This serves to identify it for storage and retrival. Operations on memories are called reads and writes, defined from the perspective of a processor or other device that uses a memory: a write instruction transfers information from other device to memory and a read instruction transfers information from the memory to other devices. A memory that performs both reads and writes is often called a RAM, random access memory. Other types of memories commonly used in systems are read-only memory.

Data Representation

The smallest unit of information is a single digit called a 'bit' (binary digit), which can be either 0 or 1. The capacity of a memory system is represented by a unit called a byte, which is 8 bits of information. Memory sizes in modern systems range from 4MB (megabytes) in small personal computers up to several billion bytes (gigabytes, or GB) in large high-performance systems.

The performance of a memory system is defined by two different measures, the access time and the memory cycle time. Access time, also known as response time or latency, refers to how quickly the memory can respond to a read or write request. Memory cycle time refers to the minimum period between two successive requests. The following terminology is used while discussing hierarchical memories:

- The registers (internal memory) are used to hold the instruction and data for the execution of the processor. Eventually the top of the hierarchy goes to the registers.
- The memory closest to the processor is known as a

cache. It is a high speed memory that is much faster than the main memory.

- The next is the main memory which is also known as the primary memory.
- The low end of the hierarchy is the secondary memory.

The secondary memory is the memory that supplements the main memory. This is a long term non-volatile memory. It is external to the system nucleus and it can store a large amount of programs and data. The CPU docs not fetch instructions of a programme directly from the secondary memory. The programme should be brought into the main memory from the secondary memory before being executed. The secondary memory is cheaper compared to the main memory and hence a computer generally has limited amount of main memory and large amount of secondary memory.

INPUT AND OUTPUT DEVICES

The main function of a computer system is to process data. The data to be processed by the computer must be input to the system and the result must be output back to the external world.

INPUT DEVICES

An input device is used to feed data into a computer. For example, a keyboard is an input device. It is also defined as a device that provides communication between the user and the computer. Input devices are capable of converting data into a form which can be recognized by computer. A computer can have several input devices.

Keyboard

The most common input device is the keyboard. Keyboard consists of a set of typewriter like keys that enable us to enter data into a computer. They have alphabetic keys to enter letters, numeric keys to enter numbers, punctuation keys to enter comma, period, semicolon, etc., and special keys to perform some specific functions.

The keyboard detects the key pressed and generates the corresponding ASCII codes which can be recognized by the computer.

Key Board

Fig. Keyboard

Mouse

Mouse is an input device that controls the movement of the cursor on the display screen. Mouse is a small device, we can roll along a flat surface. In a mouse, a small ball is kept inside and touches the pad through a hole at the bottom of the mouse. When the mouse is moved, the ball rolls. This movement of the ball is converted into signals and sent to the computer. We will need to click the button at the top of the mouse to select an option. Mouse pad is a pad over which we can move a mouse. Mouse is very popular in modern computers.

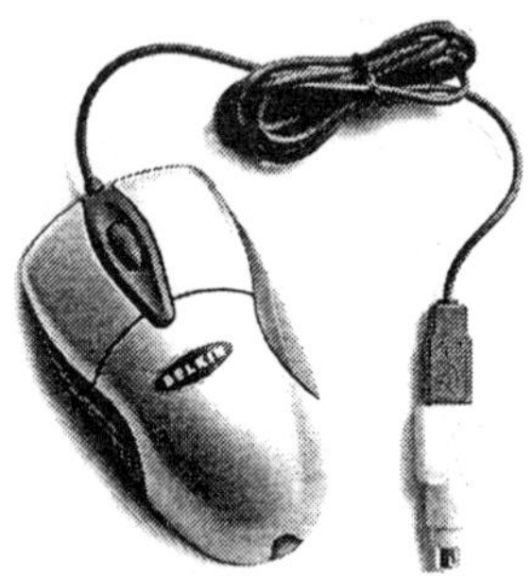

Fig. Mouse

Scanner

Scanner is an input device that allows information such as an image or text to be input into a computer. It can read image or text printed on a paper and translate the information into a form that the computer can use. That is, it is used to convert images (photos) and text into a stream of data. They are useful for publishing and multi-media applications.

Fig. Scanner

Bar Code Reader

The barcode readers are used in places like supermarket, bookshops, etc. A bar code is a pattern printed in lines of different thickness. The bar-code reader scans the information on the barcodes and transmits to the computer for further processing. The system gives fast and error-free entry of information into the computer.

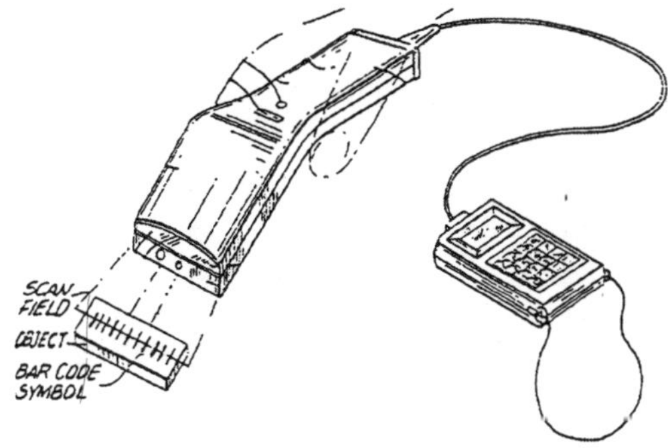

Fig. Bar Code and Reader

Digital Camera

The digital camera is an input device mainly used to capture images. The digital camera takes a still photograph, stores it and sends it as digital input to the computer. It is a modern and popular input device.

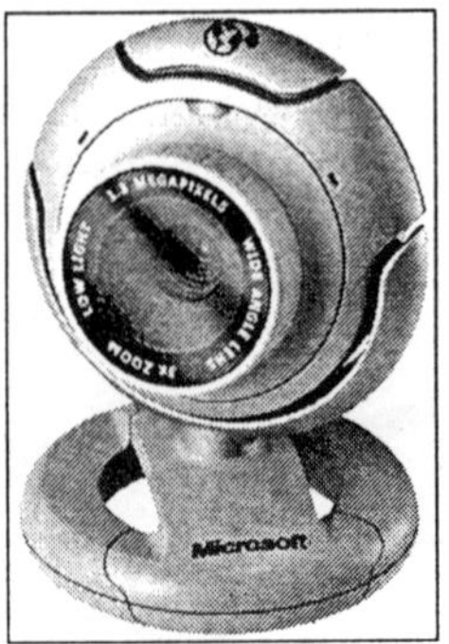

Fig. Digital Camera

Touch Sensitive Screen

Touch Sensitive Screen is a type of display screen that has a touch-sensitive panel.

It is a pointing device that enables the user to interact with the computer by touching the screen. We can use our fingers to directly touch the objects on the screen. The touch screen senses the touch on the object (area pre-defined) and communicate the object selection to the computer.

Fig. Touch Sensitive Screen

Magnetic Ink Character Recognition (MICR)

MICR is widely used by banks to process cheques. Human readable numbers are printed on documents such as cheque using a special magnetic ink. The cheque can be read using a special input unit, which can recognize magnetic ink characters.

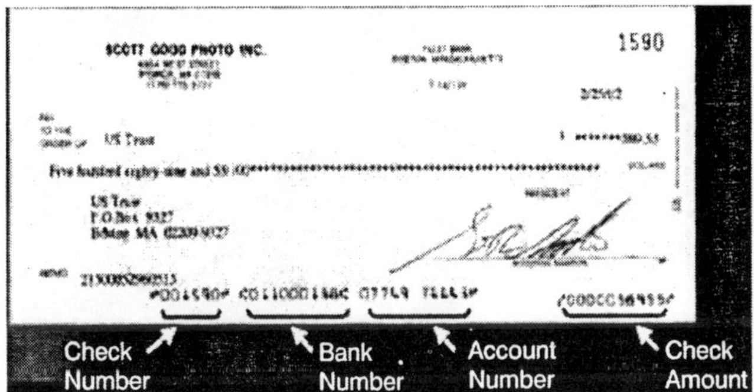

Fig. MICR Cheque

This method eliminates the manual errors. It also saves time, ensures security and accuracy of data.

Optical Character Recognition (OCR)

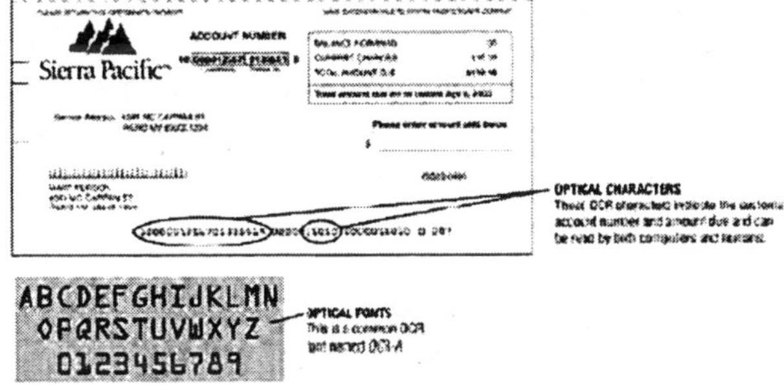

Fig. OCR Sheet

The OCR technique permits the direct reading of any printed character like MICR but no special ink is required. With OCR, a user can scan a page from a book. The computer will recognize the characters in the page as letters and punctuation marks, and stores. This can be edited using a word processor.

Optical Mark Reading and Recognition (OMR)

In this method special pre-printed forms are designed with boxes which can be marked with a dark pencil or ink. Such documents are read by a reader, which transcribes the marks into electrical pulses which are transmitted to the computer.

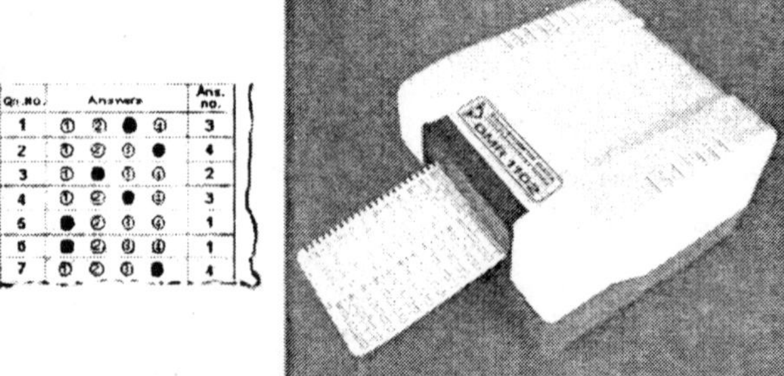

Fig. OMR Reader

They are widely used in applications like objective type answer papers evaluation in which large number of candidates appear, time sheets of factory employees etc.

Light Pen

A light pen is a pointing device shaped like a pen and is connected to a monitor. The tip of the light pen contains a lightsensitive element which, when placed against the screen, detects the light from the screen enabling the computer to identify the location of the pen on the screen.

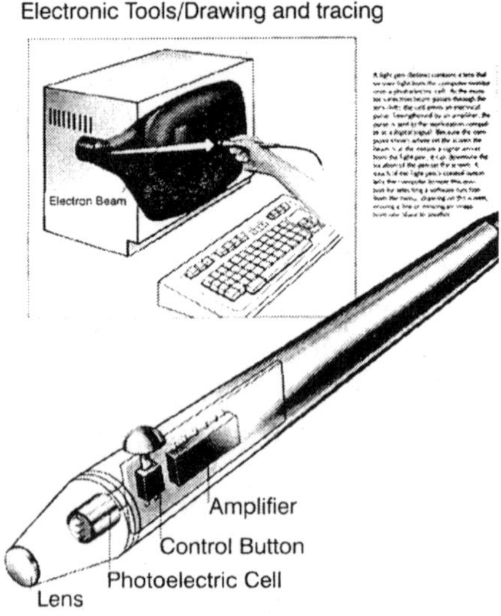

Fig. Light Pen

Light pens have the advantage of 'drawing' directly onto the screen, but this can become uncomfortable, and they are not accurate.

Magnetic Reader

Magnetic reader is an input device which reads a magnetic strip on a card. It is handy and data can be stored and retrieved. It also provides quick identification of the card's owner. All the credit cards, ATM cards (banks), petro cards, etc. stores data in a magnetic strip which can be read easily by the magnetic reader.

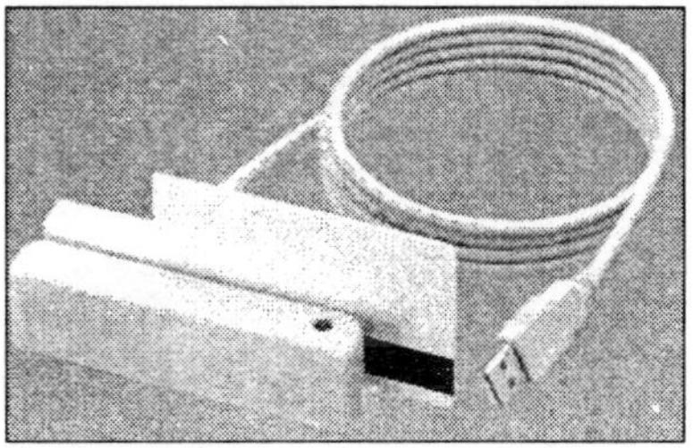

Fig. Magnetic Reader

Smart Cards

This input device stores data in a microprocessor embedded in the card. This allows information, which can be updated, to be stored on the card.

Fig. Smart Card Reader

These data can be read and given as input to the computer for further processing. Most of the identification cards use this method to store and retrieve the vital information.

Notes Taker

Notes taker is a device that captures natural handwriting on any surface onto a computer. Using an electronic pen, the notes taker displays the user's handwritten notes, memos or drawings on the computer, and stores the image for future use.

Fig. Notes Taker

Microphone

Microphone serves as a voice input device. It captures the voice data and input to the computer.

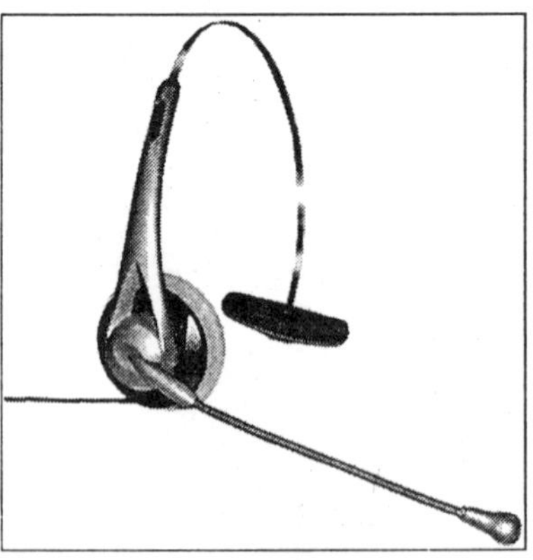

Fig. Microphone

Using the microphone along with speech recognition software can offer a completely new approach to input information into our computer. Speech recognition programs, although not yet completely exact, have made great strides in accuracy as well as ease of use.

The voice-in or speech recognition approach can almost fully replace the keyboard and mouse. Speech recognition can now open the computer world to those who may have been restricted due to a physical handicap. It can also be a boon for those who have never learned to type.

OUTPUT DEVICES

Output is anything that comes out of a computer. An output device is capable of presenting information from a computer. There are many output devices attached with the computers. But the monitors and printers are commonly used output devices.

Monitors

Monitor is a commonly used output device, sometimes called as display screen. It provides a visual display of data. Monitors are connected with the computer and are similar in appearance to a television set.

Fig. Monitor

Initially there were only monochrome monitors. But

gradually, we have monitors that display colour. Monitors display images and text. The smallest dot that can be displayed is called a pixel (picture element) The resolution of the screen improves as the number of pixels is increased. Most of the monitors have a 4: 3 width to height ratio. This is called 'aspect ratio'. The number of pixels that can be displayed vertically and horizontally gives the resolution of the monitor.

The resolution of the monitor determines the quality of the display. Some popular resolutions are 640 x 480 pixels, 800 x 600 pixels and 1024 x 768 pixels. A resolution of 1024 x 768 pixels will produce sharper image than 640 x 480 pixels.

Printers

Printer is an output device that prints text or images on paper or other media (like transparencies). By printing we create what is known as a 'hard copy'. There are different kinds of printers, which vary in their speed and print quality. The two main types of printers are impact printers and non-impact printers.

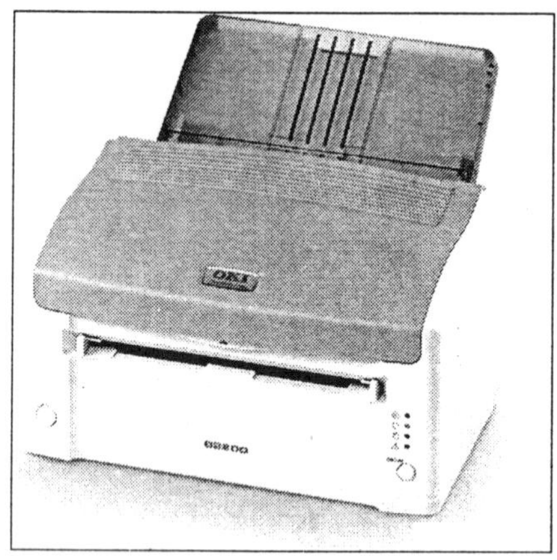

Fig. Printer

Types of Printers

Impact printers include all printers that print by striking an ink ribbon. Impact printers use a print head containing a number of metal pins which strike an inked ribbon placed between the print head and the paper.

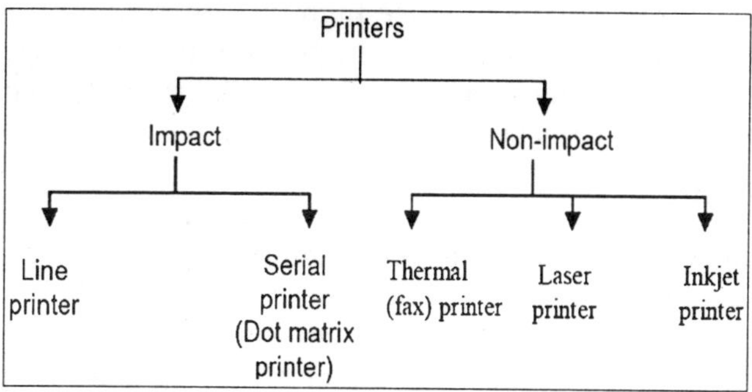

Line printers, dotmatrix printers are some of the impact printers.

Characteristics of Impact Printers

- In impact printers, there is physical contact with the paper to produce an image.
- Due to being robust and low cost, they are useful for bulk printing.
- Impact printers are ideal for printing multiple copies (that is, carbon copies) because they can easily print through many layers of paper.
- Due to its striking activity, impact printers are very noisy.
- Since they are mechanical in nature, they tend to be slow.
- Impact printers do not support transparencies.

Non-impact printers are much quieter than impact printers as their printing heads do not strike the paper. Non-impact printers include laser printers, inkjet printers and thermal printers.

Characteristics of Non-Impact Printers

- Non-impact printers are faster than impact printers because they have fewer moving parts.
- They are quiet than impact printers because there is no striking mechanism involved.

- They posses the ability to change typefaces automatically.
- These printers produce high-quality graphics
- These printers usually support the transparencies
- These printers cannot print multipart forms because no impact is being made on the paper.

Line Printer

Line printers are high-speed printers capable of printing an entire line at a time. A line printer can print 150 lines to 3000 lines per minute. The limitations of line printer are they can print only one font, they cannot print graphics, the print quality is low and they are noisy to operate. But it can print large volume of text data very fast compared to the other printers. It is also used to print on multipart stationaries to prepare copies of a document.

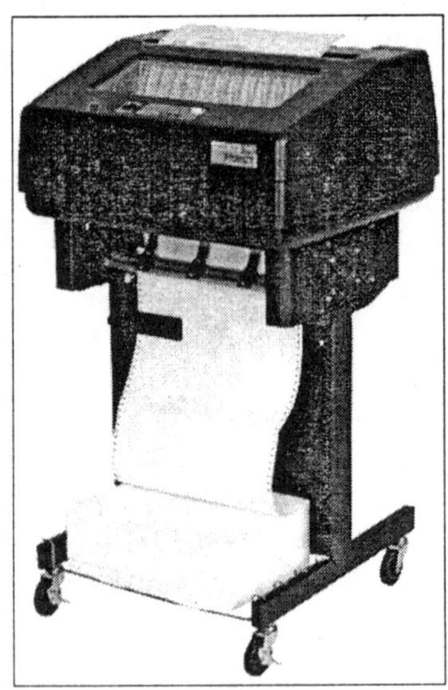

Fig. Line Printer

Dot Matrix Printer

The most popular serial printer is the dot matrix printer.

It prints one line of 8 or 14 points at a time, with print head moving across a line. They are similar to typewriters. They are normally slow. The printing speed is around 300 characters per second. It uses multipart stationaries to prepare copies of a document.

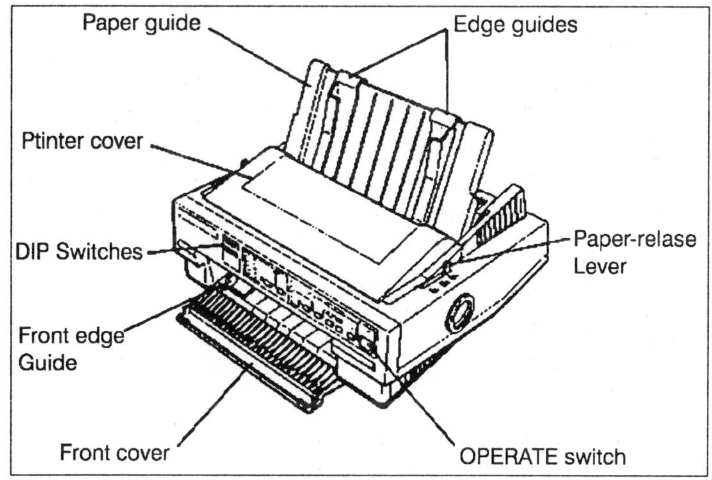

Fig. Dot Matrix Printer

Thermal Printer

Thermal printers are printers that produce images by pushing electrically heated pins against special heat-sensitive paper. They are inexpensive and used widely in fax machines and calculators

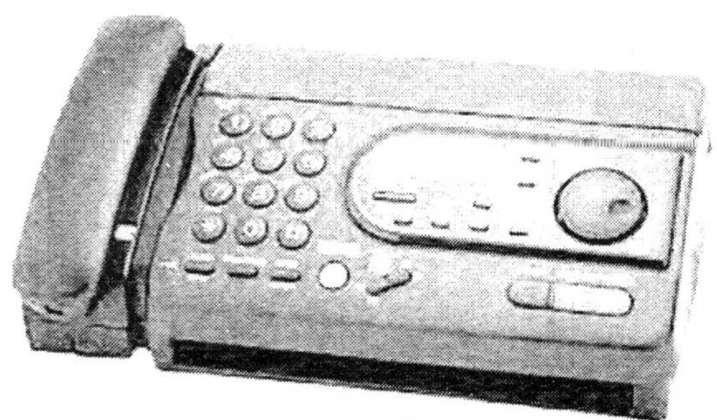

Fig. Thermal Printer

Thermal printer paper tends to darken over time due to exposure to sunlight and heat. So the printed matters on the paper fade after a week or two. It also produces a poor quality print.

Laser Printers

Laser printers use a laser beam and dry powdered ink to produce a fine dot matrix pattern. It can produce very good quality of graphic images. One of the chief characteristics of laser printers is their resolution - how many dots per inch (dpi) they lay down. The available resolutions range from 300 dpi at the low end to around 1200 dpi at the high end.

Fig. Laser Printer

Inkjet Printers

Inkjet printers use colour cartridges which combine magenta, yellow and cyan inks to create colour tones.

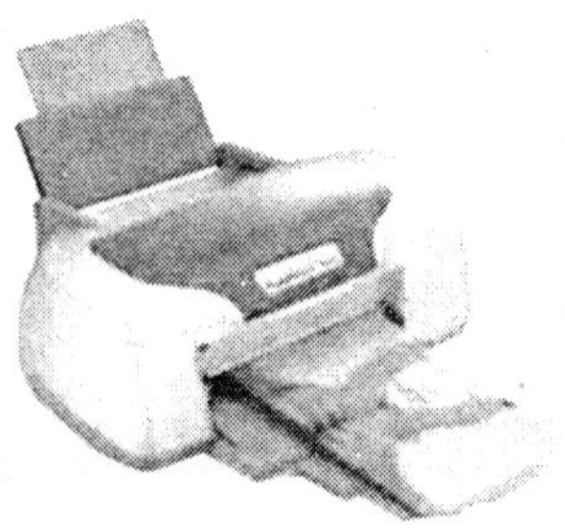

Fig. Inkjet Printer

A black cartridge is also used for crisp monochrome output. Inkjet printers work by spraying ionizing ink at a sheet of paper. Magnetized plates in the ink's path direct the ink onto the paper in the described shape.

Speakers

The computer can also give produce voice output(audio data). Speaker serves as a voice output device. Using speakers along with speech synthesizer software, the computer can provide voice output. Voice output has become very common in many places like airlines, banks, automatic telephone enquiry system etc. Users can also hear music/songs using the voice output system.

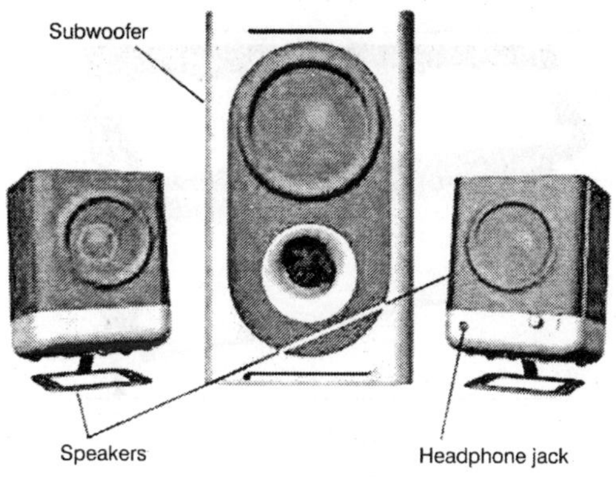

Fig. Speakers

STORAGE DEVICES

The computer may need to store data, programs etc. in a computer readable medium. This is called the secondary storage. Secondary storage is also called backup storage. Secondary storage can be used to transmit data to another computer either immediately or a latter time. This provides a mechanism for storing a large amount of data for a long period of time. Some of the commonly used storage devices are hard disks, magnetic tapes, floppy disks and CD-ROM.

To understand the physical mechanism of secondary storage devices one must have knowledge of magnetism, electronics and electro mechanical systems. The average time required to reach a storage location and obtain its contents is called its access time. In electromechanical devices with moving parts such as disks and tapes, the access time consists of a seek time required to position the read write head to a location and transfer time required to transfer the data to or from the device.

Plotters

Apart from the output devices like printers, plotters are also used to produce graphical output. Although printer output is very convenient for many purposes, the user needs to present the information graphically in order to understand its significance.

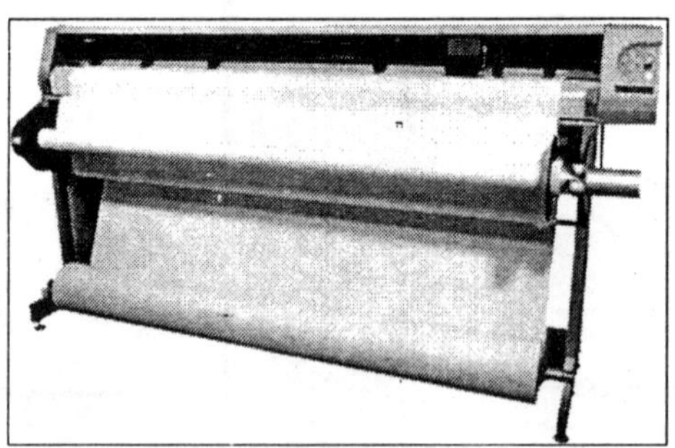

Fig. Plotters

HARD DISK

Hard disk is a magnetic disk on which we can store computer data. The hard disk is a direct-access storage medium. This means we can store and retrieve data randomly. Disk storage systems are essentially based on magnetic properties. The magnetic disk consists of high speed rotating surfaces coated with a magnetic recording medium. The rotating surface of the disk is a round flat plate.

When writing data, a write head magnetizes the particles on the disk surface as either north or south poles. When reading data, a read head converts the magnetic polarisations on the disk surface to a sequence of pulses. The read and write heads are generally combined into a single head unit. There may be more than one read/write head.

Data is arranged as a series of concentric rings. Each ring (called a track) is subdivided into a number of sectors, each sector holding a specific number of data elements (bytes or characters).

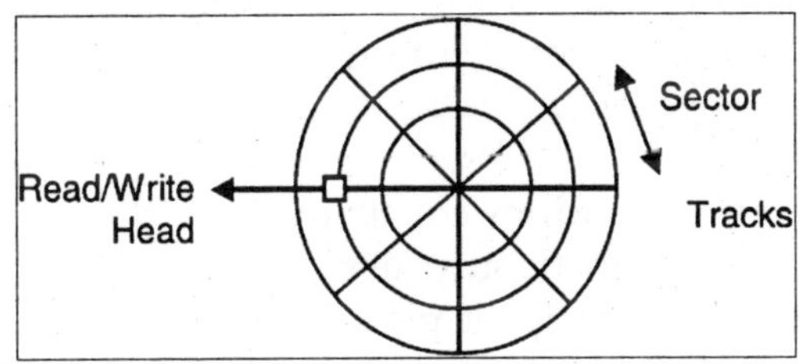

Fig. A Track Subdivided Into Sectors

The smallest unit that can be written to or read from the disk is a sector. Once a read or write request has been received by the disk unit, there is a delay involved until the required sector reaches the read/write head. This is known as rotational latency, and on average is one half of the period of revolution.

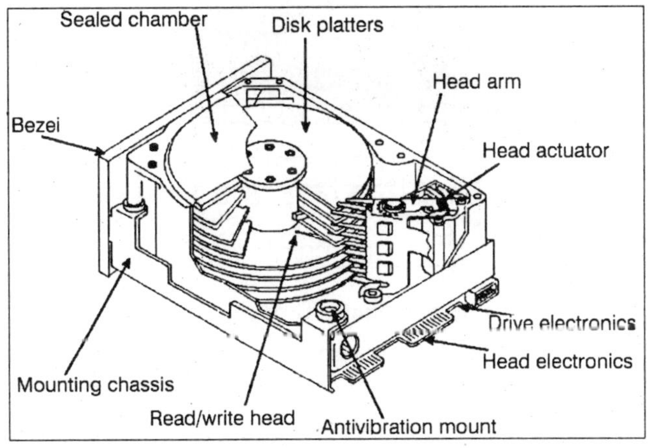

Fig. Hard Disk Drive

The storage capacity of the disk is determined as (number of tracks *number of sectors* bytes per sector * number of read/ write heads) Thus,the data is stored as magnetized spots arranged in concentric circles (tracks) on the disk. Each track is divided into sectors. The arrangement of tracks and sectors on a disk is known as its 'format'.

High data rates demand that the disk rotates at a high speed (about 3,600 rpm). As the disk rotates read/write heads move to the correct track and fetch the desired data. The storage capacity of a hard disk can be Gigabytes (GB), i.e. thousands of Megabytes of information.

Magnetic Tape

A recording medium consisting of a thin tape with a coating of a fine magnetic strip, used for recording digital data. The tape itself is a strip of plastic coated with a magnetic recording medium.

Fig. Magenatic Tape Reader

Bits are recorded as magnetic spots on the tape along several tracks. Usually, seven or nine bits are recorded simultaneously to form a character together with a parity bit. Read/write heads are mounted one in each track so that data can be recorded and read as a sequence of characters.

Data is stored in frames across the width of the tape. The frames are grouped into blocks or records which are separated from other blocks by gaps.

Magnetic tape is a serial access medium, similar to an audio cassette, and so data cannot be randomly located. This characteristic has prompted its use in the regular backing up of hard disks.

Floppy Disk

Fig. Floppy Disk

The floppy drive uses a thin circular disk for data storage. It is a soft magnetic disk. It is a thin magnetic-coated disk contained in a flexible or semi-rigid protective jacket. The disk rotates at 360rpm. A read/write head makes physical contact with the disk surface. Data is recorded as a series of tracks subdivided into sectors. The floppy disks are usually 3.5" in size. However, older floppy disks may be in use; these would be 5.25" in size or even 8" in size. A 3.5" floppy disk can hold 1.44 MB of data. Once data is stored on a floppy disk it can be 'write protected' by clicking a tab on the disk.

This prevents any new data being stored or any old data being erased. Disk drives for floppy disks are called floppy drives. Floppy disks are slower to access than hard disks and have less storage capacity. It is less expensive and are portable.

Optical Disk

Optical disks are a storage medium from which data is read and to which it is written by lasers. The optical disk is a random access storage medium; information can be easily read from any point on the disk. CD-ROM stands for Compact Disk - Read Only Memory.

Fig. Compact Disk

It is now possible to have CD-ROMs where tracks of information can be written onto them by the user. These are called read/write CD-ROMs and these are becoming a popular and cheap method for storage.

Chapter 4

Working Principle of Digital Logic

LOGIC GATES

A logic gate is an elementary building block of a digital circuit. It is a circuit with one output and one or more inputs. At any given moment, logic gate takes one of the two binary conditions low (0) or high (1), represented by different voltage levels.

A voltage level will represent each of the two logic values. For example +5V might represent a logic 1 and 0V might represent a logic 0.

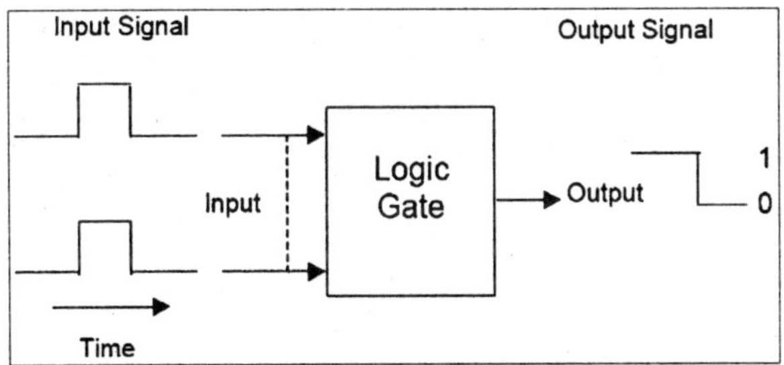

This diagram which represents a logic gate accept input signals (two or more) and produces an output signal based on the type of the gate. The input signal takes values '1' or '0'. The output signal also gives in the value '1' or '0'.

There are three fundamental logic gates namely, and, or and not. Also we have other logic gates like Nand, Nor, XOR and XNOR. Out of these Nand and Nor gates are called the universal gates, because the fundamental logic gates can be realized Through them. The circuit symbol and the truth table of these logic gates are explained here.

AND Gate

The AND gate is so named because, if 0 is called "false" and 1 is called "true," the gate acts in the same way as the logical "AND" operator. The output is "true" only when both inputs are "true", otherwise, the output is "false". In other words the output will be 1 if and only if both inputs are 1; otherwise the output is 0.

The output of the AND gate is represented by a variable say C, where A and B are two and if input boolean variables. In boolean algebra, a variable can take either of the values '0' or '1'. The logical symbol of the AND gate is:

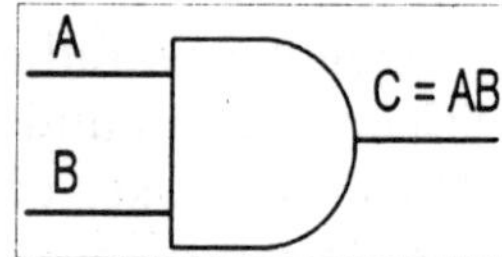

Fig. Logic symbol of AND Gate

One way to symbolize the action of an AND gate is by writing the boolean function.

C = A AND B

In boolean algebra the multiplication sign stands for the AND operation. Therefore, the output of the AND gate is C = A. B or simply C = AB. Read this as "C equals A AND B". Since there are two input variables here, the truth table has four entries, because there are four possible inputs: 00, 01, 10 and 11. For instance, if both inputs are 0,

$$C = A.B$$
$$= 0.\ 0$$
$$= 0$$

The truth table for and Gate is

Table: Truth Table for AND Gate

Input		*Output*
A	B	C
0	0	0
0	1	0
1	0	0
1	1	1

OR Gate

The OR gate gets its name from the fact that it behaves like the logical inclusive "OR". The output is "true" if either or both of the inputs are "true". If both inputs are "false," then the output is "false". In otherwords the output will be 1 if and only if one or both inputs are 1; otherwise, the output is 0. The logical symbol of the OR gate is

Fig. Logic symbol of or Gate

The OR gate output is

$$C = A \text{ OR } B$$

We use the + sign to denote the OR function. Therefore,

$$C = A + B$$

Read this as "C equals A OR B".

For instance, if both the inputs are 1

$$C = A + B = 1 + 1 = 1$$

The truth table for OR gate is

Table: Truth Table for or Gate

Input		*Output*
A	B	C
0	0	0
0	1	1
1	0	1
1	1	1

OT Gate

The not gate, called a logical inverter, has only one input. It reverses the logical state. In other words the output C is always the complement of the input. The logical symbol of the not gate is:

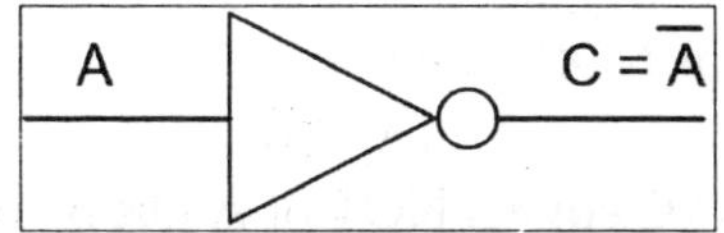

Fig. Logic symbol of not Gate

The boolean function of the NOT gate is C = NOT A

In boolean algebra, the overbar stands for NOT operation. Therefore,. $C = \overline{A}$

Read this as "C equals NOT A" or "C equals the complement of A".

If A is 0,

$$C = \overline{0} = 1$$

On the otherhand, if A is 1,

$$C = \overline{1} = 0$$

The truth table for NOT gate is

Table: Truth Table for NOT Gate

Input	*Output*
A	C
1	0
0	1

NOR Gate

The NOR gate circuit is an OR gate followed by an inverter. Its output is "true" if both inputs are "false" Otherwise, the output is "false".

In other words, the only way to get '1' as output is to have both inputs '0'. Otherwise the output is 0. The logic circuit of the NOR gate is

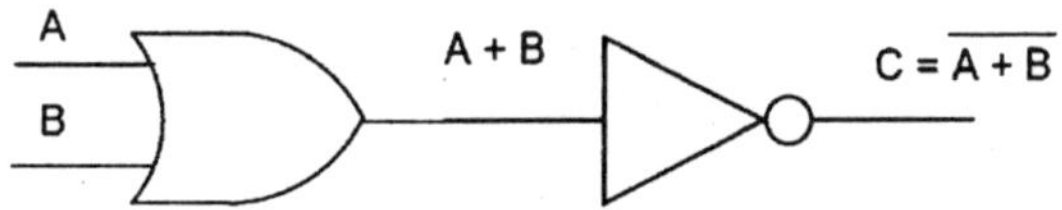

Fig. Logic Ciruit of nor Gate

Fig. Logic Sumbol of nor Gate

The output of NOR gate is

$$C = \overline{(A + B)}$$

Read this as "C equals NOT of A OR B" or "C equals the complement of A OR B"

For example if both the inputs are 0,

$$C = \overline{(0+0)} = \overline{0} = 1$$

The truth table for NOR gate is

Table: Truth Table for NOR Gate

Input		*Output*
A	B	C
0	0	1
0	1	0
1	0	0
1	1	0

Bubbled AND Gate

The Logic Circuit of Bubbled and Gate

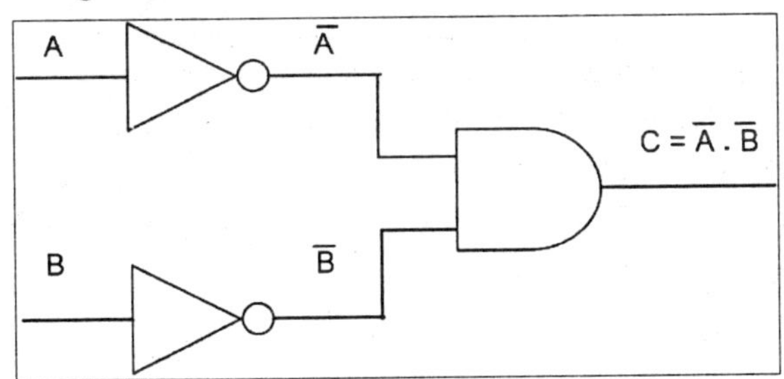

Fig. Logic Circuit of Bubbled and Gate

In the above circuit, invertors on the input lines of the and gate gives the output as

$$C = \overline{A} . \overline{B}$$

This circuit can be redrawn as the bubbles on the inputs, where the bubbles represent inversion

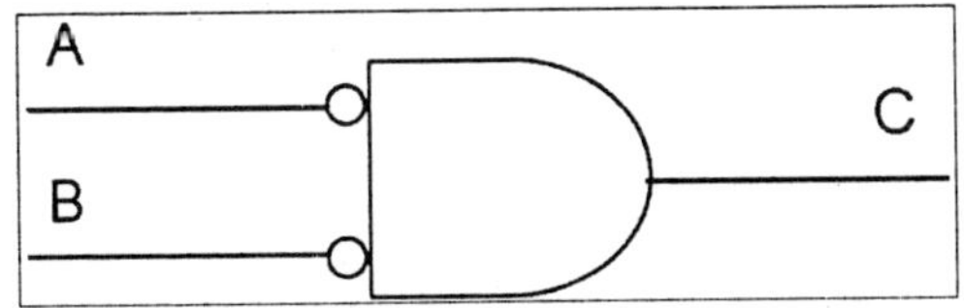

Fig. Logic Symbol of Bubbled and Gate

We refer this as bubbled and gate. Let us analyse this logic circuit for all input possibilities.

If A = 0 and B = 0 $C = (\bar{0} . \bar{0}) = 1. 1 = 1$

If A = 0 and B = 1 $C = (\bar{0} . \bar{1}) = 1. 0 = 0$

If A = 1 and B = 0 $C = (\bar{1} . \bar{0}) = 0. 1 = 0$

If A = 1 and B = 1 $C = (\bar{1} . \bar{1}) = 0. 0 = 0$

Here the truth table is

Table: Truth Table for Bubble and Gate

Input		*Output*
A	B	C
0	0	1
0	1	0
1	0	0
1	1	0

We can see that, a bubbled and gate produces the same output as a NOR gate. So, we can replace each NOR gate by a bubbled and gate. In other words the circuits are interchangeable. Therefore $(\overline{A + B}) = \bar{A} . \bar{B}$ which establishes the De Morgan's first theorem.

NAND Gate

The NAND gate operates as an AND gate followed by a NOT gate. It acts in the manner of the logical operation "AND" followed by inversion. The output is "false" if both inputs are "true", otherwise, the output is "true". In otherwords the output of the NAND gate is 0 if and only if both the inputs are 1, otherwise the output is 1. The logic circuit of NAND gate is

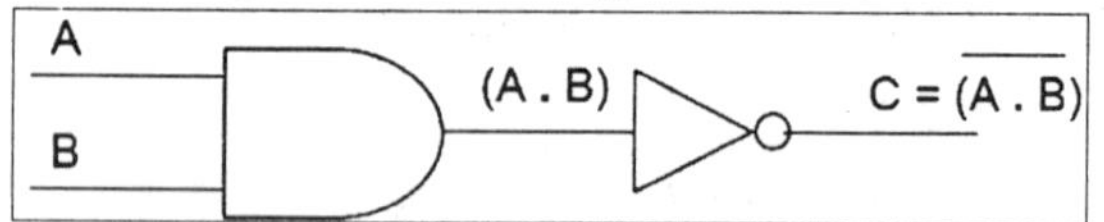

Fig. Logic Circuit of NAND Gate

The logical symbol of NAND gate is

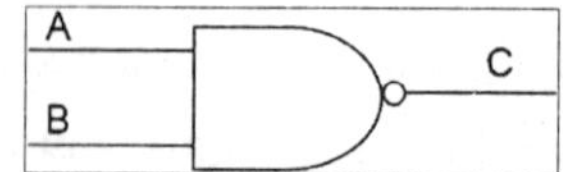

Fig. Logic Symbol of NAND Gate

The output of the NAND gate is

$$C = \left(\overline{A \, . \, B}\right)$$

Read this as "C equals NOT of A AND B" or "C equals the complement of A AND B".

For example if both the inputs are 1

$$C = \left(\overline{1 \, . \, 1}\right) = \bar{1} = 0$$

The truth table for nand gate is

Table: Truth Table for NAND Gate

Input		*Output*
A	B	C
0	0	1
0	1	1
1	0	1
1	1	0

Bubbled OR Gate

The logic circuit of bubbled OR gate is

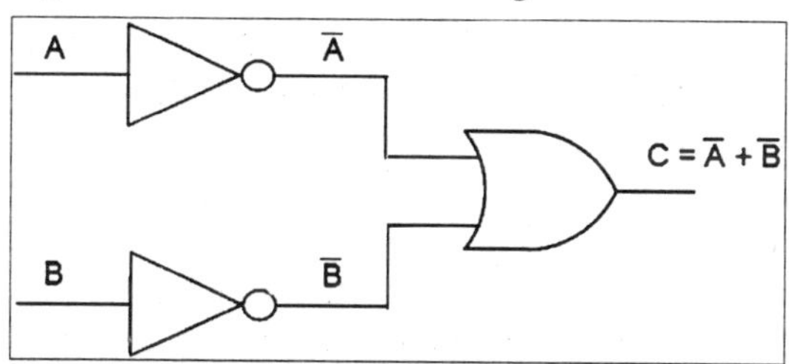

Fig. Logic Circuit of Bubbled OR Gate

The output of this circuit can be written as

$$C = \overline{A} + \overline{B}$$

The above circuit can be redrawn as the bubbles on the input, where the bubbles represents the inversion.

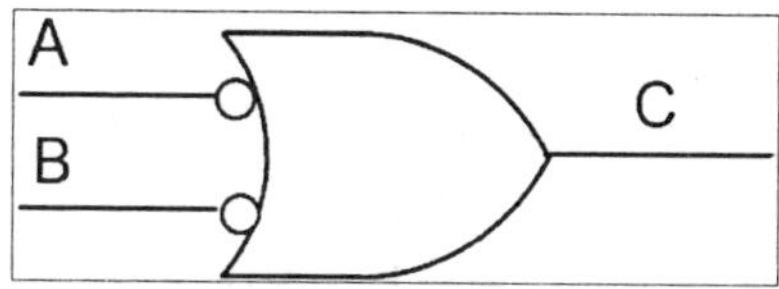

Fig. Logic Symbol of Bubbled or Gate

We refer this as bubbled OR gate. The truth table for the bubbled OR is

Table: Truth Table for Bubbled or Gate

Input		*Output*
A	B	C
0	0	1
0	1	1
1	0	1
1	1	0

If we compare the truth tables of the bubbled OR gate with NAND gate, they are identical. So the circuits are interchangeable.

Therefore $\left(\overline{A \,.\, B}\right) = \overline{A} + \overline{B}$ which establishes the De Morgan's second theorem.

XOR Gate

The XOR (exclusive-OR) gate acts in the same way as the logical "either/or." The output is "true" if either, but not both, of the inputs are "true."

The output is "false" if both inputs are "false" or if both inputs are "true."

Another way of looking at this circuit is to observe that the output is 1 if the inputs are different, but 0 if the inputs are the same. The logic circuit of XOR gate is;

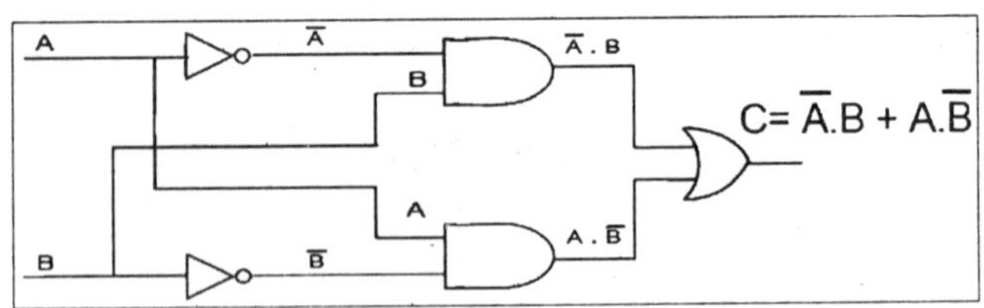

Fig. Logic Circuit of XOR Gate

The output of the XOR gate is

$$C = \overline{A}\,B + A\,\overline{B}$$

The truth table for XOR gate is

Table: Truth Table for XOR Gate

Input		*Output*
A	B	C
0	0	0
0	1	1
1	0	1
1	1	0

In boolean algebra, exclusive-OR operator is ⊕ or "encircled plus".

Hence, $C = A \oplus B$

The logical symbol of XOR gate is

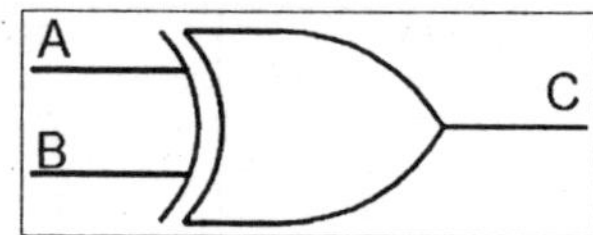

Fig. Logic Symbol of XOR Gate

XNOR Gate

The XNOR (exclusive-NOR) gate is a combination XOR gate followed by an inverter. Its output is "true" if the inputs are the same, and "false" if the inputs are different. In simple words, the output is 1 if the input are the same, otherwise the output is 0. The logic circuit of XNOR gate is

The output of the XNOR is NOT of XOR

$$C = \overline{A \oplus B}$$

$$= \overline{\bar{A}.B + A.B}$$

$$= AB + \bar{A}\bar{B} \qquad \text{(Using De Morgan's Theorem)}$$

In boolean algebra, or "included dot" stands for the XNOR.

Therefore, $C = A \odot B$

The logical symbol is

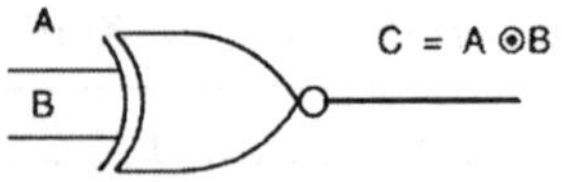

A
B
C = A ⊙B

Fig. Logic Symbol of XNOR Gate

Using combinations of logic gates, complex operations can be performed. In theory, there is no limit to the number of gates that can be arranged together in a single device. But in practice, there is a limit to the number of gates that can be packed into a given physical space. Arrays of logic gates are found in digital integrated circuits. The logic gates and their corresponding truth tables are summarized in the following table.

Table: Summary of Logic Gates

Logical Gates	*Symbol*	*Truth Table*
AND	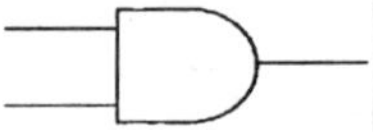	A B AB 0 0 0 0 1 0 1 0 0 1 1 1
OR		A B A+B 0 0 0 0 1 1 1 0 1 1 1 1
NOT	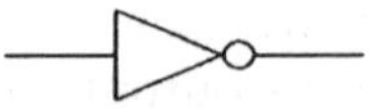	A $\overline{A}$ 0 1 1 0
NAND	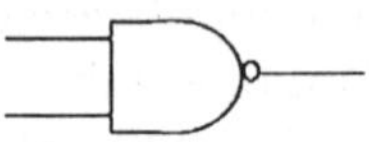	A B $\overline{AB}$ 0 0 1 0 1 1 1 0 1 1 1 0
NOR	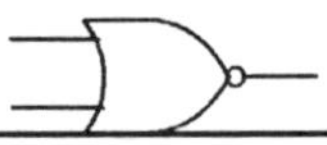	A B $\overline{A+B}$ 0 0 1 0 1 0 1 0 0 1 1 0
XOR	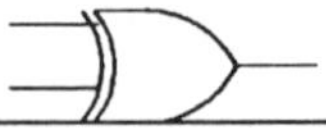	A B A+B 0 0 0 0 1 1 1 0 1 1 1 0
XNOR	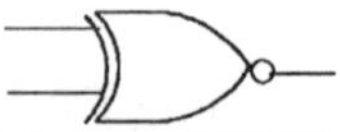	A B A B 0 0 1 0 1 0 1 0 0 1 1 1

Universality of NAND and NOR gates

We know that all boolean functions can be expressed in terms of the fundamental gates namely AND, OR and NOT.

In fact, these fundamental gates can be expressed in terms of either NAND gates or NOR gates. NAND gates can be used to implement the fundamental logic gates NOT, AND and OR. Here A and B denote the logical states (Input).

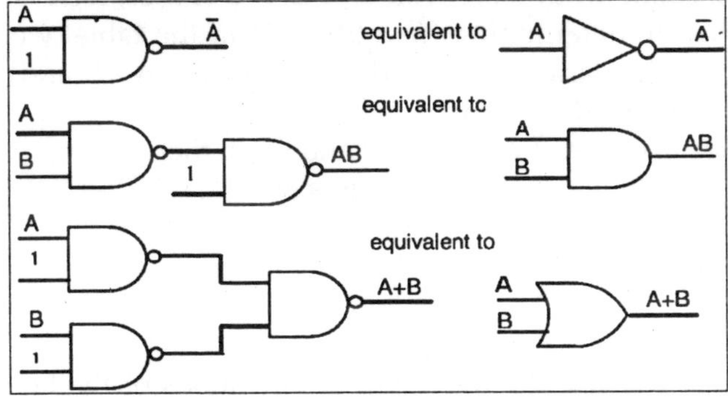

Fig. Universality of NAND Gates

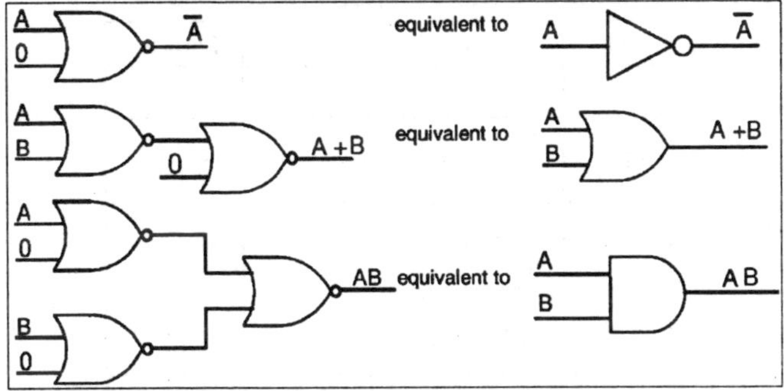

Fig. Universality of NOR Gates

CONVERSION OF BOOLEAN FUNCTION

To build more complicated boolean functions, we use the AND, OR, and NOT operators and combine them together.

Also, it is possible to convert back and forth between the three representations of a boolean function (equation, truth table, and logic circuit). The following examples show how this is done.

Converting a Boolean Equation to a Truth Table

Truth table lists all the values of the boolean function for each set of values of the variables. Now we will obtain a truth table for the following boolean function

$$D = (A \cdot B) + \overline{C}$$

Clearly, D is a function of three input variables *A*, *B*, and C. Hence the truth table will have $2^3 = 8$ entries, from 000 to 111. Before determining the output D in the table, we will compute the various intermediate terms like $A \cdot B$ and $\overline{C}$ as shown in the table below.

For instance, if A = 0, B = 0 and C = 0 then

$$\begin{aligned} D &= (A.\ B) + \overline{C} \\ &= (0.\ 0) + \overline{0} \\ &= 0 + \overline{0} \\ &= 0 + 1 \\ &= 1 \end{aligned}$$

Here we use the hierarchy of operations of the boolean operators NOT, AND and OR over the parenthesis.

The truth table for the boolean function is

Input			*Intermediate*		*Output*
A	B	C	A • B	$\overline{C}$	D
0	0	0	0	1	1
0	0	1	0	0	0
0	1	0	0	1	1
0	1	1	0	0	0
1	0	0	0	1	1
1	0	1	0	0	0
1	1	0	1	1	1
1	1	1	1	0	1

Converting a Boolean Equation to a Logic Circuit

The boolean function is realized as a logic circuit by suitably arranging the logic gates to give the desired output for a given set of input.

Any boolean function may be realized using the three logical operations NOT, AND and OR. Using gates we can realise boolean function. Now we will draw the logic circuit for the boolean function.

$$E = \overline{A} + \left(B \cdot \overline{C}\right) + \overline{D}$$

This boolean function has four inputs A, B, C, D and an output E. The output E is obtained by ORing the individual terms given in the right side of the boolean function. That is, by ORing the terms

$$\overline{A}, (B \cdot \overline{C}) \text{ and } \overline{D}.$$

The first term $\overline{A}$, which is the complement of the given inputA, is realized by

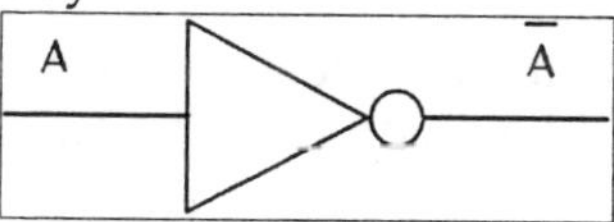

The second term is $(B \cdot \overline{C})$. Here the complement of C is AND with B. The logic circuit is realized by

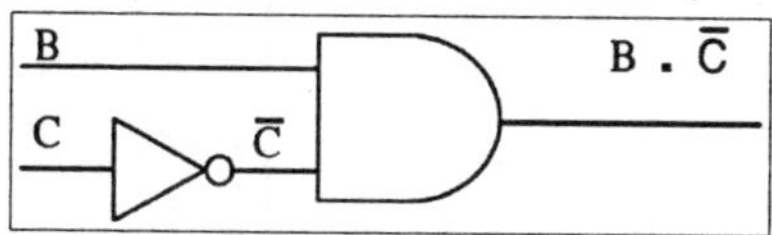

The third term, which is the complement of D is realized by

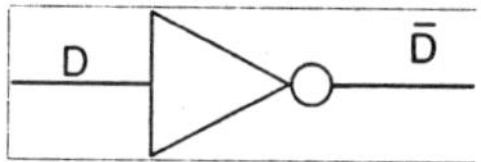

The output D is realized by ORing the output of the three terms. Hence the logic circuit of the boolean equation is

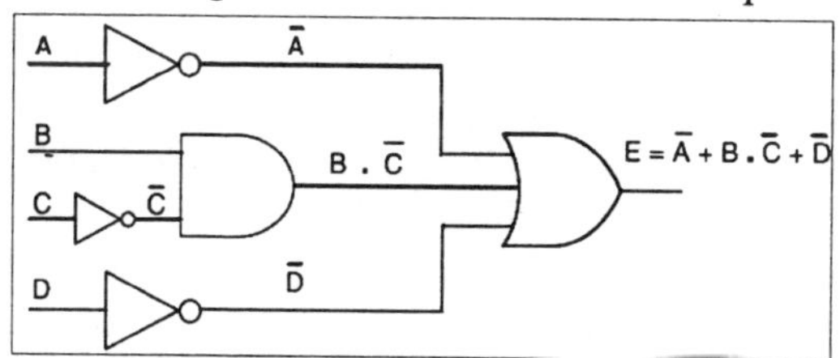

Converting a Logic Circuit to a Boolean Function

As a reversal operation, the realization of the logic circuit can be expressed as a boolean function. Let us formulate an expression for the output in terms of the inputs for the given the logic circuit To solve this, we simply start from left and work towards the right, identifying and labeling each of the signals that we encounter until we arrive at the expression for the output.

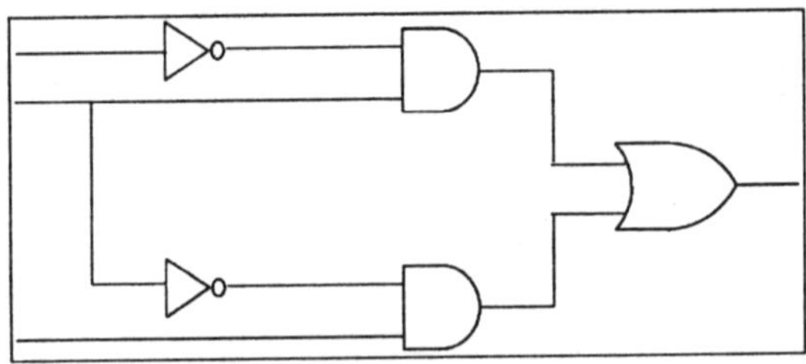

The labeling of all the signals is shown in the figure below. Let us label the input signals as A, B, C and the output as D.

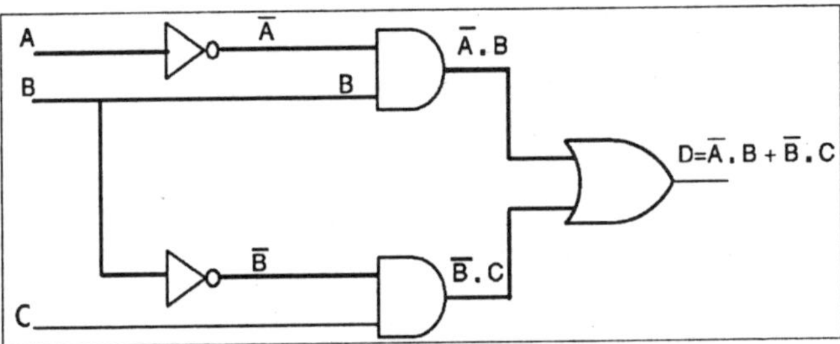

Hence the boolean function corresponding to the logic circuit can be written as.

$$D = \overline{A} \bullet B + \overline{B} \bullet C$$

Converting a Truth Table to a Boolean Function

There are many ways to do this conversion. A simplest way is to write the boolean function as an OR of minterms. A minterm is simply the ANDing of all variables, and assigning bars (NOT) to variables whose values are 0.

For example, assuming the inputs to a 4-variable boolean function as A, B, C, and D the minterm corresponding to the input 1010 is: $A \bullet \overline{B} \bullet C \bullet \overline{D}$.

Notice that this minterm is simply the AND of all four variables, with B and D complemented. The reason that B and D are complemented is because for this input, B = D = 0. As another example, for the input 1110, only D = 0, and so the corresponding minterm is $A \bullet B \bullet C \bullet \overline{D}$.;

- For example let us write a boolean function for the following truth table

Input			*Output*
A	B	C	D
0	0	0	1
0	0	1	0
0	1	0	1
0	1	1	0
1	0	0	1
1	0	1	0
1	1	0	1
1	1	1	0

- To do this problem, we first circle all of the rows in the truth table which have an output D = 1. Then for each cirlced row, we write the corresponding minterm. This is illustrated in the table below.

Input			*Output*	
A	B	C	D	Minterms
0	0	0	1	$\bar{A} \bullet \bar{B} \bullet \bar{C}$
0	0	1	0	
0	1	0	1	$\bar{A} \bullet B \bullet \bar{C}$
0	1	1	0	
1	0	0	1	$A \bullet \bar{B} \bullet \bar{C}$
1	0	1	0	
1	1	0	1	$A \bullet B \bullet \bar{C}$
1	1	1	0	

Finally, the boolean expression for D is obtained by Oring all of the minterms as follows:

$$D = (\bar{A} \cdot \bar{B} \cdot \bar{C}) + (\bar{A} \cdot B \cdot \bar{C}) + (A \cdot \bar{B} \cdot \bar{C}) + (A \cdot B \cdot \bar{C})$$

Design of Logic Circuit

There are many steps in designing a logic circuit. First, the problem is stated (in words). Second, from the word description, the inputs and outputs are identified, and a block diagram is drawn. Third, a truth table is formulated which shows the output of the system for every possible input. Fourth, the truth table is converted to a boolean function. Fifth, the boolean function is converted to a logic circuit diagram. Finally, the logic circuit is built and tested.

Let us consider the design aspects of a 2-input/single output system which operates as follows: The output is 1 if and only if precisely one of the inputs is 1; otherwise, the output is 0.

Step 1: Statement of the problem. Given above.

Step 2: Identify inputs and outputs. It is clear from the statement of the problem that we need two inputs, say A and B, and one output, say C. A block diagram for this system is:

Step 3: Formulate truth table. The truth table for this problem is given below. Notice that the output is 1 if only one of the inputs is 1. otherwise the output is '0'.

Input		*Output*
A	B	C
0	0	0
0	1	1
1	0	1
1	1	0

Step 4: Convert the truth table to a boolean function. Identify the minterms for the rows in the truth table which have an output '1'

Input		*Output*	*Minterm*
A	B	C	
0	0	0	
0	1	1	A B
1	0	1	A B
1	1	0	

By ORing the minterms, we obtain the boolean function corresponding to the truth table as

$$D = (\overline{A} \bullet B) + (A \bullet \overline{B})$$

Step 5: Realization of the Boolean function into a Logic Circuit Diagram. The logic circuit diagram corresponding to this boolean function is given below.

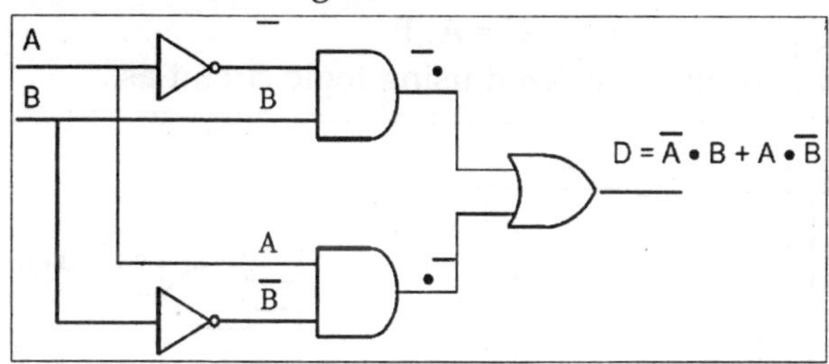

Half Adder

The circuit that performs addition within the Arithmetic and Logic Unit of the CPU are called adders. A unit that adds two binary digits is called a half adder and the one that adds together three binary digits is called a full adder.

A half adder sums two binary digits to give a sum and a carry. This simple addition consists of four possible operations.

$$0 + 0 = 0$$
$$0 + 1 = 1$$
$$1 + 0 = 1$$
$$1 + 1 = 10$$

The first three operations produce a single digit sum, while the fourth one produces two digit sum. The higher significant bit in this operation is called a carry. So the carry of the first three operations are '0', where the fourth one produces a carry '1'.

The boolean realization of binary addition is shown in the truth table. Here A and B are inputs to give a sum S and a carry C

Input		*Sum*	*Minterms*	*Carry*	*Minterms*
A	B	S	of S	C	of C
0	0	0	–	0	
0	1	1	$\overline{A}.B$	0	
1	0	1	$A.\overline{B}$	0	
1	1	0		1	A.B

The boolean functions corresponding to the sum and carry are

$$S = \overline{A} \cdot B + A \cdot \overline{B}$$
$$C = A.\ B$$

Which can be realized using logic circuit as,

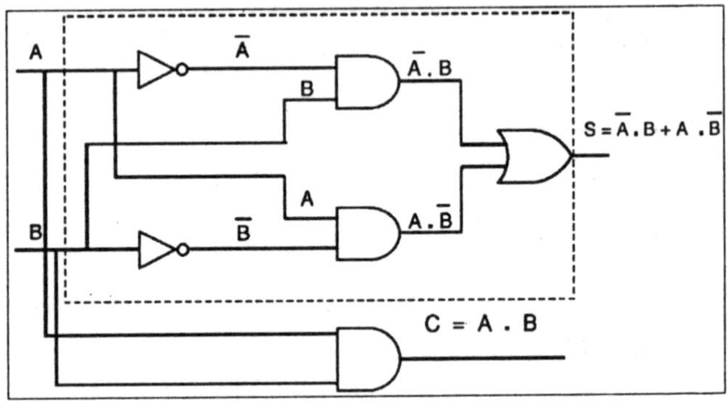

Fig. Logic Circuit of Half Adder

whic is further simplified as

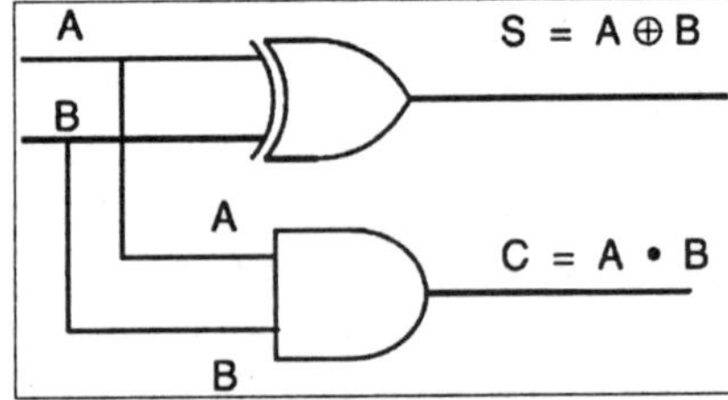

In a half adder, an AND gate is added in parallel to the XOR gate to generate the carry and sum respectively. The 'sum' column of the truth table represents the output of the XOR gate and the 'carry' column represents the output of the AND gate.

Full Adder

A half adder logic circuit is a very important component of computing systems. As this circuit cannot accept a carry bit from a previous addition, it is not enough to fully peform additions for binary number greater than 1.

In order to achieve this a full adder is required. A full adder sums three input bits. It consists of three inputs and two outputs. Two of the inputs represent the two significant bits to be added and the third one represents the carry from the previous significant position.

Here A, B referred as the inputs, C1 as carry input from the previous stage, C2 as carry output and S as sum.

Table: Truth Table for Full Adder

Input			*Output*	
A	B	C_1	C_2	S
0	0	0	1	0
0	0	1	0	1
0	1	0	0	1
0	1	1	1	0
1	0	0	0	1
1	0	1	1	0
1	1	0	1	0
1	1	1	1	1

The carry bit C_2 is 1 if both *A* and *B* are 1, or exactly one of *A* and *B* is 1 and the input carry, C_1 is 1. The sum bit *S* is 1 if there exist odd number of '1's of the three inputs. S is the XOR of the three inputs. Hence, the full adder can be realized as shown below. By ORing the minterms of the full adder truth table, the sum and carry can be written as

$$S = \bar{A}\bar{B}C_1 + \bar{A}B\overline{C_1} + A\bar{B}\overline{C_1} + ABC_1$$

$$C_2 = \bar{A}\bar{B}C_1 + A\bar{B}C_1 + AB\overline{C_1} + ABC_1$$

Consider

$$(A \oplus B) \oplus C_1 = (\bar{A}B + A\bar{B}) \oplus C_1$$

$$= \overline{(\bar{A}B + A\bar{B})}C_1 + (\bar{A}B + A\bar{B})\bar{C}_1$$

$$= \left(\overline{(\bar{A}B)} + \overline{(A\bar{B})}\right)C_1 + (\bar{A}B + A\bar{B})\bar{C}_1$$

$$= ((A+\bar{B})+(\bar{A}+B))C_1 + (\bar{A}B + A\bar{B})\overline{C_1}$$

$$= \cancel{A\bar{A}C_1} + ABC_1 + \bar{A}\bar{B}C_1 + \cancel{B\bar{B}C_1} + \bar{A}B\overline{C_1} + A\bar{B}\overline{C_1}$$

(Since, $A\bar{A} = B\bar{B} = 0$) $= S$

Also

$$C_2 = \overline{A}BC_1 + A\overline{B}C_1 + AB\overline{C_1} + ABC_1$$
$$= (\overline{A}B + A\overline{B})C_1 + AB(C_1 + \overline{C_1})$$
$$= (A \oplus B)C_1 + AB$$

Hence

$$S = (A \oplus B) \oplus C_1 \text{and}$$
$$C_2 = (A \oplus B)C_1 + AB$$

To realise the full adder we need two 2-input XOR, two 2-input AND gates and a 2-input OR gate.

Hence the full adder can be realized as.

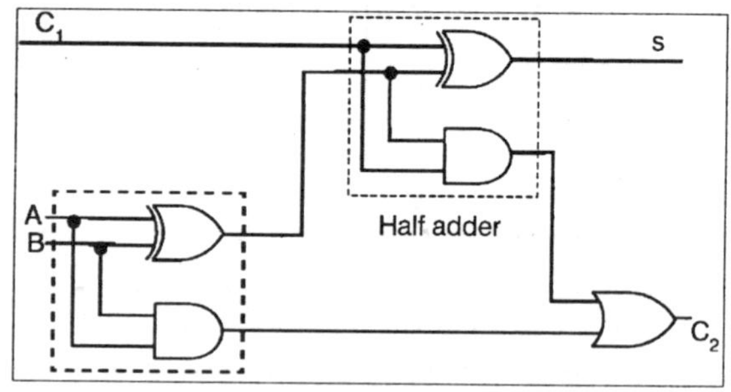

Fig. Logic Circuit of Full Adder

Notice that the full adder can be constructed from two half adders and an OR gate. If the logic circuit outputs are based on the inputs presented at that time, then they are called combinational circuit.

The half adder and full adder circuits are the examples for the combinational circuits. On the other hand, if the logic circuit outputs are based on, not only the inputs presented at that time, but also the previous state output, then they are called sequential circuits.

There are two main types of sequential circuits. A synchronous sequential circuit is a system whose output can be defined from its inputs at discrete instant of time. The output of the asynchronous sequential circuit depends upon the order in which its input signals change at any instance of time. The flip-flop circuit is an example of sequential circuit.

THE FLIP-FLOP

A flip flop is a circuit which is capable of remembering the value which is given as input. Hence it can be used as a basic memory element in a memory device. These circuits are capable of storing one bit of information.

Basic Flip-flops

A flip-flop circuit can be constructed using either two NOR gates or two NAND gates.

A common example of a circuit employing sequential logic is the flip-flop, also called a bi-stable gate. A simple flip-flop has two stable states. The flip-flop maintains its states indefinitely until an input pulse called a trigger is received. If a trigger is received, the flip-flop outputs change their states according to defined rules, and remain in those states until another trigger is received.

Flip - Flop Circuit using NOR Gates

By cross-coupling two NOR gates, the basic operation of a flip-flop could be demonstrated. In this circuit the outputs are fed back again to inputs.

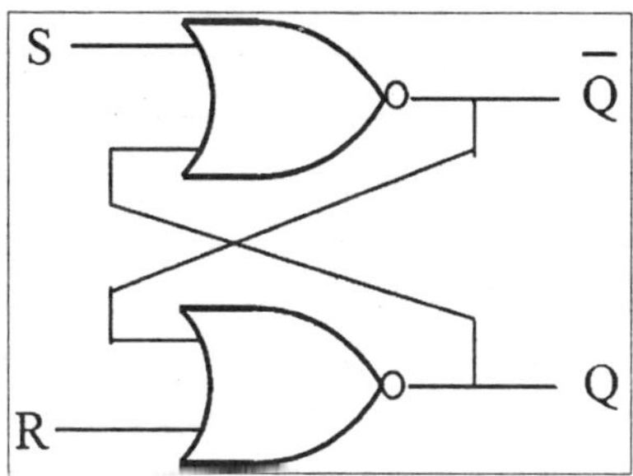

Fig. Flip Flop Circuit using NOR Gates

The flip-flop circuit has two outputs, one for the normal value Q and another for the complement value It also has two inputs S (set) and R (reset). Here, the previous output states are fed back to determine the current state of the output.

The NOR basic flip-flop circuit operates with inputs normally at '0' unless the state of the flip-flop has to be changed. As a starting point, we assume S = 1 and R = 0. This makes $\overline{Q}$ = 0. This $\overline{Q}$ = 0 is again given along with R = 0 to make Q = 1.

ie. when S = 1 and R = 0 make Q = 1 and $\overline{Q}$ = 0.

When the input S returns to '0', the output remains the same, because the output Q remain as '1' and $\overline{Q}$ as '0'.

ie. when S = 0 and R = 0 make Q = 1 and $\overline{Q}$ = 0 after S = 1 and R = 0.

In a similar manner the reset input changes the output Q = 0 and Q = 1.

We assume S = 0 and R = 1. This make Q = 0. This Q = 0 is again given along with S = 0 to make $\overline{Q}$ = 1.

ie. when S = 0 and R = 1 make Q = 0 and $\overline{Q}$ = 1.

When the reset input returns to 0, the outputs do not change, because the output Q remains as '0' and $\overline{Q}$ as '1'.

ie. when S = 0 and R = 0 make Q = 0 and Q = 1 after S = 0 and R = 1.

This can be tabulated as

S	R	Q	$\overline{Q}$	
1	0	1	0	
0	0	1	0	(after S = 1 and R = 0)
0	1	0	1	
0	0	0	1	(after S = 0 and R = 1)

When '1' is applied to both S and R, the outputs Q and $\overline{Q}$ become 0. These facts violate the output Q and $\overline{Q}$ are the complements of each other. In normal operations this condition must be avoided.

Thus a basic flip-flop has two useful states. When Q = 1 and $\overline{Q}$ = 0, it is called as set state. When Q = 0 and $\overline{Q}$ = 1, it is called as reset state.

Flip - Flop Circuit using NAND Gates

In a similar manner one can realise the basic flip-flop by cross coupling two NAND gates.

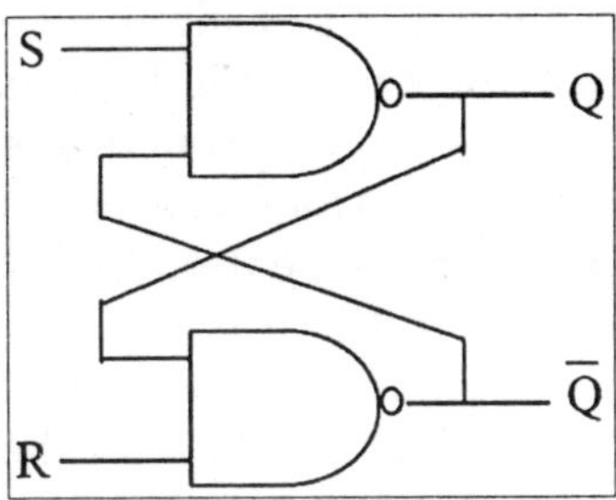

Fig. Flip Flop Ciruit using NAND Gates

The corresponding truth table is given as

S	R	Q	$\bar{Q}$	
1	0	1	1	
1	1	0	1	(after S = 1 and R = 0)
0	1	1	0	
1	1	1	0	(after S = 0 and R = 1)

The NAND basic flip-flop circuit operates with inputs normally at '1' unless the state of the flip-flop has to be changed. A momentary '0' to the input S gives Q = 1 and $\bar{Q}$ = 0. This makes the flip-flop to set state. After the input S returns to 1, a momentary '0' to the input R gives Q = 0 and $\bar{Q}$ = 1. This makes the flip-flop to reset state. When both the inputs become 0, ie., S = 0 and R = 0, both the outputs become 1. This condition must be avoided in the normal operation.

There are several kinds of flip-flop circuits, with designators such as D, T, J-K, and R-S. Flip-flop circuits are interconnected to form the logic gates that comprise digital integrated circuits (ICs) such as memory chips and microprocessors.

ELECTRONIC WORKBENCH

Electronic workbench is a simulation tool for electronic circuits. It allows to design and analyse circuits without using actual instruments. The workbench's click-and-drag operation make editing a circuit fast and easy. It is a windows compatible tool and follows the normal conventions of windows. The completed circuit can be simulated within the workbench by the use of simulated test and measurement equipment which are wired into the circuit. The circuit diagrams and the output of the simulated circuits can be printed or exported to other tools such as word processors for inclusion in other documents. The electronic workbench can be used for analogue, digital or mixed mode circuits. MultiSim is a electronic workbench which is used for design and analysis of circuits. It offers a single, easy-to-use graphical interface for the design needs. It also provides the advanced functionality we need to design from specifications.

OBJECTIVES AND EXPECTATIONS

Even though the Multisim is designed with much functionality, we use the tool to help us get familiar with the basic digital features.

- To learn how to build and test some simple digital logic gates using Multisim.
- To know how to build and simulate simple combinational logic circuits using the logic converter.

Building a Simple Digital logic Gate

- Start MultiSim from the Programs group in the Start menu.

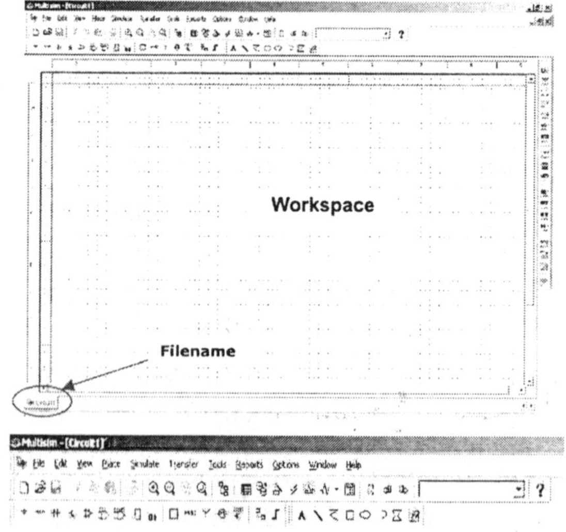

Fig. MultiSim Main Screen

- Assign a name to our file by following the steps given below. Choose File > Save As, under the File Name box to save the new workspace as circuit1. Press OK. The filename will then appear in the lower left hand corner of the workspace.

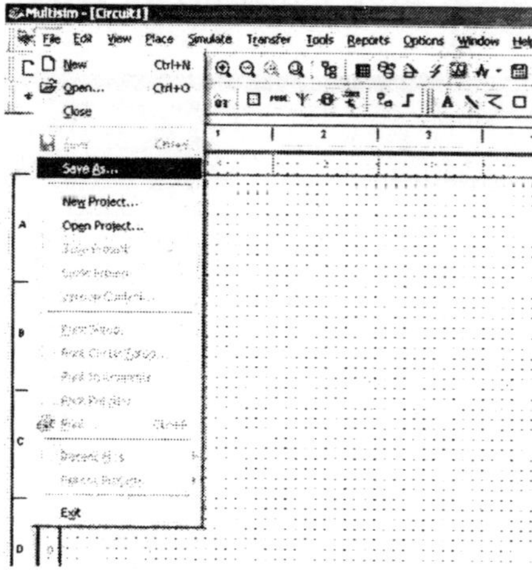

Fig. File Menu

- Click on the Place menu, then click on the Component, which shows the list of components in the component library.

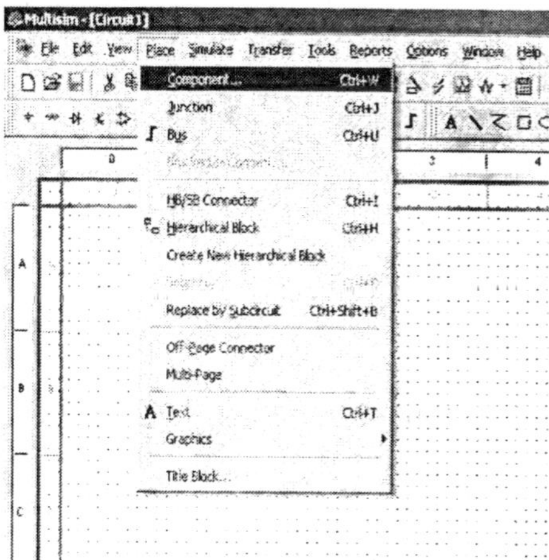

Fig. Place Menu

A ghost image of the component appears on the circuit window showing exactly where the component is placed.
One can use the appropriate database, group and component drop-down list to select the desired component.

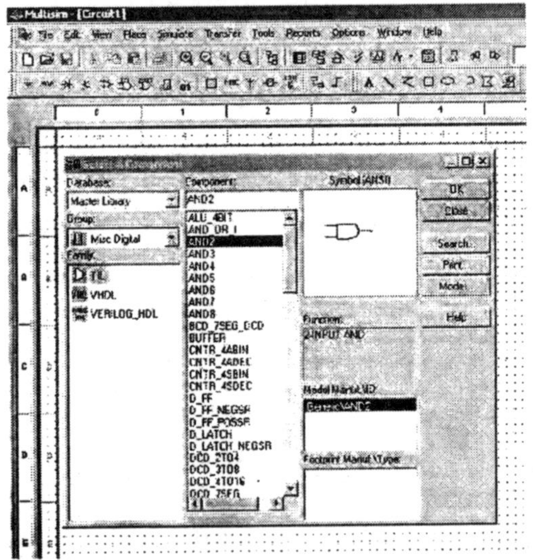

Fig. Component Window

- Click on any one of the logic gates available in the 'select a component' dialog box and drag it to place it in the workspace.
  Double click on the logic gate to change the properties of it and label the gate.

Placing Components

Components like logic gates are placed in the workspace by:

- Selecting component from Place menu.
- Right clicking on the workspace and select place components or Ctrl+W.

Selecting Components

Click on the component to highlight it.Once highlighted

the options in the 'Circuit ' menu will apply to that component. To select several components drag a box around them. All selected components will be highlighted.

To get help, just click on the logic gate using the left mouse button and choose help.

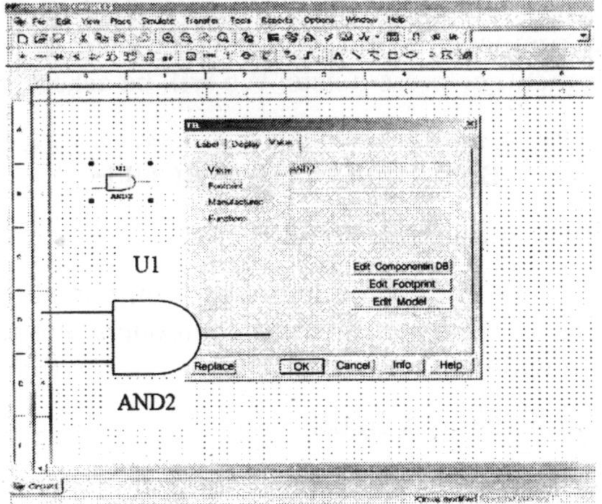

Fig. Selecting a Component

Building a Simple Combinational Logic Circuit Here the general steps to build a circuit by dragging the components like gates, wires, etc. are discussed.

Copying Components

To copy a component select it and then choose 'Copy' from the 'Edit' menu (or <cntrl> C). Then select paste (or <cntrl> V). Copies of the component will appear in the middle of the drawing area. They can then be moved to their required positions.

Modifying Components

- Select the components and then choose the available options from the 'CIRCUIT' menu.
- Double click on the component. A window will be opened which gives the parameters for the component which can be customized. Change the values as required and then click on 'Accept'.

Moving Components

To move components on the drawing select it and drag it to a new position and drop it. Any wires connected to it will be dragged with it.

Deleting Components

Select components and then select 'Delete' or 'Cut' from the 'EDIT' menu or press delete. We will be asked to confirm the delete.

BUILDING THE CIRCUIT

Placing Interconnecting Wires

Click on the end of the leg of the component. Drag the wire directly to the leg of the next component and then drop it. The wire will then route itself neatly.

Opening an Existing Circuit

Select 'Open' from the File Menu and then enter the filename in the dialogue box that opens. Consider a logical circuit by connecting two NOT gates with an AND gate. Place the NOT gate and AND gate on the workspace by selecting the respective components from the 'select a component' dialog box. Copy NOT gate.

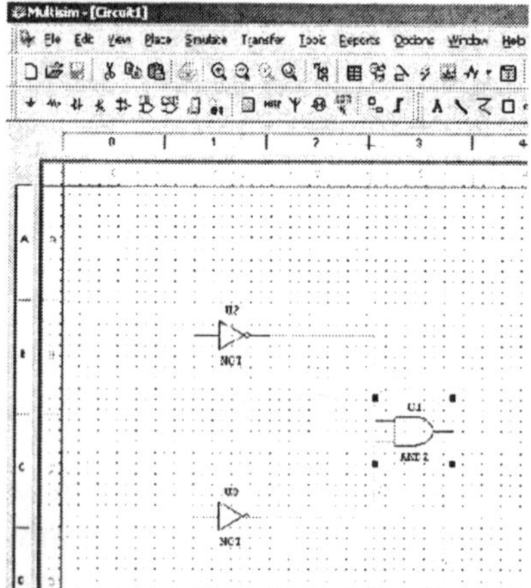

Fig. Construction of a Logic Circuit

Printing the Circuit

Select 'Print' from the File Menu and then select the item(s) to print from the dialogue box that is opened.

Saving the Circuit

To save a new circuit or rename an old one, select 'Save As' from the File Menu and complete the details in the dialogue box that opens. To save an existing circuit select 'Save' from the 'File' Menu

THE LOGIC CONVERTER

MultiSim provides a tool called the logic converter from the instrument bin. With the logic converter, one can carry out several conversions of a logic circuit representation:

1. Logic Circuit → ruth Table
2. Truth Table → Boolean Expression
3. Truth Table → Simplified Boolean Expression
4. Boolean Expression → Truth Table
5. Boolean Expression → Logic Circuit
6. Boolean Expression → NAND-gate only logic circuit

One can connect it to a digital circuit to derive the truth table or Boolean expression the circuit represents.

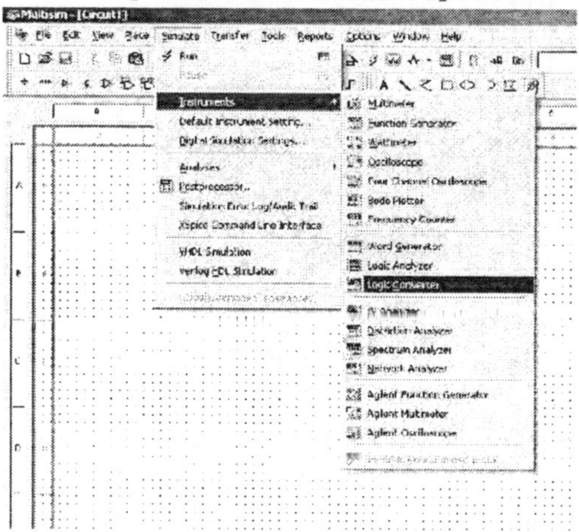

Fig. Logic Convertor

One can also use it to produce a logic circuit from a truth

table or boolean expression. To open the logic converter, click on the simulate menu, instruments and then logic converter.

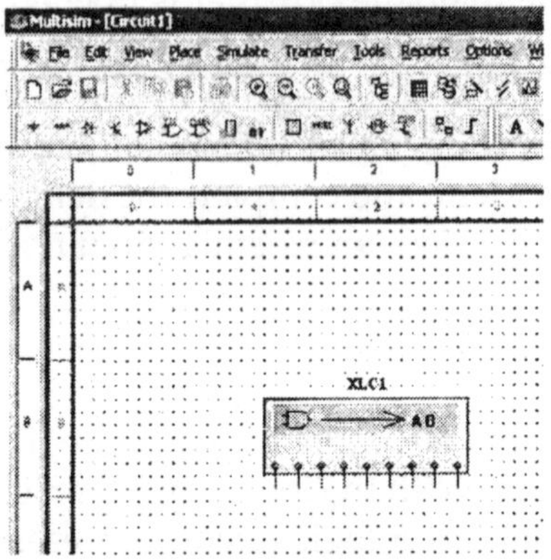

Fig. Logic Convertor on the Workspace To use the Logic Converter, Double-click on the Logic Converter Icon.

The figure shows the logic converter that we have placed in the workspace.

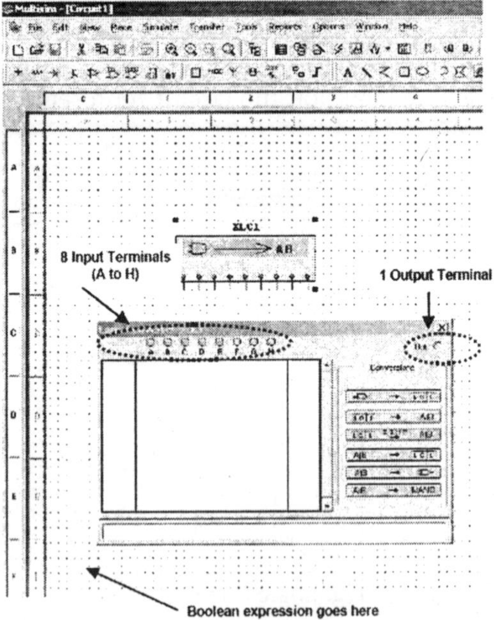

Fig. View of Logic Convertor

The little circles in the bottom are the inputs and output terminals. There are 8 input terminals and 1 output terminal available for use. That means if we want to use the logic converter to carry out the conversions, an individual circuit is limited to 8 inputs and 1 output.

Notice that the 8 input terminals are labeled as A to H and the output terminal is labeled as 'Out'. The converting options available in the logic converter are as follows:

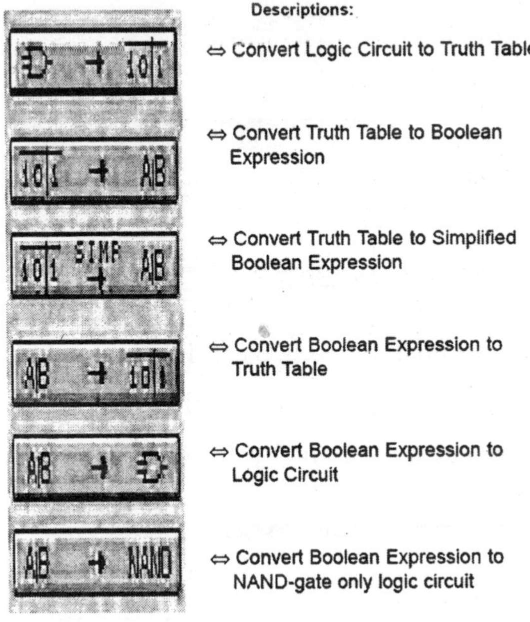

Descriptions:

⇔ Convert Logic Circuit to Truth Table

⇔ Convert Truth Table to Boolean Expression

⇔ Convert Truth Table to Simplified Boolean Expression

⇔ Convert Boolean Expression to Truth Table

⇔ Convert Boolean Expression to Logic Circuit

⇔ Convert Boolean Expression to NAND-gate only logic circuit

Converting a Truth Table to a Boolean Expression

Once we have a truth table, the logic converter can transform it into a boolean function in the form of an algebraic expression.

To create a Truth table

- Drag a logic converter to the workspace and open it.
- Click the number of inputs we want, from A to H at the top of the logic converter.
- The inputs are present in standard binary count format. In this case select A, B and C.

- The values in the output column are set to '?'. Click the output values once to change as '0' and twice to change as '1'.

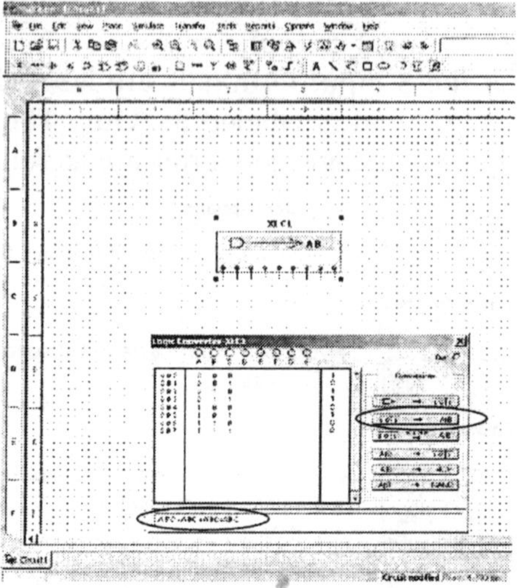

Click the Truth Table to Boolean Expression button.

Converting a logic Circuit To a Truth Table

- Construct the circuit by drawing the components (logic circuit).

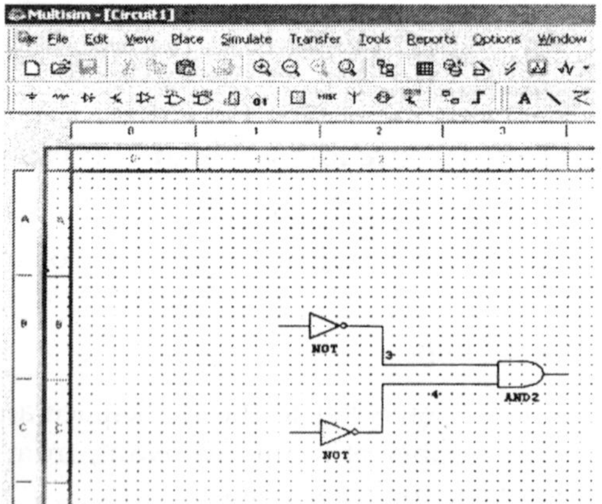

- Connect the inputs of our circuit to the input terminals on the logic converter and single output of the circuit to the output terminal on the logic converter

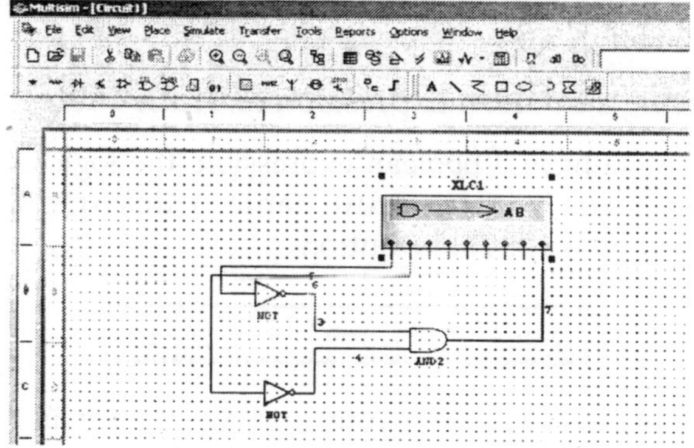

The boolean expression will be displayed at the bottom of the logic converter. In this case:

A'B'C' + A'BC' + A'BC + AB'C

Note the primes, representing inversion. A' means NOT A, or $\overline{A}$

Converting a Truth Table to a Simplified Boolean Expression

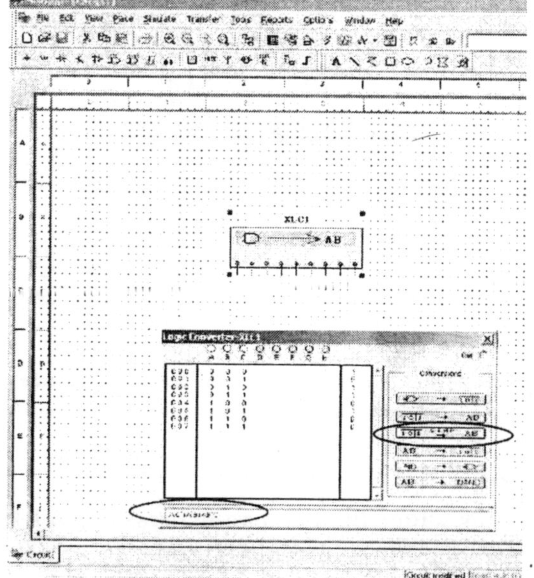

Some expressions can be recalculated in a simpler form. ·To try to simplify the expression, click the 'simplify' button using the previous truth table. In this case, the expression can be simplified to A'C' + A'B +AB'C

Converting a Boolean Expression to Truth Table

Once we have a boolean expression, the logic converter can transform it into a truth table. Click the 'Boolean Expression to Truth Table' button

after entering the Boolean expression A' + BC + B' in the logic converter. The truth table will be displayed in the logic converter as shown below.

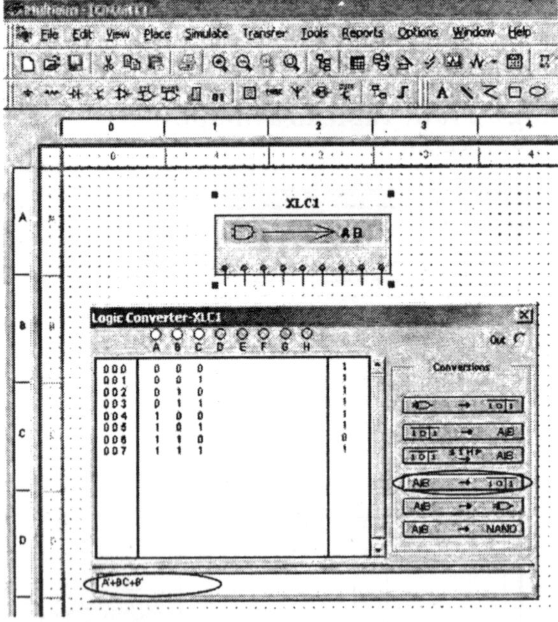

Converting a Boolean Expression to a Circuit

To do this, enter the boolean expression, A'B+B'C+ABC and click the 'Boolean to Circuit' button.

The resulting circuit will appear in the workspace.

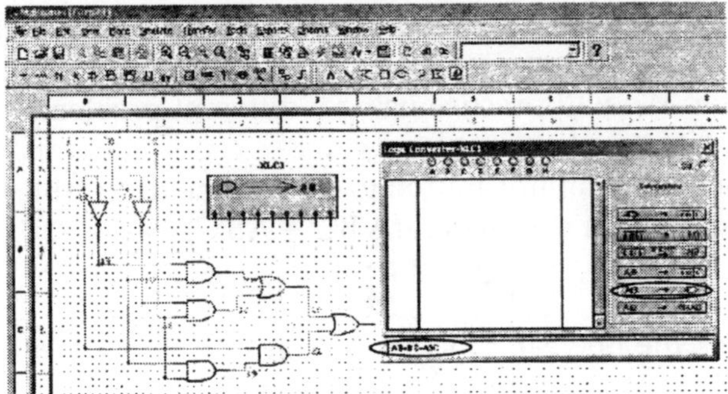

Converting Boolean Expression to NAND-gate only logic circuit

To realise the logic circuit using NAND-gates for the same boolean expression A'B+B'C+ABC, click

The resulting circuit will appear on the workspace.

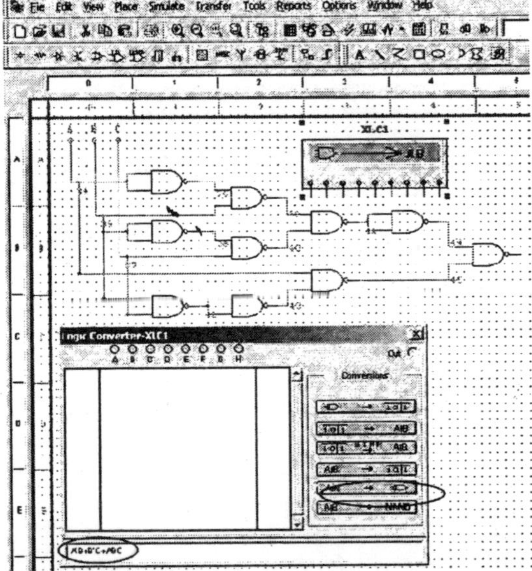

Creating a Circuit from a Truth Table

This is the most useful conversion for a circuit designer. Normally, we will have translated the client's specification into a truth table, and have then to produce a logic gate circuit to do the job.This requires two conversions using the logic converter. We will practice using a different problem.

- Create a truth table.

Click the 'simplify' button to convert the truth table to the simplest Boolean expression (A'BC' + AB'C)

Click the Boolean to Circit Button

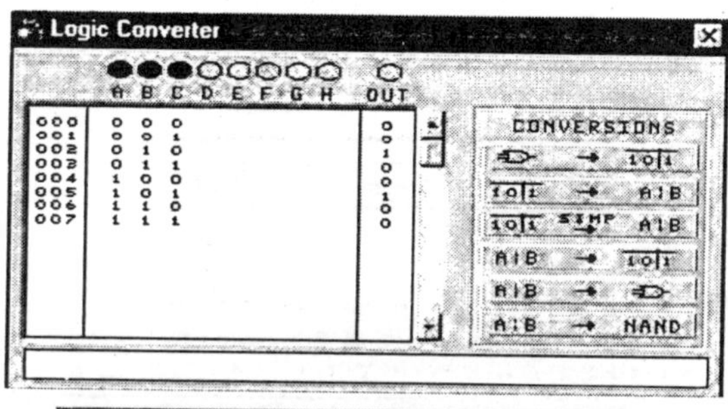

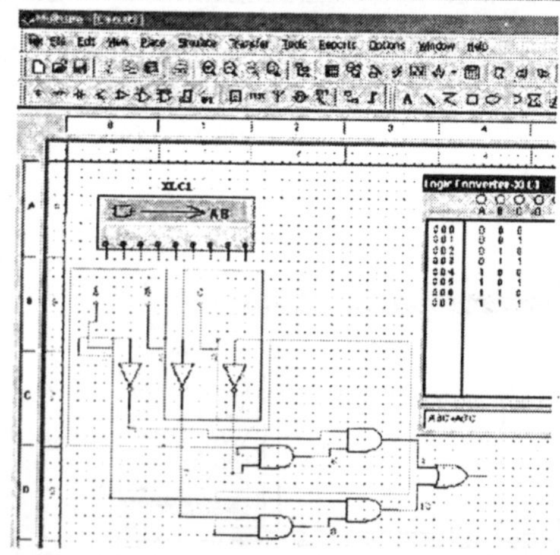

The resulting circuit will appear, selected, on the

workspace. If we want to move it, point to one component and drag the circuit.

The following table summarizes all possible scenarios that one can encounter:

Table: Quick Guide to convert a Digital Circuit using the Logic Converter

From	To	Options
Truth Table	Boolean Expressions	10|1 → A|B
	Simplified Boolean Expressions	10|1 SIMP→ A|B
	Logic Circuit	10|1 → A|B A|B →
	NAND-gate only logic circuit	10|1 → A|B A|B → NAND
Boolean Expressions	Truth Table	A|B → 10|1
	Logic Circuit	A|B →
	NAND-gate only logic circuit	A|B → NAND
	Simplified Boolean Expressions	A|B → 10|1 10|1 SIMP→ A|B
Logic Circuit	Truth Table	→ 10|1
	Boolean Expressions	→ 10|1 10|1 → A|B
	Simplified Boolean Expressions	→ 10|1 10|1 SIMP→ A|B

Chapter 5

Operating System

When a computer is devoid of any software it is just like dead bodies. The computer software and hardware have been intrinsically linked with each other. One of them cannot do anything useful by itself without help from the other.

There are two types of software, one is the System Software and the other is the Application Software. System Software looks after the functions of the computer. This is just like involuntary actions controlling involuntary muscles such as digestive system of the animal. System software makes efficient use of the computing resources and normally provides a uniform base for different apllications. It is there to operate, control and extend the processing capabilities of computers. Application software helps the user to do his/her work.

This is similar to the voluntary actions controling voluntary muscles like hand etc. Moving a hand is a voluntary action. The Operating System comes under the System Software category. The actual work is undertaken only by the hardware.

In order to do useful work on a computer, one has to access the hardware, but one can access the hardware directly, only in the first generation computers. In the subsequent generations of computers direct access is denied. The architecture of the computers at the machine level is primitive and very hard to programme. What is the reason for the denial of the access? If the access is not denied, unless the user is hard working, one of the two alternatives can happen.

- The user may be forced to conclude that computer is not for him/ her.

- The user may damage the computer hardware.

This leads us to a natural question. Who will access the computer hardware directly if the user is denied such permission? The answer is the Operating System. The Operating system provides so many facilities with which a user comfortably uses their computers. This resembles the life of modern man, who cannot tolerate power cut even for five minutes.

Apart from being complicated, trying to deal with I/O(Input/Output) opeations can prove truly frustrating. The average user wants to have a simple high-level abstraction to deal with. If we see an object, a lot of Impulses are triggned on inside our brain. At the end we are shown an image of the object. If an average person is asked to explain the activities that happen inside the brain, he/she will not dare to even open his eyes.

The brain provides a convenient highly sophisticated abstraction. It merely provides the image of an object without letting people know about the activities that happen inside the brain. In this case eye is an interface between the object and the part of the brain that processes visual data. In a similar fashion the Operating System hides from a person know the complexity of the hardware and allows the user to use the name of the files for reading and writing.

The Operating System adds extended capabilities to a machine with which it is easier to programme than the underlying hardware.

The Operating System manages the resource. Modern computers are highly complex machines. They get more complex day by day. So it is very difficult to manage such a complex system but the Operating System manages the complex system in an efficient way.

It provides special routines called device drivers to support the specific behaviour of individual device. In this view the primary task of the Operating System is to keep track of who is using which resource, to grant resource requests, to account for usage and to mediate conflicting requests from different programs and users.

The Operating System is to provide an orderly and controlled allocation of resources among the various programs competing for them. The Operating System is the intermediary between the user and computer hardware. When the Operating System was first introduced, the primary goal of the Operating System was mainly to optimize resources. The secondary goal was to make the computer environment, user-friendly. Now providing the user-friendly environment is the main aim of the operating system.

The Operating System acts as the manager of resources such as CPU time, memory space, file storage, I/O devices. Since there may be many conflicting requests, Operating System allocates resources in an optimal manner. That is, Operating System allocates resources in such a manner so as to achieve the maximum best possible result.

The Operating System also provides the means for the proper use of hardware, software and data in the operation of the computer system. The Operating System is like a supervisor in a company providing an excellent environment in which the other people can perform useful work.

Operating System assumes yet another responsibility, that of serving as a control programme. A control programme controls the execution of user programs to prevent errors and improper use of the computer. It is especially concerned with the operation and control I/O devices.

It is hard to define Operating System. There are several definitions for Operating System. One of the definitions is that Operating System is one programme running at all times on the computer. The another, somewhat more widely accepted definition is that an Operating System is an interface between the user and hardware.

The Operating System's goals are to:

- Execute user programs in a user-friendly atmosphere.
- Make the computer system convenient to use.
- Optimize computer hardware.

Any Operating system should be easy to use. Now-a-days people are hard pressed for time, so they cannot undergo any training for making use of the Operating System. The idea of using facilities available in the Operating System should be intuitive. The Operating System should allow developing application programs easier. Otherwise people cannot concentrate on the application development; instead, they have to spend lot of time in concentrating on the peculiarities of the Operating System. The Operating System should be portable. That is, the Operating System should run in almost all hardware platforms.

If there is a new version of the Operating System, it should not confuse the people who used the earlier version and also it should run software that ran successfully in earlier versions. The Operating System should provide data security; it should not allow one user to write on the file/files of the other user and thus spoiling the contents of the owner of the file/files.

The Operating System should provide data confidentiality. That is, the Operating System should not allow unauthorised people to access the data of the other people. If this is possible then the scientific and technological institutions and banks will have a nightmarish existence. The vendor who provided the Operating System should undertake the service facility also. The vendor should be accessed easily. Otherwise that Operating System will attain notoriety.

The Operating System should work in a network as well as distributed environment. The Operating System should make system administration more efficient.

The Operating system should provide the help facility. There are people who do not like to get help from the other people; this will prick their self-esteem. Instead they may try to get help from the system. The help facility should mainly concentrate on people like them. There should be different levels of help to satisfy the needs of different levels of users. According to John Von Neumann architecture application, programme and data should reside in main memory. In those days programs dealt mainly with scientific problems.

For solving these types of problems, software libraries are created. These libraries complicated the normal user of that time. Therefore, the computer operator job is created. But this prevented the programmer to remove the errors (debug) immediately. Programmers had to wait for nearly six hours for debugging their programs.

HISTORY OF THE OPERATING SYSTEM

In the beginning, programs were run one at a time. In order to use CPU more efficiently, jobs of similar nature were grouped and made to run in batches. But after programme execution, the computer operator manually restarted the next programme. To avoid the delay due to manual operation, Automatic Job Sequencing mechanism was introduced.

This is called Resident Monitor and this may be the first elementary Operating System. If scientific applications had been used in a computer, the CPU (Central Processing Unit) was busy with the programme, but if business problems had been handled, I/O system was busy and the CPU was kept idle.

In order to make the CPU busy, the I/O operations were done in an inexpensive computer, the contents of card reader was transferred in a magnetic tape and which in turn was placed in the computer that performed the business operation. In those days data were stored in cards, called punched cards. Another attempt was made to keep the CPU busy for most of the time.

A buffer was (and still is) allowed to store Input, when the CPU needed the data, buffer sent the data immediately. The next input might be ready in the buffer before the CPU processed the earlier data. When the processing was completed, the CPU sent the output to the buffer. When the data were ready, an interrupt mechanism interrupted the CPU. The CPU having taken the necessary actions and resumed its original work.

At the same time, Direct Memory Access (DMA) mechanism was also created, which allowed transferring data to and from memory without the intervention of the CPU. Spooling (is a way of dealing with dedicated I/O devices in the multiprogramming system.) allowed (and still allows) reading a set of jobs in disk system from the card reader. When printing work had to be undertaken, the print image was copied into the disk system and when conditions were favourable the print image was sent to the printer.

Spooling is superior to the buffer, because in spooling I/O operations can be overlapped with the working of other jobs but that is not possible with the buffer. While executing one job, the OS, reads next job from card reader into a storage area on the disk and outputs printout of previous job from disk to the printer. Spooling allowed the CPU to choose a particular job for execution leading to the concept called the Job Scheduling. The job scheduling led to the concept known as the Multiprogramming.

In multiprogramming, memory is divided into many partitions. Multiprogramming allows many programmers to load their programs in the different partitions. Each programmer is made to believe his/her programme is the only programme running. Multiprogramming was followed by Time-sharing concept. Here the CPU allocated a fixed time for each programme. In the next cycle, the programme that had been considered earlier was taken once again. This process continued until all the programs were executed.

MAJOR FEATURES OF THE OPERATING SYSTEM

Types

As per the number of users, there are two types of the Operating Systems. They are:

- Single user Operating System.
- Multi-user Operating System.

Single user Operating System: At a time, only one user can operate the system. MS Disk Operating System is an example of single user Operating System.

Multi-user Operating System: More than one user can operate the same system simultaneously. The multi-user Operating System is based on the concept of time-sharing. Unix is an example of multi-user Operating System.

Input/Output

Application software does not allocate or de-allocate the

storage area on the disk for different files belonging to various users. If the application software is allowed to allocate or de-allocate, two or more users may try to write on the same sector of disk, resulting in confusion.

Even a single user may try to write in some sector, which may contain valuable information. In order to avoid such an awkward situation, only the Operating System is empowered to make such an allocation or de-allocation. This arrangement safeguards the loss of data. Such safeguading of data is called Data Security. From the above discussion, one may come to the conclusion that the Operating System alone should be empowered to instruct the hardware to write data from memory onto a Pre-specified location on the disk. In fact Input/ Output operation code of the Operating System constitute a sizeable code of the Operating System.

The application programme is not allowed to read data from the disk. Otherwise any user can access any type of sensitive information. There may not be any secrecy.

For example, banks will have precarious existence. An application programme can do all the operations with the exception of input/output operations. When the application programme is translated into the machine code, the request for reading or writing will not be translated into the machine code, instead a system call is given. (A set of extended instructions providing an interface between the Operating System and the user programs, is called a System Call.)

The Operating System will then generate suitable input/ output command to the hardware to replace this system call. We cannot fool the system by writing the I/O code in machine language. User code will not be entertained for input/output at any circumstance. This arrangement not only helps in protecting the data integrity, but also, it saves the user from writing a lot of code to execute I/O operations. Thus it saves from reinventing the wheel.

It is enough, if the programmer concentrated in logical behaviour of the programme. The Operating System does the spadework for the arrival of application programme and the Operating System which is in the back ground, when needed comes into forefront and does its work gracefully after that it relegates itself to the background.

Printer

Ideally we can expect computers to create truly paperless society. Appropriate networking and Infrastructure must be provided for this. As of today computers consume a lot of papers. Usage of printers is rampant. How does the Operating System help for printing? The Operating System makes the programmer's life much easier as far as the printing work is concerned. Even a small document takes a few minutes to complete the printing work.

Now for printing a document, the Operating System first makes a temporary copy of the file and then hands over the control back to the application. Spooling is a way of dealing with dedicated I/O devices in a multiprogramming system. To print a file, a process first generates the entire file to be printed and puts in the spooling directory. (Directory is a container for storing files on other sub-directories). Then the special process having permission to use printer's special file is allowed to print the files in the directory. If two users print two documents, in the absence of overlapping of the two documents.

This is similar to overlapping of the signals from two radio stations. This unwanted behaviour is completely eliminated by spooling. Each document's print image will be written on to the disk at two different locations of the spool file.

While printing, the printer is not allowed to print the original document; instead it is allowed to print the contents of spooler programme. Multiprocessor systems have more than one CPU in close communication with the others. In a tightly coupled system the processors share memory and a clock; communication usually takes place through the shared memory.

MOST DESIRABLE CHARACTERS OF THE OPERATING SYSTEM

User Interface

The Operating System should concentrate on the user

interface. The only way that we can see this world is through our eyes.

Similarly the only way that we can interact with a computer is through the user interface. People may be attracted to the computer in the beginning. If the interface is not user-friendly, only persistent people may continue with their work with the computer.

The other people slowly move away from the computer with the intention of not returning to the computer forever. One can judge, from the immense popularity of the GUI (Graphical User Interface) based interface, the importance of well designed well thought interface. The GUI is window based. The vivid colours attract children. Novices are attracted by the help pop up messages. Icons give iterative usage of the particular application.

Now Linux is also available as windows based Operating System. The user interface of the Operating System should be appealing to the senses. The human brain is good in pattern recognition. Human brain learns through association. All these factors should be taken into account, when user interface is improved. In addition to the above, the following points should also be considered when User Interface is designed.

- Interface should be designed in such a manner as to master the interface. As already stated, people are hard pressed for time.
- The speed of response should play a vital role in designing the user interface. The speed of response is nothing but the time taken to execute a particular task.
- The user interface should reduce the number of errors committed by the user. With little practice, the user should be in a position to avoid errors.
- The user interface should be pleasing to the senses. Vivid colours, enchanting music may achieve this.
- The user interface should enable the people to retain this expertise for a longer time.
- The ultimate aim of any product is to satisfy the customer. The user interface should also satisfy the customer.

Interface developers should also take the following considerations into account. Interfaces mainly should satisfy the end users. The other users such as programmers may work even in an unfriendly environment. The interface should not heavily burden the memory of users. Menus, minimal typing work will be an added advantage of the Operating System.

MEMORY MANAGEMENT

The Operating System should provide memory management techniques also. Any error in the user programme should not be allowed to spoil the entire memory. So the Operating System divides the main memory into user memory and reserved memory.

If some errors creep into the user programme then only user memory may be affected however the reserved memory is always in an unaffected condition.

User memory is divided into many partitions to accommodate various jobs. Therefore the number of jobs accommodated cannot exceed the number of partitions. Naturally the size of the user programme should be less than that of the available main memory. This is like cutting the feet to the size of the shoe (if the size of the shoe is inadequate).the Operating System provides virtual (imaginary) memory to include the entire programme.

Operating System should manage the devices also. It is not uncommon for several processes to run simultaneously. In order to achieve successful operation, the processes should effectively communicate with each other. This interprocess communication is made possible by the Operating System.

Process management

Process management undertakes the allocation of processors to one programme. The Operating System controls the jobs submitted to the system (CPU). Several algorithms are used to allocate the job to the processor. Algorithm is a step-by-step method to solve a given problem.

- FIFO
- SJF

- Round Robin
- Based on Priority

FIFO (First In First Out)

This algorithm is based on queuing. Suppose we are standing in a queue to get our notebook corrected from our teacher. The student who stands first in the queue gets his/her notebook corrected first and leaves the queue. Then the next student in the queue gets it corrected and so on. This is the basic methodology of the FIFO algorithm.

Now, let us deal with this FIFO a little more technically. The process (A process is basically a programme in execution) that enters the queue first is executed first by the CPU, then the next and then the next and so on. The processes are executed in the order in which they enter the queue.

SJF (Shortest Job First:)

This algorithm is based on the size of the job.

Take two jobs A and B.

A = 5 kilo bytes

B = 8 kilo bytes

Kilo literally means 1000 but here kilo means 1024. A byte consists of eight bits. A bit can store either TRUE (1) or FALSE (0). First the job A will be assigned processor time after which B gets its turn.

Round Robin

Jobs are assigned processor time in a circular method. For example take three jobs A, B, C. First the job A is assigned to CPU then job B and after B job C and then again A,B and C and so on.

Based On Priority

In this method each job is assigned a Priority. The higher Priority job is awarded favorable treatment. Take two jobs A and B. Let the priority of A be 5 and priority B be 7. Job B is assigned to the processor before job A. The allocation of processors by process management is also known as the CPU

Scheduling. The objectives of the CPU Scheduling should be to maximize:

- The CPU utilisation
- The number of jobs done in a unit time (throughput) and to minimise the time taken. before the execution of the job and to run the job.

Let us consider e-mail, which allows to:-

- Represent the information electrically
- Carry information from source to destination
- Manage the flow of such information

The telecommunication industry provides all the above facilities. The information that may be sent by network may be voice, data, video, fax etc. Web camera unites the parents and their children who are away from each other. Now the size of LAN has grown. We can see a LAN with more than 1000 computers connected to it. Through telecommunication links, LAN can access remote computers. The size and complexity of the network grow day by day. It is not a mean achievement to manage them. The Operating System shoulders the burden (responsibility) of managing the nets.

Security Management

The biggest challenge to the computer industry is to safeguarding one's data from unauthorized people. The Operating System provides three levels of securities to the user. They are:

- File access level
- System level
- Network level

In order to access the files created by other people, we should have the requisite permission. Permissions can either be granted by the creator of the file or by the administrator of the system. System level security is offered by the password in a multi-user environment. Both windows XP professional and Linux offer the password facility. Network security is an elusive one. People from all over the world try to provide such a security. All the above levels of security are provided only by the Operating System.

Fault Tolerance

The Operating Systems should be robust. When there is a fault, the Operating System should not crash, instead the Operating System have fault tolerance capabilities.

Application Base

Operating System should provide a solid basis for running many popular applications.

Distributed Operating System

If we want to make use of the Network, we must know the machine address and the variety of services provided by that machine. But Distributed Operating System ensures that the entire network behaves as a single computer. Getting access to the remote resources is similar to access to local resources. The user's job is executed in an idle machine and the result is communicated to the user machine.

The user is under the illusion that everything is done only in his/her computer. In a distributed Operating System a user is not aware of multiplicity of machines.

The future of the Operating System may be Distributed Operating System since all the computers become a part of one or other network. But the virus attacks discourage people to get connected to the net. From the above one can appreciate the importance of the Operating System.

Chapter 6

Computer Communications

Communication is the desire of man. When human voice became inadequate, ancient civilizations devised drum codes and smoke signals to send information to far off distances. These primitive methods have given way to sending messages through electronic pulses.

A stand-alone computer communicates very efficiently by connecting it with other computers. Data in a computer is transmitted to another computer located across continents almost instantaneously using telephone, microwaves or radio links. The long distance communication link between a computer and a remote terminal was set up around 1965. Now networking has become a very important part of computing activity.

NETWORK

A large number of computers are interconnected by copper wire, fibre optic cable, microwave and infrared or through satellite. A system consisting of connected nodes made to share data, hardware and software is called a Computer Network.

SOME IMPORTANT REASONS FOR NETWORKING

- Sharing of resources: Primary goal of a computer network is to share resources. For example several PCs can be connected to a single expensive line printer.
- Sharing information: Information on a single computer can be accessed by other computers in the

network. Duplication of data file on separate PCs can be avoided.

- Communication: When several PCs are connected to each other, messages can be sent and received. From a remote location, a mobile salesman can relay important messages to the central office regarding orders. Relevant databases are updated and the business commitments are fulfilled.

Applications of Network

The following are the areas where computer networks are employed.

- Electronic data interchange
- Tele-conferencing
- Cellular telephone
- Cable Television
- Financial services, marketing and sales
- Reservation of Airlines, trains, Theatres and buses
- Telemedicine
- ATM
- Internet banking

Several educational institutions, businesses and other organizations have discovered the benefits of computer networks. Users can share data and programmes. They can co-operate on projects to maximize the usage of available expertise and talent.

Benefits of Network

- Effective handling of personal communications
- Allowing several users to access simultaneously Important programs and data:
- Making it easy for the users to keep all critical data on shared storage device and safeguard the data.
- Allowing people to share costly equipment.

The computer communication should ensure safe, secure and reliable data transfer.

Safe: The data received is the same as the data sent

Secure: The data being transferred cannot be damaged either will fully or accidentally.

Reliable: Both the sender and the receiver knows the status of the data sent. Thus the sender knows whether the receiver got the correct data or not.

Types of Network

The following are the general types of networks used today.

- Local Area Network (LAN)
- Metropolitan Area Network (MAN)
- Wide Area Network (WAN)

A network connecting systems and devices inside a single building or buildings close to each other is called Local Area Network (LAN). Generally LANs do not use the telephone network. They are connected either by wire or wireless. Wired connection may be using twisted pairs, coaxial cables or Fibre Optic cables. In a wireless LAN, connections may be using infrared or radio waves. Wireless networks are useful when computers are portable. However, wireless network communicates slowly than a wired network.

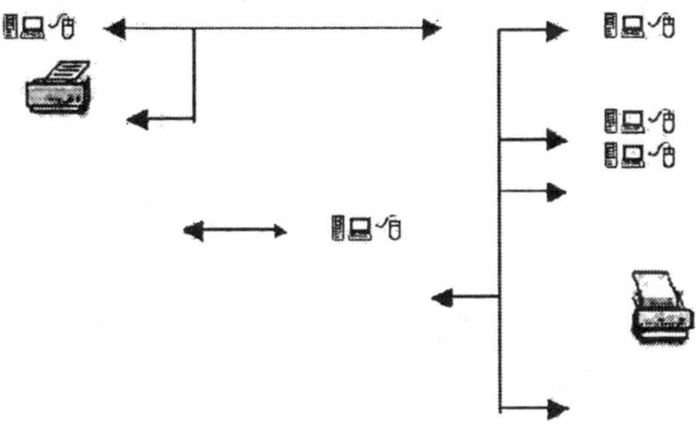

Fig. Local Area Network

The number of Computers in the network is between two to several hundreds. LAN is generally used to share hardware, software and data. A computer sharing software package and hard disk is called a file server or network server.

A Network that spans a geographical area covering a Metropolitan city is called Metropolitan Area Network (MAN) A WAN is typically two or more LANs connected together across a wide geographical area. The individual LANs separated by large distances may be connected by dedicated links, fibre optic cables or satellite links.

Star Network

In a star network all computers and other communication devices are connected to a central hub. Such as a file server or host computer usually by a Unshielded Twisted Pair (UTP) cables.

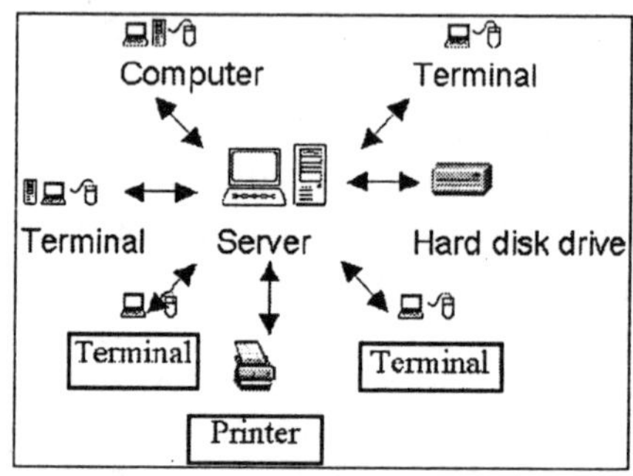

Fig. Star network

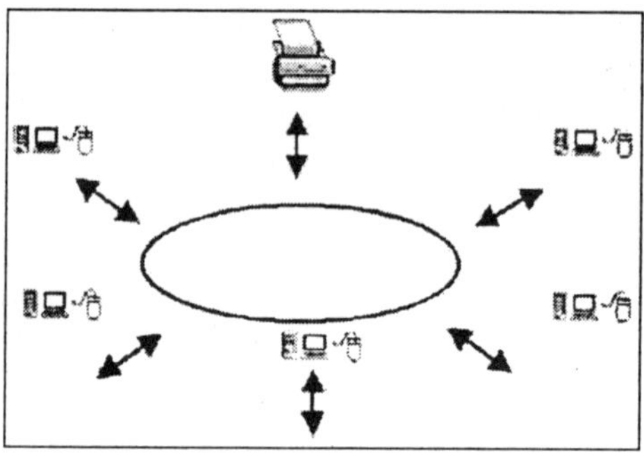

Fig. Ring Network

NETWORK TOPOLOGY

The network topology is the structure or layout of the communication channels that connects the various computers on the network. Each computer in the network is called a node. There are a number of factors that determine the topology suitable for a given situation. Some of the important consideration is the type of nodes, the expected performance, type of wiring (physical link) used and the cost. Network can be laid out in different ways.

The five common topologies are star, ring, bus, hybrid and FDDI.

Ring Network

In a ring network computers and other communication devices are connected in a continuous loop. Electronic data are passed around the ring in one direction, with each node serving as a repeater until it reaches the right destination. There is no central host computer or server.

Bus Network

In a bus network all communication devices are connected to a common cable called bus. There is no central computer or server. The data transmission is bidirectional.

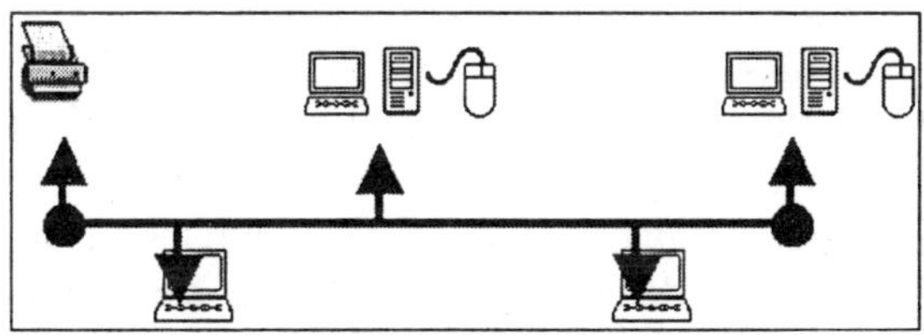

Fig. Bus Network

Hybrid Network: A hybrid network is a combination of the above three networks suited to the need.

FDDI Network: A FDDI network (pronounced as fiddy short for Fibre Distributed Data Interface) is a high-speed network using fibre optic cable. It is used for high tech purposes such as electronic images, high-resolution graphics and digital video. The main disadvantage is its high cost.

BASIC ELEMENTS IN NETWORKING

All networks require the following three elements:

- *Network services*: Network services are provided by numerous combinations of computer hardware and software. Depending upon the task, network services require data, input/output resources and processing power to accomplish their goal.

- *Transmission media*: Transmission media is the pathway for contacting each computer with other. Transmission media include cables and wireless Technologies that allows networked devices to contact each other. This provides a message delivery path.
- *Protocols*: A protocol can be one rule or a set of rules and standards that allow different devices to hold conversations.

COMMON NETWORK SERVICES

The following common network services are available.

File Services

Those are the primary services offered by the computer networks. This improves the efficient storage and retrieval of computer data. The service function includes.

- *File Transfer*: Rapidly move files from place to place regardless of file size, distance and Local operating system.
- *File Storage and data migration*: Increasing amount of Computer data has caused the development of several storage devices. Network applications are well suited to control data storage activity on different storage systems. Some data becomes less used after certain time. For example higher secondary examination result posted on the web becomes less used after a week. Such data can be moved from one storage media (say hard disc of the computer) to another, less expensive media (say an optical disk) is called data migration.
- *File update synchronization*: Network service keeps track of date and time of intermediate changes of a specific file. Using this information, it automatically updates all file locations with the latest version.
- *File Archiving*: All organizations create duplicate copies of critical data and files in the storage device.

This practice is called file archiving or file backup. In case of original file getting damaged, Computer Operator uses the Network to retrieve the duplicate file. File archiving becomes easier and safe when storage devices are connected in the Network.

Print Services

Network application that control manage access to printers and fax equipments. The print service function includes

- *Provide multiple access* (more than one user, use the network): Reduce the number of printers required for the organization.
- *Eliminates distance constraints*: Take a printout at a different location.
- *Handle simultaneous requests*: queue print jobs reducing the computer time.
- *Share specialized equipments*: Some printers are designed for specific use such as high-speed output, large size formals or colour prints. Specialised equipments may be costlier or may not be frequently used by the user, when numerous clients are using the network, printer use is optimized.
- *Network fax service*: Fax service is integrated in the network.

The computer in the network sends the digital document image to any location. This reduces the time and paper handling.

Message services

Message services include storing, accessing and delivering text, binary, graphic digitized video and audio data. Unlike file services, message services deal actively with communication interactions between computer users applications, network applications or documents.

Application Services

Application services are the network services that run

software for network clients. They are different from file services because they allow computers to share processing power, not just share data.

Data communication is the process of sending data electronically from one location to another. Linking one computer to another permits the power and resources of that computer to be tapped. It also makes possible the updating and sharing of data at different locations.

Co-ordinating Data Communication

The device that coordinates the data transfer is called Network interface card (NIC). NIC is fixed in the computer and communication channel is connected to it. Ethernet, Arcnet and token ring are the examples for the NIC. Protocol specifies the procedures for establishing maintaining and terminating data transfer.

In 1978, the International Standards organization proposed protocol known as open system interconnection (OSI). The OSI provided a network architecture with seven layers. Figure gives the seven layers and the respective functions. This architecture helps to communicate between Network of dissimilar nodes and channels.

FORMS OF DATA TRANSMISSION

Data is transmitted in two forms

- Analog data transmission
- Digital data transmission

Analog data transmission is the transmission of data in a continuous waveform.

The telephone system, for instance, is designed for analog data transmission. Analog signals are sometimes modulated or encoded to represent binary data.

Digital data transmission is the widely used communication system in the world. The distinct electrical state of 'on' and 'off' is represented by 1 and 0 respectively. Digital data transmission as shown in Figure is faster and more efficient than analog. All computers understand and work only in digital forms

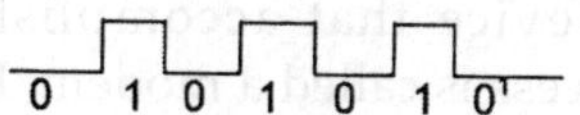

Fig. Digital Data Transmission

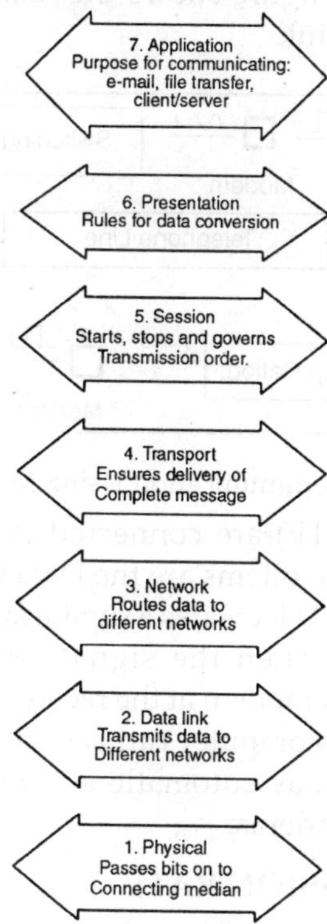

Fig. Seven Layers of Protocols

MODEM

Computers at different parts of the world are connected by telephone lines. The telephone converts the voice at one end into an electric signal that can flow through a telephone cable. The telephone at the receiving end converts this electric signal into voice. Hence the receiver could hear the voice. The process of converting sound or data into a signal that can flow through the telephone wire is called modulation.

The reverse process is called demodulation. The telephone instrument contains the necessary circuit to perform these activities. The device that accomplishes modulation - demodulation process is called a modem. It is known that the electrical and sound signals are analog - which continuously vary with time. The figure shows the relationship of modem to communication Link

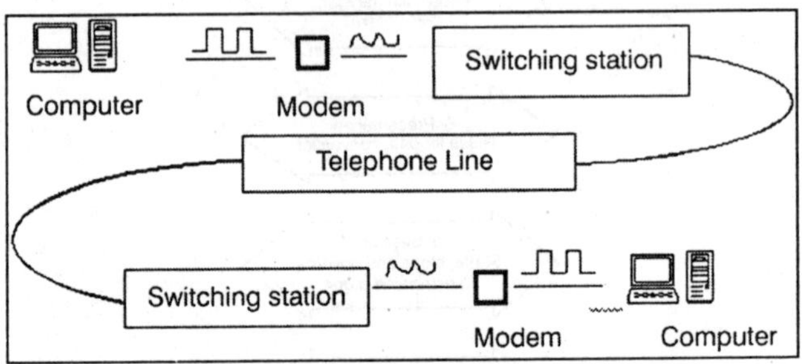

Fig. Communication Using Modem

Equipments (DTE) are connected through modem and Telephone line. The modems are the Data Circuit Terminating Equipments (DCE). DTE creates a digital signal and modulates using the modem. Then the signals relayed through an interface. The second modem at the receiving end demodulates into a form that the computer can accept. A modem that has extra functions such as automatic answering and dialing is called intelligent Modems.

DATA TRANSMISSION RATE

The speed at which data travel over a communication channel is called the communication rate. The rate at which the data are transferred is expressed in terms of bits per second (bps)

SIMPLEX

Simplex Mode

In simplex mode, data can be transmitted in one direction as shown in the figure. The device using the simplex mode of transmission can either send or receive data, but it cannot do both. An example is the traditional television broadcast, in which the signal is sent from the transmitter to the TV. There is no return signal. In other words a TV cannot send a signal to the transmitter.

Transmission Mode

When two computers are in communication, data transmission may occur in one of the three modes.

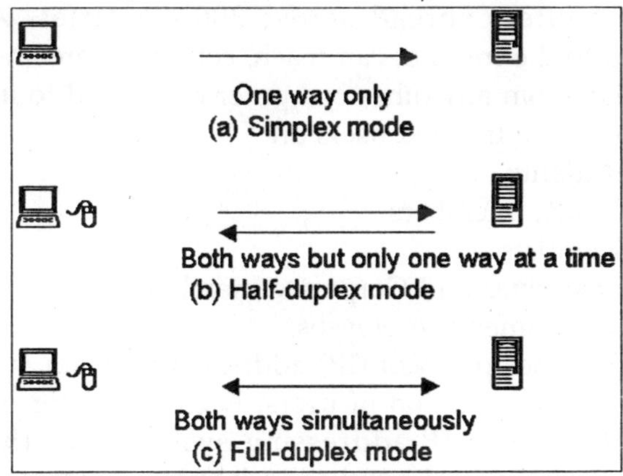

Fig. Transmission modes

Half Duplex Mode

In Half duplex mode data can be transmitted back and forth between two stations. But at any point of time data can go in any one direction only. This arrangement resembles traffic on a onelane bridge. When traffic moves in one direction, traffic on the opposite direction is to wait and take their turn. The common example is the walky-talky, wherein one waits for his turn while the other talks.

Full Duplex Mode

In full duplex mode a device can simultaneously send or receive data. This arrangement resembles traffic on a two-way bridge, traffic moving on both directions simultaneously. An example is two people on the telephone talking and listening simultaneously. Communication in full duplex mode is faster. Full duplex transmission is used in large computer systems.

Products like "Microsoft Net Meeting' supports such two way interaction

INTERNET

Several networks, small and big all over the world, are connected together to form a Global network called the Internet. Today's Internet is a network of about 50 million or more computers spread across 200 countries. Anyone connected to the Internet can reach, communicate and access information from any other computer connected to it.

Some of the Internet users are

- Students
- Faculty members
- Scientists
- Executives and Corporate members
- Government employees.

The Internet protocol (IP) addressing system is used to keep track of the million of users. Each computer on net is called a host. The IP addressing system uses the letter addressing system and number addressing systems.

COMMUNICATION PROTOCOL

Internet is a packet-switching network. Here is how packetswitching works: A sending computer breaks an electronic message into packets. The various packets are sent through a communication network-often by different routes, at different speeds and sandwiched in between packets from other messages.

Once the packets arrive at the destination, the receiving computer reassembles the packets in proper sequence. The packet switching is suitable for data transmission. The software that is responsible for making the Internet function efficiently is TCP/IP. TCP/IP is made up of two components. TCP stands for transmission control protocol and IP stands for Internet Protocol.

TCP breaks up the data to be sent into little packets. It guarantees that any data sent to the destination computer reaches intact. It makes the process appear as if one computer is directly connected to the other providing what appears to be a dedicated connection.

IP is a set of conventions used to pass packets from one host to another. It is responsible for routing the packets to a desired destination IP address.

Who Governs The Internet

The Internet as a whole does not have a single controller. But the Internet society, which is a voluntary membership organization, takes the responsibility to promote global information exchange through the Internet technology. Internet Corporation for Assigned Names and Numbers (ICANN) administers the domain name registration. It helps to avoid a name which is already registered.

Future of Internet

The popularity of Internet is growing ever since its evolution 20 years ago. This will bring out

- New standard protocol
- International connections
- Consumer civilization
- Data sharing in research and Engineering

Uses of Internet

The following are some of the popular Internet tools, used by the million of the users.

World Wide Web

Web is a multimedia portion of the Internet. It consists of an interconnection system of sites or servers all over the world that can store information in the multimedia form. The Multimedia sites include text, animated graph, voice and images. The World Wide Web is the most graphically inviting and easily navigable section of the Internet.

It contains several millions of pages of information. Each page is called a web page. A group of related web pages linked together forms a web site. The first page of the website is called a Home page. The Home page usually contains information about the site and links to other pages on that site. Every web page has a unique address called the Uniform Resource Locator or URL. The URL locates the pages on the Internet. An example of URL is,

http:// www.country-watch.com/India

Where http stands for Hypertext Transfer Protocol (HTTP). This protocol is meant for transferring the web files. The www portion of the address stands for "world wide web" and the next part countrywatch. com is the domain name. Generally, the domain name will be followed by directory path and the specific document address separated by slashes.

Looking for information on the Internet is called surfing or browsing. To browse the Internet, a software called web browser is used. Web browser translates HTML documents of the website and allows to view it on the screen. Examples of web browsers are Internet Explorer and Netscape Navigator. The mouse pointer moves over a underlined or highlighted words and images change to a hand icon. This is called an hyperlink. This indicates the link to other sites. To go to one of the linked sites, just click the mouse on the hyperlink.

E-mail: The World Wide Web is getting a lot of attention due to its main attraction of Electronic mail. Electronic mail is usually used to exchange messages and data files. Each user is assigned an electronic mail box. Using mail services, one can scan a list of messages that can be sent to anyone who has the proper email identification. The message sent to any one resides in the mailbox till it is opened. Many other features of standard mail delivery are implemented in email.

Usenet News Groups: Electronic discussion groups. User network abbreviated as usenet is essentially a giant disbursed bulletin board. Electronic discussion groups that focus on specific topic forms, computer forums.

Mailing list: Email based discussion groups combining E-mail, news groups and mailing lists send messages on a particular subject. Automatically messages reach the mailbox of that group.

FTP: File Transfer Protocol, abbreviated as FTP is used for the net user for transferring files around the world. The transfer includes software, games, photos, maps, music and such other relevant materials.

Telnet: Telnet is a protocol that allows the user to connect to a remote computer. This feature is used to communicate a microcomputer with mainframe.

Getting Connected to Internet

To use an Internet in the simplest way, we need

- A Computer
- A Telephone line
- A Modem
- Internet Service Provided or ISP

The ISPs are the companies which allows the user to use the Internet for a price. One has to register with the ISP for an Internet account. ISP provides the following:

- *User name*: An unique name that identifies the user
- *Password*: A secret code that prevents other users from using our account
- *E-mail Address*: Unique address that we can send or receive E-mails.

Fig. Dialogue Box for Connecting to the Internet

- *Access Telephone Number*: Internet users can use this number to connect to the service provider. Figure shows dialog boxes on the computer screen wherein the user name (Govt. Higher Secondary School, Chennai -600 003 abbreviated as a ghssch3), a password (alpha numeric of word length 8 characters appearing as 'x') and access telephone number are entered. By clicking on the dial button, the modem establishes a connection with the ISP.

There are two ways to look for the information on the Web. If the URL of the website is known, enter it on the address bar. If URL is not known, then 'Search Engines' will help us to get the information.

Search Engines are tools that allow the user to find specific document through key words or menu choices. Some of the popular Search engines are Yahoo, Lycos, AltaVista, Hotbot, Google and Askjeeves.

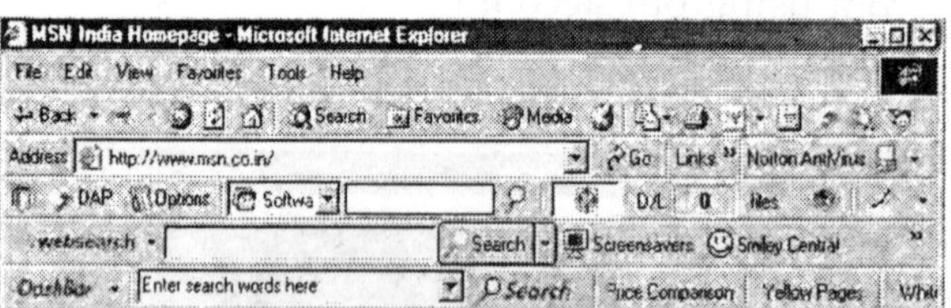

Fig. Entering the URL

Internet explorer helps to use the net more effectively with the navigation buttons on the toolbar. Internet explorer helps to use the net more effectively with the navigation buttons on the toolbar.

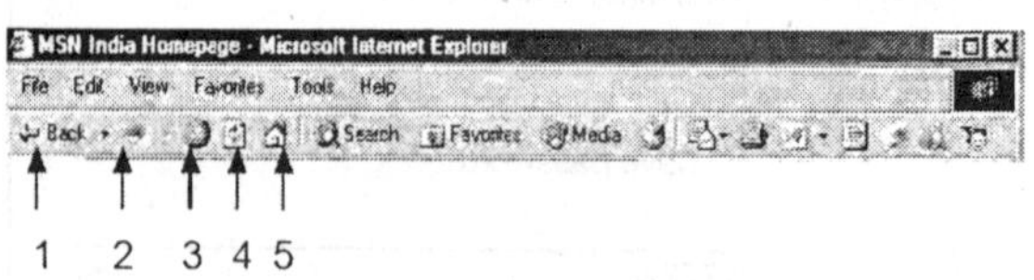

Fig. Navigation Buttons

- *Back Button*: This button helps to go back to the previous link. The small triangle adjacent to it displays a dropdown list of several recently used pages. Instead of pressing the back button several times, select a page from the list.

- *Forward Button*: This is a similar to the back button. One can jump forward by one page or several pages.
- *Stop Button*: After clicking on a link, some times we may realise that the link is not necessary. The click stop button and move back without wasting time.
- *Refresh Button*: Sometimes a page may take longer time or may not load properly. Click on the refresh button, helps reload the page faster.
- *Home Button*: While following the hyperlink, it is very easy to get lost. The home button reverts to the home page of the website.

Popular Uses of the Web

Research: The web provides research materials from libraries, research institutions, encyclopedia, magazines and newspapers. Some sample sites www.encarta.com the Internet Public Library site *www.ipl.com* and Library of Congress *www.loc.gov*.

Chatting: Some websites proved chat rooms to interact with an individual or a group.

Free-wares: Some sites provide free download of software's, tutorials and benchmarks.

Education online: Educational institutions offer courses via the web. Student can attend and interact in a class from home using a computer.

Online services: Online shopping, online booking for travels and entertainments managing investments are the upcoming areas of Internet that reaches every home.

Job searches: The digital revolution is changing everything it touches and the job market is no exception. Several web sites are assisting people in finding internship, jobs and helps companies to fill job vacancies. There are sites relating to specific job and profession also. Some of these sites charge a fee for the services while others are free.

Intranet and Extranet

Many organizations have Local Area Network that allows

their computers to share files, data, printers and other resources. Sometimes these private network uses TCP/ IP and other Internet standard protocols and hence they are called intranet. All the Internet services such as web pages, email, chat; usenet and FTP are provided on the intranet to serve the organization.

Creating a web page on the intranet is simple because they use only Word-Processing Software One of the main consideration of the intranet is security. The sensitive company data available on the intranet is protected from the outside world.

Taking intranet technology a few steps forward extranets are useful in the business world. Intranet connecting selected customers, suppliers and offices in addition to the internal personnel, is called extranet.

By using extranet business organizations can save telephone charges. For example a can manufacturing company can extend their intranet to their dealers and customers for support and service.

Chapter 7

Introduction to Windows XP

WINDOWS XP

Windows XP Professional is a user-friendly operating system designed for popular use. The most important advantage of using Windows is its GUI (pronounced as "*gooyee*"). It is said that the right side brain is good in processing the pictures and is the seat of creative thinking and intuitive ideas whereas the left side brain is good at logical thinking.

It is believed, before the introduction of GUI, users of OS, mainly used their left side brain, keeping their right side brain idle. It is felt, Windows effectively uses the left and right side of the brain.

Many other operating systems (including MS-DOS) use Command Line Interface (Interface lets any one connected with the machine. Actually interface is a (virtual) connection between two entities.

For example, T.V remote is an interface which connects a user and a T.V). In this kind of interface, we have to remember cryptic commands and type them without mistakes. To make things worse some operating systems are case-sensitive also (LS, Ls, lS or ls are not same).

A simple spelling mistake or missed space will result in an error. Windows displays all the information on the screen and all we have to do is to point and select using the mouse, with its GUI. A picture is worth a thousand of words, as they say. Windows XP Professional combines all the positive aspects of its Microsoft predecessors.

This satisfies all the users who want to prevent frequent crashing of software and want to use easy techniques

Evolution of the Windows Operating System

Windows XP is the latest version in the series of Windows products in the Operating System.The Apple introduced the concept of Windows but Microsoft popularised the Windows concept. The first version which become reasonably popular was Windows 3.0. For the first time, Windows came with file management utilities and other system tools.

Soon, several applications that were meant to be used with Windows appeared in the market. Within a few years, Windows started being used in offices, homes and business establishments. Windows 3.0 was followed by Windows 3.1, which offered better features. Windows 3.1 used a window called Programme Manager to launch applications. Almost at the same time, Microsoft introduced Windows 3.11 for workgroups.

Now, Windows could be used on a LAN-based networking environment. None of these products was an actual operating system of its own. They were just programs that worked with MS-DOS. The next major development came with the introduction of Windows 95. Unlike earlier versions of Windows, Windows 95 was a complete operating system. Now, Windows was no longer restricted by the conventions of MS-DOS.

It was easier to start applications in Windows 95. The Programme Manager of Windows 3.1 was hidden from the user. This was replaced by new ways of starting applications and opening documents.

It also gave the user better facilities to manage application windows, new context-sensitive short-cut menus, improved networking features and so on.

After Windows 95, came Windows 98 with a bang. Windows 98 offered many new utilities at that time, improved the performance and support of the latest hardware technologies of that time. It also provided several features and utilities that allowed easy access to the internet.

In the meantime Microsoft produced Windows NT(New Technology) independent of 9x(95 or 98) versions. Windows NT family produced Windows NT versions 3.5,3.51,4 each of which came in a workstation version and a server version.

Some users thought

Windows 9x crashed often, that is they felt Windows 9x lacked stability. Some others thought Windows NT lacked compatibility. That is they cannot run some of their favourite programs in NT which could run successfully in Windows 9x. The windows 9x line gave a new offspring Me (Millennium edition) which provided some of the much needed stability.

NT line of development resulted in Windows 2000 professional. Windows 2000 professional increased the compatibility of its parent.

The never tiring Microsoft development team, at last brought the stability of NT and the compatibility of 9x, under one roof, which resulted in Windows XP Professional through Windows XP home.

Windows XP professional is designed to satisfy the insatiable demand of the business community but its immediate predecessor, Windows XP home targetted home users. At the time of writing this book, Microsoft is to introduce windows 2003. The never ending race of ever increasing demand and the quest for satisfying them may continue leading to the vocation of more and more sophisticated with user-friendly products.

The Mouse

If we want to extract work from the computer, we have to input data. The input can normally be provided by the keyboard and the Mouse.

We know the keyboard. If we want to move from one window to another, unless we know the keyboard combinations, it will be very difficult to move one window to another by using keyboard. But the mouse intuitively provides the idea.

As we have learnt in the earlier section, Windows XP uses

GUI. That is, all information is displayed on the screen. We can use it by simply pointing to it and selecting. To do this we use the mouse. The mouse is an input device that we move on a flat surface (usually a mouse pad.). When we move the mouse, a pointer moves on the screen.

This pointer, called the Mouse Pointer, is used to point to things on the screen. The mouse has either two or three buttons on the top. The left button is the most often used. Described below are mouse actions that we need to know to use Windows XP effectively.

Note: Click on and Click are used interchangeably for example we can write Click on the button or Click the button.

- *Move*: Moving the mouse is simply dragging the mouse on the mouse pad so that the mouse pointer moves in the direction we want, without touching the buttons. This action allows we to point to things on the screen.
- *Click*: Clicking is used to select objects on the Windows screen. To click, ensure that the mouse is pointing to what we want and press the left button of the mouse once and release the button immediately.
- *Double-click*: Double-click is most often used to start applications. To double-click, point to what we want and press the left button of the mouse twice in quick succession.

  We should get used with Double-click; because new comers to the computer field find it difficult to cope with Double-click in the beginning.
- *Click and Drag*: This mouse action is used to move an object from one place to another. When we click and drag an object, the object moves along with the mouse pointer. To click and drag, hold the left button of the mouse down and move the mouse to the place wherever we want.

Mouse after Right Click

The right click: Right Mouse button gains a lot of

significance now-a-days. If we right click on an item, we will be provided with a context sensitive menu (context sensitive menu changes its contents depending on the situation). This is also called short-cut menu. We can experiment with that menu.

The context sensitive menu provides almost all the facilities offered by menu as well as toolbars. We can change left mouse button into right mouse button and vice versa. In this case the left click becomes the right click and vice versa. This action may be helpful to the left handed people.

Moving the Mouse Pointer Via the Keyboard

Again we can create the effect of all the above operations by keyboard operations. In the beginning, people are very much attracted by the use of mouse, but when they have to write lengthy programs, changing mouse and keyboard frequently is irksome. Therefore those people who are experts in typewriting prefer to make use of keyboard to bring the effect of mouse click. The following keys can duplicate the mouse operations. If we want to use our keyboard to do the work of the mouse, we have to follow these steps:

- Click the Start button
- Select the Control Panel in the menu and click it.
- Choose the Accessibility Options icon and click on it.
- It opens a screen, click on Accessibility Option under pick a Control Panel icon.
- Open the Mouse tab.
- Activate use MouseKeys check box if it is not already activated.

Windows XP allows we to move the mouse pointer by using the arrow keys on numeric keypad of the keyboard.

Note 1: Make sure that we have Num Lock turned on.

Note 2: MouseKeys do not work with the separate arrow-key keypads found on most modern keyboards.

Besides the basic arrow movements, we can also use the numeric keypad keys outlined here. The following table gives we the equivalent keys for mouse operations.

Key Equivalent Mouse Action

Key	Equivalent Mouse Action
5	Click
+	Double-click
/	Select the left mouse button
*	Select both mouse buttons
-	Select the right mouse button
Insert	Lock the selected button
Delete	Release the selected button

These keys can be used as follows:

- To double-click an object, use the arrow keys to move the pointer over the object, press the slash key (/) to select the left mouse button, and press the plus sign (+) to double-click.
- To right-click an object, use the arrow keys to move the pointer over the object, press the minus sign (-) to select the right mouse button, and press 5.
- To drag-and-drop an object, use the arrow keys to move the pointer over the object, press the slash key (/) to select the left mouse button, press Insert to lock the button, use the arrow keys to move the object to its desired destination, and press Delete to release the button and drop the object.
- To click an object, use the arrow keys to move the pointer over the object, press the slash key (/) to select the left mouse button (if it isn't selected already), and press 5 to click.
- To right-drag-and-drop an object, use the arrow keys to move the pointer over the object; press the minus sign (-) to select the right mouse button; press Insert to lock button; use the arrow keys to move the object to its destination; and then press Delete to release the button to drop the object, and display the context menu.

Use MouseKeys when Num Lock is on. These options determine the relationship between MouseKeys and the Num Lock key. When On is activated (this is the default), for example, Windows XP will use MouseKeys whenever we have Num Lock is on. If we then turn off Num Lock, we can use the regular arrow keys. Show MouseKey status on screen: When this check box is activated, Windows XP displays the MouseKeys icon in the system tray. Double-clicking this icon opens the Accessibility Properties dialog box.

LOGGING IN

If the computer is not already turned on, turn on the computer. If we are the lone user we will be taken into the Windows XP desktop directly. We can continue our work.

Suppose there are multi-users, we will be shown a welcome screen similar to what is shown in figure. The aim of logging in is to take we to Windows XP desktop.

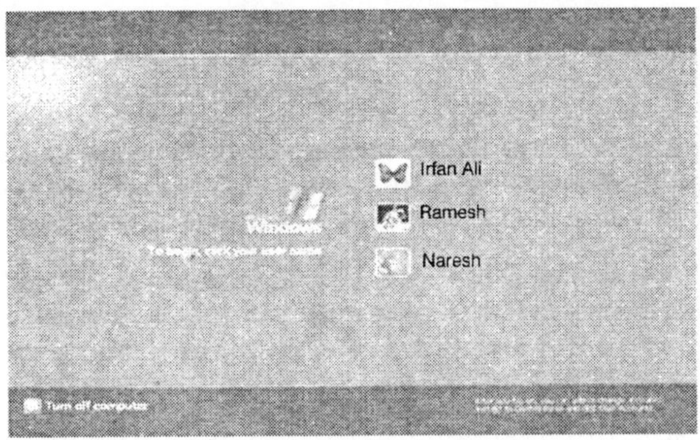

Fig. Logging Screen

We can select our account by clicking the appropriate icon or username. (Icon is a small picture/ image representing an application, Icon literally means a statue.) If we do not have a user account, do not worry, there is guest account which we can make use of. We all know PC means Personal Computer. A single person or his family used a computer earlier which made them to store his/ their data secretly.

When many different people start to work in the same computer, secrecy cannot be maintained. We cannot afford to provide each one with a computer. Such proposition is a costly affair. How about making the people to believe that they are working in their own computers even though they work in the same computer?

We can select our account by clicking the appropriate icon

or username. (Icon is a small picture/ image representing an application, Icon literally means a statue.) If we do not have a user account, do not worry, there is guest account which we can make use of. We all know PC means Personal Computer.

A single person or his family used a computer earlier which made them to store his/ their data secretly. When many different people start to work in the same computer, secrecy cannot be maintained. We cannot afford to provide each one with a computer. Such proposition is a costly affair. How about making the people to believe that they are working in their own computers even though they work in the same computer?

Note: Windows XP is used to refer Windows XP Professional Suppose we do not have password we will be taken directly to the Windows XP. Suppose we do have a password (otherwise it will defeat the purpose of having User Account. User Accounts determine who the actual users are.

Others may enter in to the system as Guest user) an entry box appears, click the entry box and enter our password into it. Caution must be taken to enter our password because it is case sensitive. Our 'A' is different from 'a'. Our password is determined by the administrater. The administrater governs the computer.

Consult our teacher for further details. This trick is achieved by a user account. If we have a user account in Windows XP Professional, we will be provided with a separate My Computer, My Documents, and some other folders. The only drawback is that our work can be watched by the administrator or administrators, he/ she/ they has/ have special powers to control the activities related to that personal computer with Windows XP Professional. If we have forgotten our password (which we cannot afford, especially if we are the administrator, in this case nobody can help we) and if we select the help icon for hint, the password hint appears (if we have one).

If we commit mistake while we enter our password, we will be prompted to enter our password again, with some help from the computer. When we are in the welcome screen, Ctrl + Alt + Del key combinations, provide we the dialog box for entering the username and password. If we successfully enter our password, we will be taken to Windows XP Desktop. If our computer is on a network, we may be shown a dialogue window that requests our ID and Password. Provide them.

Logging Off and Shutting Down

Logging off is the process of closing the desktop and returning to the Windows Log In screen.

Suppose we want to come out of our work, we can do either of the following two. We can close our session or we can shut down the computer. Suppose we want to Log off without shutting down the computer, follow the following steps:

- Save all unsaved documents
- Click the Start button (or press Winkey or Ctrl + Esc; Winkey pronounced as Win-key that lies between Ctrl and Alt keys, the Start menu will be displayed.
- Click the Log off button (or press L or l key) Log Off is at the bottom of the Start menu.
- We will be shown Log off Windows. Click Log off button (or press L or l key).

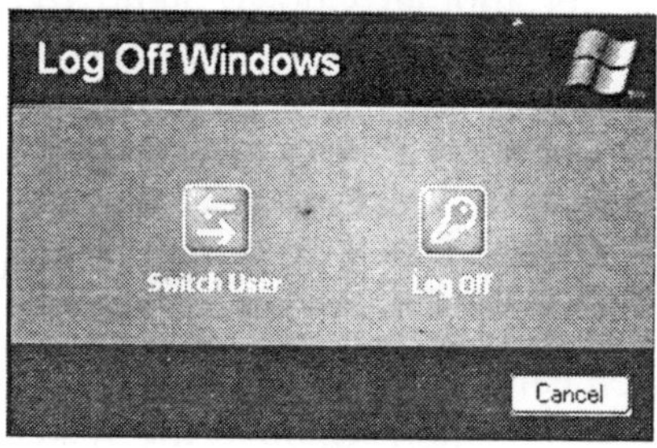

Fig. Log Off Screen

Note: Do not try to use Switch User button. It may lead to dangerous consequences. It may lead to fatal error; we should restart wer computer. We may lose unsaved data in this process. Suppose we want to shut down the computer we have to follow these steps,alert the other users at that time.

- Save all unsaved documents
- Click the Start button.

- Click Turn Off Computer button (or press U or u key).We will be Shown Turn Off Computer Window with three options, along with cancel.
- If we have changed our mind not to shut down the computer click Cancel, button at the bottom.
- If we want to shut down the computer click Turn Off button (or press U or u key).

Some computers especially new ones will automatically shut down the computers. Other computers will show us. 'It is now Safe to Turn off your computer' message (It is specific to the Configuration).

We can switch off the computer. Alternatively we can press the power key from the keyboard, if that key is available in our computer. We can also Turn Off the computer by the key combinations of Alt+F4 and then click Turn Off button. Another method for turning off is given in customizing the Taskbar.

- Suppose we have dual operating system, if we want to switch over to the other operating system then we can click Restart button. This will be useful when we install new software also.
- There is yet another Choice Stand By. This may be very useful for notebook computer. This action will save power. If we have Hibernate facility, we can make use of it. Place the cursor on Stand By button and press Shift key, Stand By will change into Hibernate. If we click the Hibernate button (Shift + Click Stand By) and Switch off computer, the computer can be started comparatively quickly, in the next time, when we open the system.

Working with Windows XP

When we switch on our computer, Windows XP automatically starts loading from the Hard disk, if it is our default operating system. While loading, it performs a series of diagnostic tests to check the memory and hardware components such as keyboard, disk drives etc. Once the diagnostic tests are over, Windows XP starts loading files and graphics necessary for the GUI interface. This takes a few minutes, after which it displays a screen.

Fig. The Desktop

The opening screen of Windows XP is called the Desktop. The desktop of our computer may look different from what is seen in This is because Windows XP allows we to change the appearance of the desktop. Our computer may or may not be connected to other computers.

Computers that are not connected to any other computers are called Stand-alone computers. Two or more computers can be connected together to form a network. If our computer is in a Network, we have to do some more actions to Start our computer.

The Desktop

In Windows XP, the basic working platform is the Desktop. Let us understand the desktop with an example. When we study, we use a table, don't we? Usually, we keep all the books and note books that we may need on the table in front of we. We may also keep our pencil box, colour box, a dictionary and a few other things on the table.

When we want a particular notebook, we simply reach out to that notebook and pick it up. Window's desktop is very similar to the tabletop. All the programs in our computer are available on the desktop. Here, instead of our hand, we use the mouse pointer to point to things and select them.

The desktop has several Icons. Each icon has a label telling we the name of the application it represents. My Computer, My Documents, My Recent Documents are some of the standard icons that we can see on the Windows desktop. Each of these icons represents an application that is frequently used. For example, My Computer allows we to see the contents of our computer, install and use new software and hardware. Apart from the standard icons provided by Windows, we can also create icons for the applications that we use frequently and place them on the desktop.

The desktop also contains the Taskbar The taskbar is usually a narrow strip, present at the bottom of the screen. On the left, it has the Start button. When we click on the Start button, the Start menu appears on the left side of the screen. Using the Start menu, we can start any application that we have currently installed. Next to the Start button is the Quick Launch Toolbar.

One advantage of using Windows XP is the easy access it provides to the Internet, through the quick launch toolbar which contains icons that allow we to select some commonly used Internet-related applications. On the extreme right is the Systems Tray that contains the Clock and icons for other utilities. The empty space between the Quick Launch Toolbar and the Systems Tray is used to display buttons for the applications currently being used.

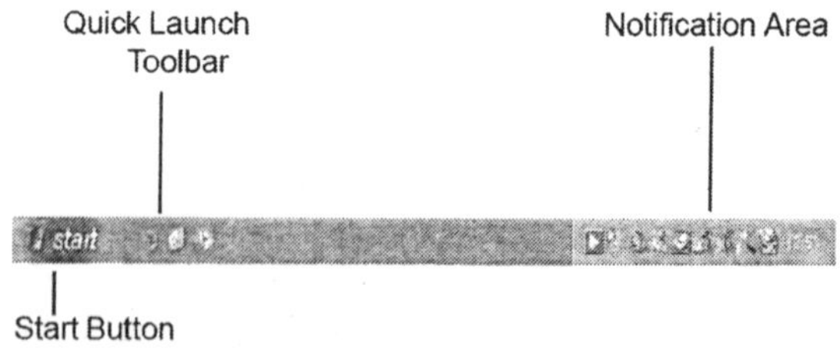

The Start Menu

The Start menu acts as a launch pad for most of the things we want to do with Windows XP. Using this menu, we can start applications, change the settings of our computer, find files, get help and do much, much more. The Start menu appears when we click on the Start button on the taskbar.

We can have two different Start menus, one is our usual Start menu and another one is Classic Start menu, which is explained later.

Fig. The Start Menu

We can select an option from this menu by using the mouse. As we move the mouse pointer over the options, they get highlighted.

Simply click the mouse when the option we want is

highlighted. All Programs on the Start menu has an arrow on the right.

A right arrow, whether we are in Start menu or Classic Start menu indicates the presence of one or more levels of submenu. A submenu is shown in Figure.

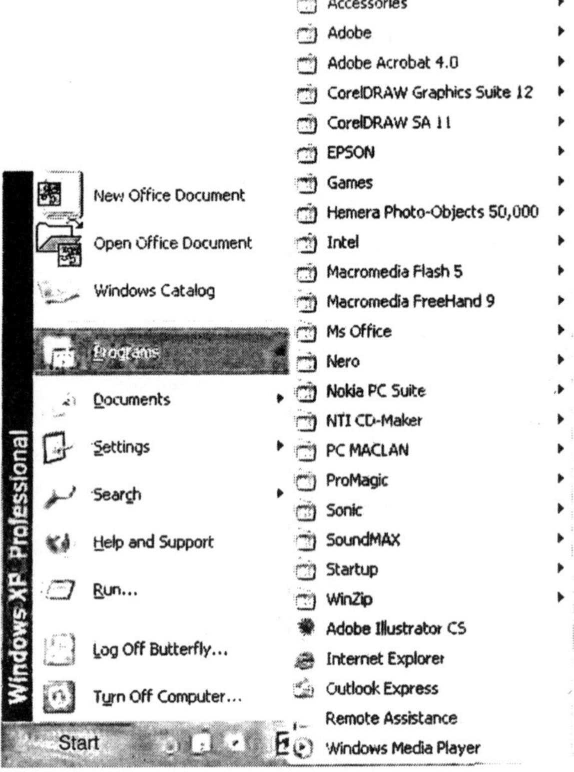

Note: The particulars in the screen may differ from our screen but the general features are the same.

To select an option on the submenu, slide the mouse pointer sideways. One option on the submenu will get highlighted.

Now, move the mouse pointer up and down till the option that we want is highlighted and click.

Note that some of the options in the submenu also have

an arrow. Selecting these options will display another submenu as shown in Figure.

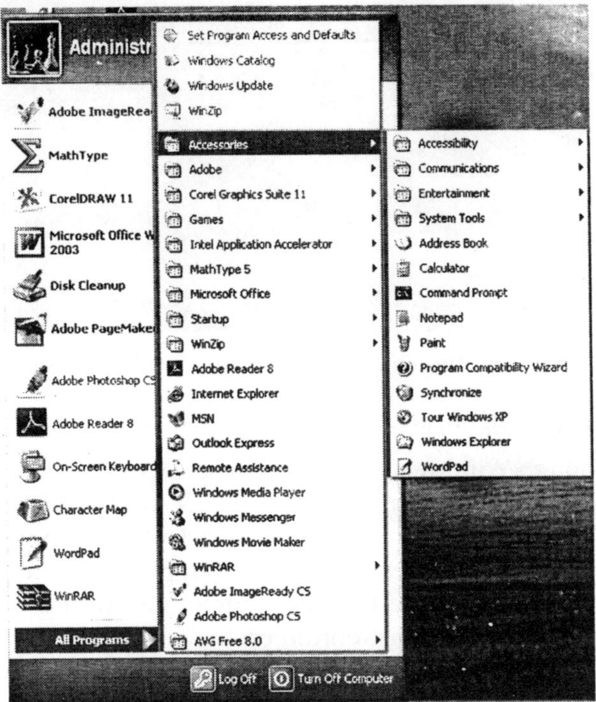

Fig. Start, Programs, Accessories Menus

Starting an Application

Windows XP allows we to start an application in many ways. The most frequently used ones are:

- Using icons on the desktop
- Using the Start menu

Using icons on the Desktop: The easiest way to start an application is to use its icon on the desktop.

When we want to start an application, look for its icon on the desktop.

If we find the icon, double-click on it to start the application. For example, to start the card game Solitaire, look for its Short-cut on the desktop and double-click on it.

The game appears on the screen as shown in Figure.

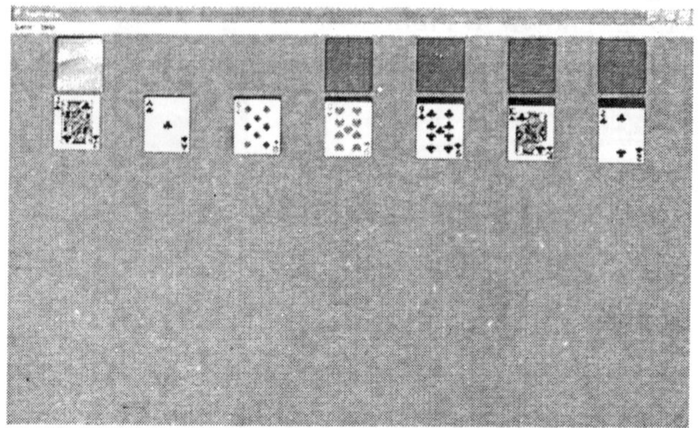

Fig. Application Started Using an Icon on the Desktop

Using the Start Menu

Though Windows XP gives we a few icons on the desktop and allows we to create our own icons for other frequently used applications; it is not possible to have icons for all applications on the desktop. To start applications, for which icons are not available on the desktop; we can use the Start menu. Click on the Start button on the taskbar and select the option that we want from any one of the menus or submenus that appear.

For example, to start the card game Solitaire (If we have not made a Shotcut), click on the Start button, and then click on All Programs. Select Games from the submenu, which appears, then click on Solitaire.

We can also perform the above operation by keyboard operations alone.

- Press Ctrl + Esc, or Window Key
- Press P, this will highlight All Programs (Character P is underlined.
- Press the Enter key, submenu will be displayed.
- Press G
- In the final submenu press S and Enter key.

Now we are in the card game Solitaire. Suppose we want to select an item of Microsoft in the submenu of programs, repeated use of M(or m) key will take we to different items that start with letter m (M). After the desired item is selected then follow these steps as given above.

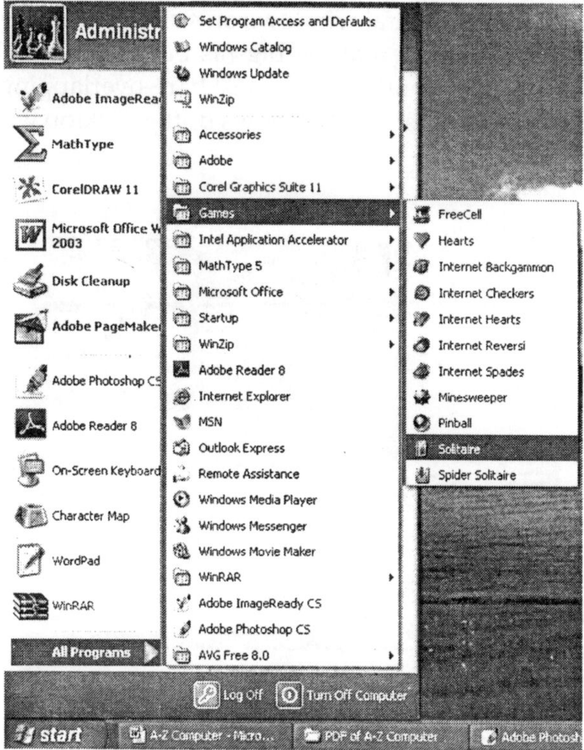

Fig. Using the Start Menu to Start Solitaire

WINDOWS

When we are using a table to study, we keep all the books we need on the table. Each book occupies some space on the table. Smaller books occupy less space and bigger books take up more space.

The books may even overlap each other partially or completely. We can use these books by moving them around, closing some, opening others and so on.

By doing this, we can ensure that the book we want is easily available to us. Windows XP allows we to work with different applications in the same way. When we start an application, it occupies a rectangular area on the desktop. This rectangular area is called a window.

We can have several windows on our desktop at the same time. These windows may be big (as big as the desktop) or small (as small as a button on the taskbar), overlapping others or one beside the other. Figure shows us the desktop with three windows.

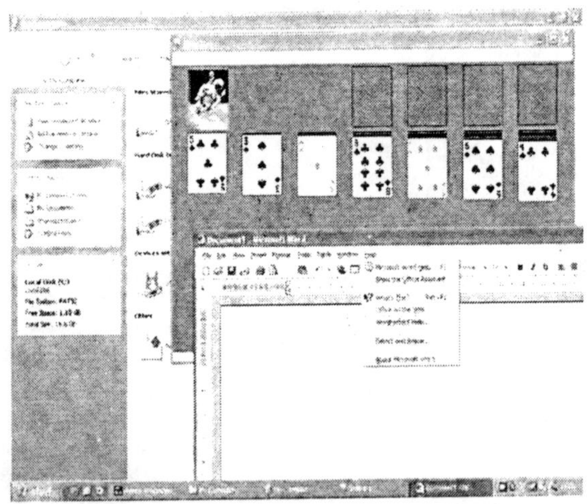

Fig. Desktop with three windows

Parts of a Window

To work efficiently with windows, it is important to learn to manage them well. Windows XP allows us to move them around, change their size, and hide them from our view and so on. Let us use the application WordPad, to manage windows well. WordPad is one of the applications that comes as part of Windows XP. It is a simple word processor - we can enter and store text using it. To start WordPad, click on Start All Programs Accessories WordPad.

The above command means first click the Start button, then click All Programs in the menu, then click Accessories from the ensuing submenu, and finally click Wordpad in the last submenu that appears.

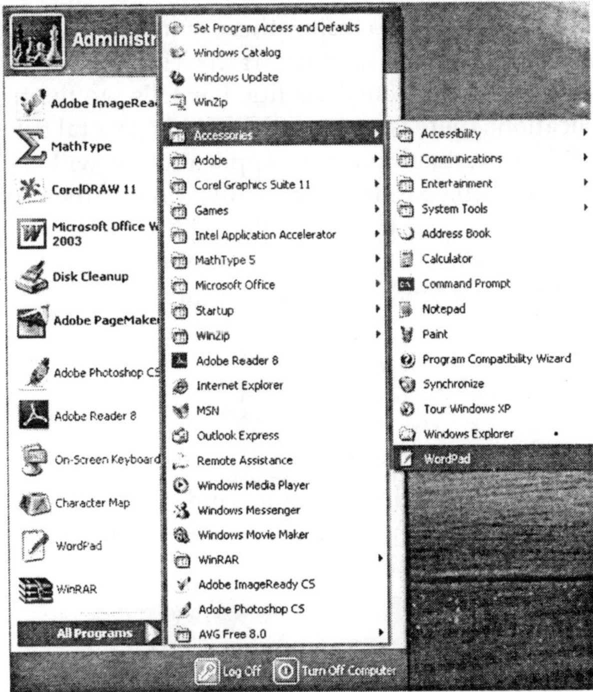

Fig. Starting WordPad

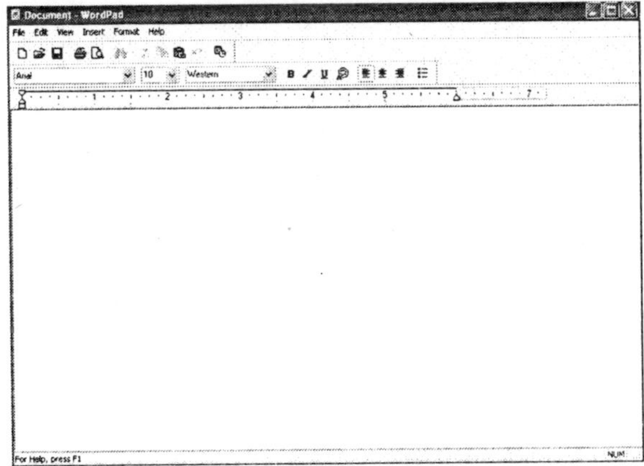

Fig. WordPad window

The Wordpad window opens. Windows XP is designed in such a way that all windows are similar. The methods used for sizing, moving and closing these windows are also the same. At the top of each window is the Title Bar.

As the name indicates, the title bar tells we the name of the application. There is an execption to this general rule. Even though Windows Explorer is an application, it will not show its name in the title bar. It also contains three of the following four Sizing buttons, at the top of the right corner.

Minimize Button: The minimize button is used to reduce the size of the window to a button on the taskbar.

Remember that minimizing a window does not close a window. It simply hides it from we. Figure shows the WordPad window minimized.

Fig. Minimized WordPad window

Maximize Button: Clicking on this button enlarges the window to fill the entire desktop.

Fig shows the Word Pad window maximized.

Fig. Maximized WordPad window

Restore Button: This button is used to restore the win dow to its original size (that is, to the size before we maximized it).

Fig. Restored Wordpad window

Close Button:

This button is used to close a window.

Re member that closing a window will remove its contents from memory and screen.

Below the title bar is the Menu Bar. This displays the different menus available to us. When we click on a menu option, say Edit, all the sub-options appear as a drop-down menu. We can select any one of them by pointing to it with the mouse pointer and clicking it.

Fig. Edit Menu

One or more Toolbars appear below the menu bar. Toolbars consist of icons representing shortcuts for the most frequently used commands.

For example, to save a file, we can click on the File menu and select Save from the drop-down list. An easier method would be to click on the Save icon on the toolbar. (Ctrl + S (or Ctrl +s) combinations also will save the file). If we save for the first time, we will be prompted to enter the name of the file.

Moving a Window

Often, while working with multiple windows, we need to move a window to different area of the desktop to see one of the underlying windows. We do so by clicking and dragging the title bar of the window. Note: We cannot drag a Window when it is either maximized or minimized.

Changing the size of a Window

Every window has a Border that can be used to change its size. Point to the window border with the mouse. The mouse pointer changes into a double-headed arrow. Click and drag this arrow to increase or decrease the size of window.

To change the length and breadth of the windows simultaneously, we have to move the mouse pointer to either of the bottom corners of the window. Now, the mouse pointer changes into a double headed arrow as said above. Click and drag the arrow to increase and decrease the length and breadth of the window simultaneously.

Windows Dialog Boxes

Windows XP is an inter-active operating system. Its GUI attempts to display as much information on the screen as possible. It uses dialog boxes to display the information and allows us to either type in our response or select from a list of choices. Listed below are some of the controls used in dialog boxes.

Text Boxes: Text boxes are used to allow the user to enter some data. Every text box is accompanied by a prompt or label that tells us what should be entered in that box. Figure shows a window with a text box.

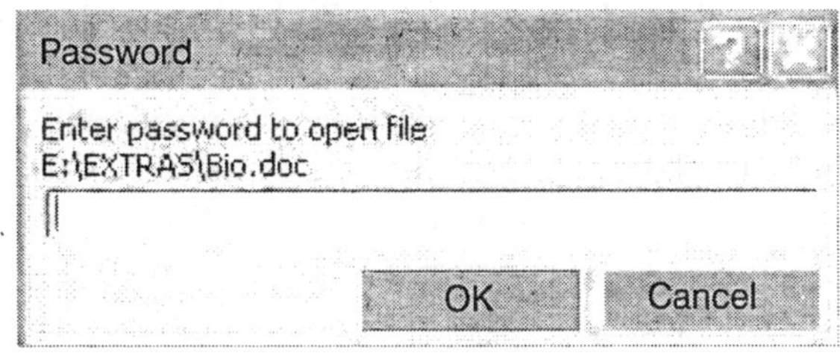

Fig. A Window with a Text Box

List Boxes: These boxes display a list of choices. We can select the one we want by simply clicking on it

Fig. A List Box

Drop-down List Boxes: These are list boxes which have a small black inverted triangle at one end. When we click on this triangle, a list of options drops down in front of us. We can select an item from this list by clicking on it. This is used when there is limited space.

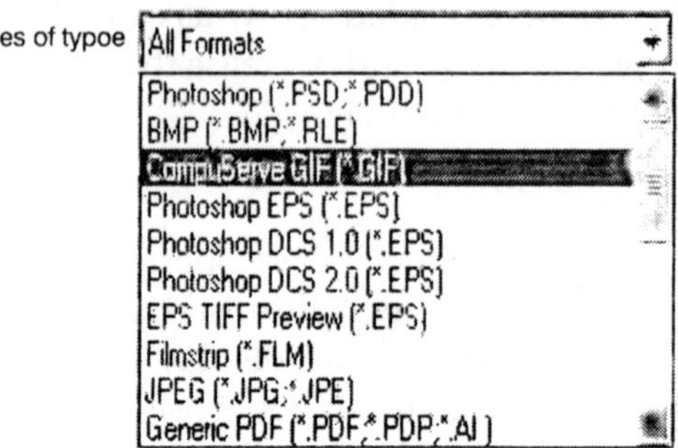

Fig. A Drop-down List Box

Radio Buttons: Figure displays a dialog box with 2 Radio buttons. These buttons are used to display multiple options. We can select one by clicking on the small white circle to the left of the option. A black dot appears at the centre of the circle to indicate a selected option. In radio button option, we can select only one of the buttons.

If we select a second radio button, the previously selected button is automatically deselected. If we have to answer multiple choice questions with several options in which we have only one correct answer then Radio Buttons are the suitable candidates.

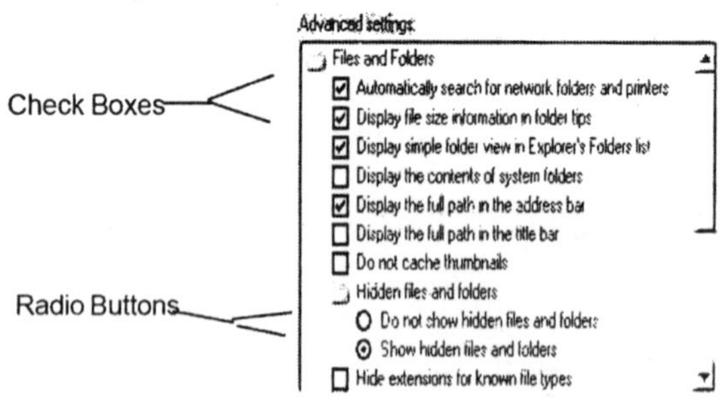

Fig. Radio Buttons and Check Boxes

Check Boxes: These boxes are used to enable or disable

options. The options in these boxes have small white squares to their left. Clicking on a square enables the option and clicking on it again disables it. A tick mark in this square indicates that the option is enabled and a blank square indicates that the option is disabled. We can select any number of check boxes in the given option.

Buttons: The OK and Cancel buttons are the most frequently used buttons in Windows XP. When we click on a button, the related command is carried out. For example, if we click on the OK button in a dialog box, Windows will accept our choices and close the dialog box. Clicking on Cancel will make Windows ignore the changes and close the dialog box. Some buttons are also used to display another dialog box.

Tabs: Tabs are used to display different sets of options in dialog boxes. Figure display a dialog box with five tabs. Clicking on each, displays an entirely different set of options. Figure shows the dialog box with the second tab Desktop selected. In Figure, the third tab, Screen Saver has been selected.

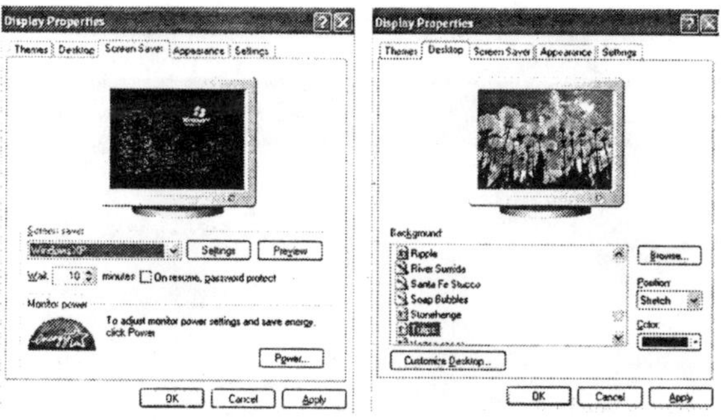

Fig. (a) Desktop Tab is Selected (b) Screen Saver Tab is Selected

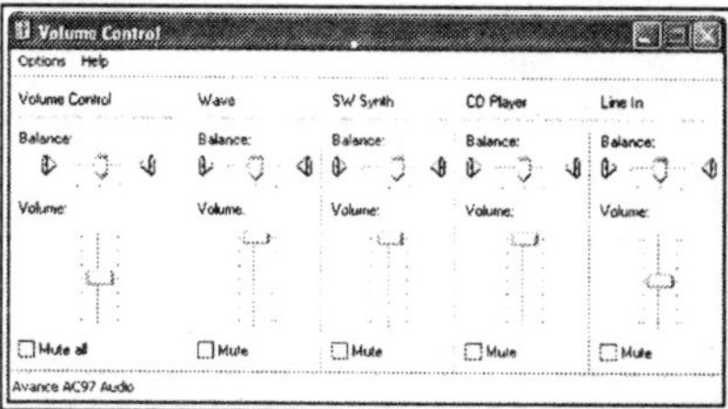

Fig. Sliders

Help and Support Centre

Even though this Chapter tries to help us to make use of Windows XP Professional, it is impossible to include all the facilities available in Windows XP Professional in a tiny Chapter. How can we access the remaining facilities offered by Windows XP Professional ? As we know, self-help is the best help. The Microsoft provides lot of help in its Help and Support Centre in Windows XP.

Actually Windows "Me" introduced Help and Support System by substantially improving the help methods available in earlier versions of Windows. Windows Me, by combining many more external resources, introduced a Web-style interface to replace old-type Helpfile interface of the earlier versions of Windows.

Windows XP improved the help facilities of Windows Me remarkably.

If we have an Internet connection, we need not use Internet Explorer to access the Microsoft knowledge Base. We can search it directly from Help and Support System.

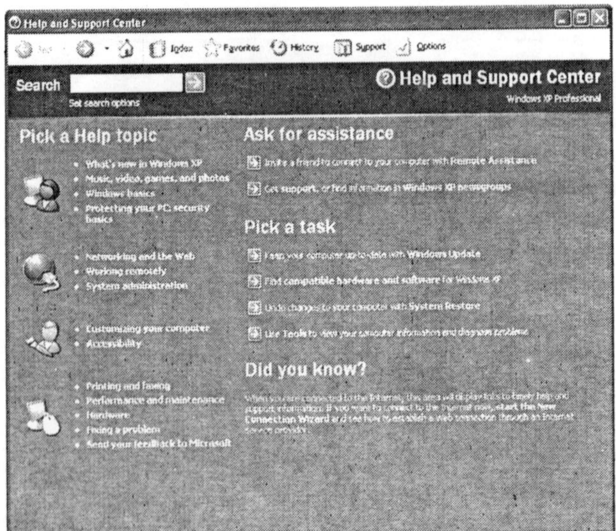

Fig. Home page for Help and Support Centre

Microsoft knowledge Base is an online database of

questions and answers Start Help and Support (or press F1 key when we are in Windows XP) will provide with the help relevant to the programme. Always make use of Winkey + F1 key combinations in order to avoid ambiguity.

This will take we to the Help and Support Centre of XP without fail, wherever we are. The Home page may slightly be different from what we see here because of customization (Customization is the process of changing default setting to suit our needs and tastes).

Except in dialog boxes, each Help and Support Centre window has a title bar, which shows Help and Support Centre as the title along with the Minimize, Maximize and Close buttons.

There is no Menu bar. It has a Toolbar, taking us to go around (navigate or travel) the Help topics. So it is called Navigating toolbar. Below the Navigating toolbar appears the Search bar.

Below this bar, information is provided. If we are lucky enough, we can get the desired help by clicking a topic from Pick a Help Topic which may solve our problem.

If we pick a topic from the Ask for Assistance that will take we either to Remote Assistance or to Support and Windows XP news groups. Any one of these may solve our problem if we have a Internet connection. But beginners may find it difficult to understand the help provided by the above. So they should be content only with what they have with internal assistance.

We should make familiar with Pick a Task and "Did you Know?" by ourself. If the item for which we need help may not be available at the home page, then enter the word or phrase into the search text box. Then press ENTER key or click the Go button (a) situated to the right of Search text box.

Suppose we have entered "view pictures" in the Search text box, Help and Support Centre displays Search Results pane on the left side and adds a toolbar containing Add to favorites, Change view, Print and Locate in Contents buttons in the right pan. Search results are shown below this Toolbar. This Help page is context sensitive.

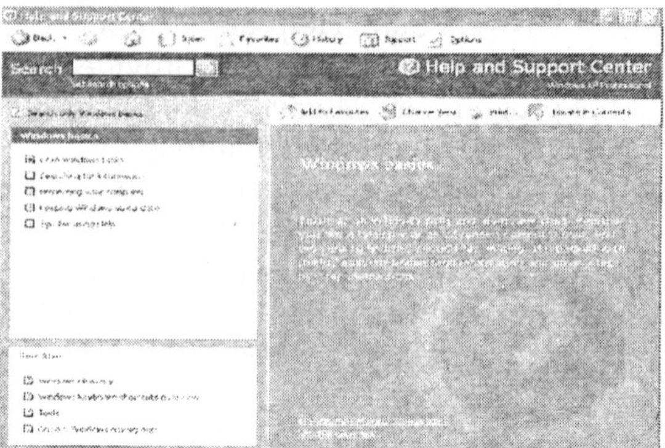

Fig. Windows Basics Help

If we have not customized the search results pane, it is divided into Suggested Topics, Full Text Search Matches and Microsoft knowledge Base. If we do not want to make use of Microsoft Knowledge Base or if we do not have Internet connection, we can hide Microsoft Knowledge Base. We can see only the first two options, the procedure for hiding Microsoft Knowledge Base will be given later.

Suggested Topics: Suggested Topics are keyword matches (these topics contain the word/ words that we have entered in the Search text box as keyword/ keywords). These topics are further classified into Pick a Task and Overviews, Articles and Tutorials.

Full-Text Search Matches: Full-text matches are topics that contain the word/ words we entered into the Search text box, into the body of the text of the help topics. Here the word/ words will not be treated as keyword/ keywords.

Microsoft Knowledge Base: The results found in this category are from Microsoft Knowledge Base. Use it if we like. We should have Internet connection; in order access this knowledge base.

If we want to display the help content, first click the category and click a search result of interest, the result is displayed in the right pane. Some help text pages will have highlighted and colored text. We see their uses below.

Highlighted text: The matched word/ pharse with what we had entered is highlighted. The highlighting serves no other purpose. If we click on those highlighted word/ pharse nothing happens. If highlighted words occur often in a text, it is an annoying experience. We can get rid off those highlighting if do not like it. We will be shown the procedure later.

Blue underline text: If we click the blue underline text, it will open the item associated with the text.

Green underlined text: If we click on this term it will provide the definition of the term. Already we have seen that three or four activated useful buttons on the right pane. Now we are going to see their usefulness.

Add to Favorites: If we see a help page and if we feel that will be useful to we for future reference, just click Add to Favorites button, that page is immediately copied and Windows XP Professional will announce that our wish is fulfilled. If we want to see the contents, we click Favorites in the navigation bar. In the left pane under the Favorites heading, opens what we have stored so far.

If we double click any one of the topic, the contents will be displayed in the right pane (we can also single click on any one of the topic and click Display button at the bottom). We can use rename or remove buttons as usual.Rename is used to change the default name. This topic is explained later.

Change View: In order to reclaim more space, we can hide the left pane by clicking the Change View button. If we again click Change View button, the left pane will appear once again. We can also perform the above action manually. We can drag the right pan to the left, so that a right pan may occupy the entire screen.

Print: We can print the help pages with this button.

Locate in Contents: If we click the Locate in Contents, it will display a table of contents for help and support in the left pane. The heading of the current help page is highlighted.

Help Index Button

Use if we know the first letter or first few letters of an item to be searched. We may feel a list that starts with that letter/letters may be helpful. If it is the case we click Index button on the toolbar. The left pane turns into an index.

Under this we can find Type in the keyword to find prompt, below this, there is the text area. We enter a letter or few letters into the text area, the index will automatically change to word/ words that started with the entered letters. We can click the appropriate entry from the list and then click the Display button or double click the desired item. If necessary use the vertical scroll bar available at the right end of the left pane.

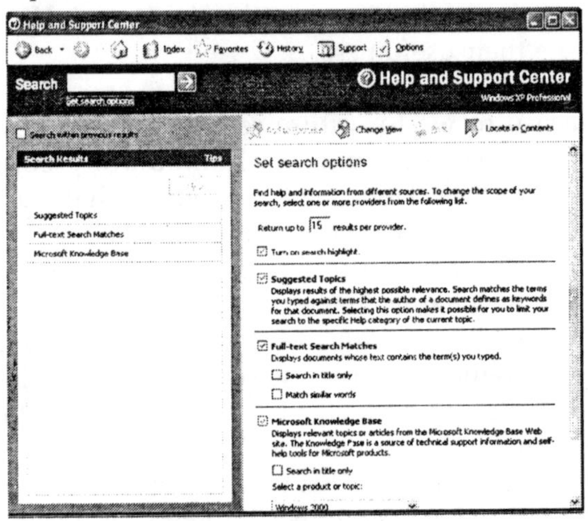

Fig. View Folders Help

Now concentrate on the navigation bar, Back: This is the first button in the navigation bar from left, after navigating to another page in help, if we want to move to the previous help page, clicking Back button will take we to the previous page. This process can be repeated until the back button is disabled. This button is disabled in the beginning.

Forward: This is the second button in the navigation bar from left. After we click the back button the forward button is enabled. We move forward by clicking the Forward button until it is disabled. This button is disabled in the beginning.

Home: This is the third button from left in the navigation bar. If we want to return to the home page, click on the Home button. Y o u have already seen Index and Favorites buttons available in the navigation bar.

History: This stores a list of help pages we have visited recently, in the left pane. As usual double clicking any title will redisplay that help page in the right pane.

Support: It provides the other forms of technical supports available from Microsoft.

Options: This button is helpful in cutomizing the Help and Support Centre.

- Click the Options button on the navigation bar. Help and Support Centre displays the Options screen.
- Click Set search options in the left pane. Help and Support Centre displays the set search options in the screen.
- If we want to change the number of search results provided by Help and Support Centre, we change the number in Return up to 15 results per provider by a number less than 100. The default value is 15.
- If we want to get rid off search highlights then deselect it. We make the other desired changes. If we do not want to access Microsoft Knowledge Base again we deselect it.
- Similarly by clicking change Help and Support Centre options in the left pane we can make the other changes.

Getting Help Online

If we want to get help from Microsoft's web site, first of all we need an Internet connection and web browser. Microsoft website includes support for all the products, not just windows XP. Suppose we want to have help for " view folder " we have to give the command as XP + view + folder. The blank spaces should be replaced by +signs. XP indicates, we want to get help from windows XP in order to get help we have to undergo the following steps.

- Make sure we are on line and use our web browser to go to http://search. microsoft. com.
- In the Search text box that appears, we type XP + view + folder in Choose a Microsoft.com location, enter United State. Click the Go button. After some time the results will be displayed.

Customizing Windows XP

One of the most attractive features of Windows XP is that it allows we to customize the desktop. We can change the appearance of the desktop by changing the background, adding icons, moving icons, moving and resizing the taskbar and so on. We can also add Screen Savers.

Customizing the Taskbar

The Taskbar is usually at the bottom of the desktop. But we can move it easily to any of the four sides of the desktop, unless it is locked. To do so, point the mouse pointer to any empty area on the taskbar. If we have opened many windows, then there will not be empty space on the taskbar. In this case we can make use of the space occupied by the clock.

Click and drag the taskbar to wherever we want it to be. Figure shows a broad taskbar at the Top. We can also change the size of the taskbar. Point to the edge of the taskbar. The mouse pointer will change into a double-headed arrow. Click and drag the mouse to increase or decrease the size of the taskbar.

Fig. A Broad Taskbar

Taskbar Settings: Right click on the empty area of the taskbar. If there is no empty area right click on the clock. From short cut menu, by selecting Toolbars, we can add or delete tools. If we click Address, Address toolbar is created and increase its size by dragging with mouse. Then we can enter any command, that will be executed either directely or accessing the Internet. we can arrange the windows with Cascade Windows, Tile Windows Horizontally and Tile Windows Vertically.

Show the Desktop is an substitute for Show Desktop button. With clicking Task Manager Shutting down, we can perform Turn off, Restart, Hybernate, Stand by and Switcher user the computer. If we want to make the position of Task bar fixed, click Lock the Taskbar, then a tick mark appears against it.

Now the taskbar cannot be moved. If we click on Properties, we will be shown Taskbar and Start Menu Properties. It opens under the Taskbar tab, we customize it to suit our needs and tastes. If we open Taskbar and Start Menu properties under Start Menu tab, and if we want to change

Start Menu into Classic Start menu, click Classic Start menu's Radio button, and click ok. A screen similar to the starting screen of Windows 98 will be shown.

Fig. A Screen Similar to the Starting Screen of Windows 98

Changing the Wallpaper

Wallpaper is the background display that appears on our desktop. We can choose from several standard Wallpapers that are available as part of Windows XP. We can also use a picture that we have drawn, scanned or copied from somewhere. To do so, right-click anywhere in the blank area of the desktop. The menu shown in Figure pops up.

Fig. Choose Properties to Change Wallpaper, Screen Savers etc.

Click on Properties. The Display Properties dialog box appears. Select Desktop tab (second from left) which will present a figure similar to the one shown below.

Fig. Display Properties Dialog Box

Browse through the list of wallpapers and click on the one we want. A preview in the top half of the window shows we how the wallpaper will look. Click on Apply and then on OK.

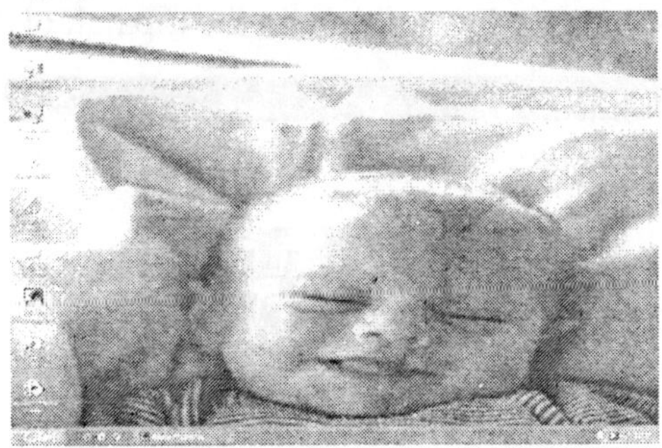

Fig. Desktop with Setup Wallpaper.

Using Screen Savers

In old monitors, if we left the images on the screen unchanged for long, the characters would burn-in, leaving a permanent impression on the screens. To avoid this screen savers were used. Constantly moving technology has improved so much that screen savers are no longer necessary.

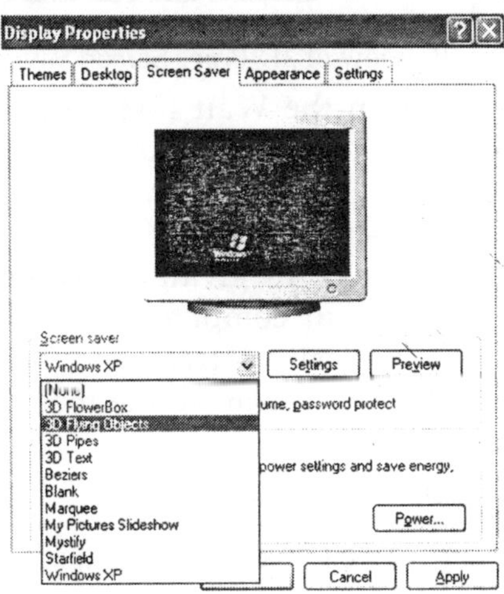

Fig. List of Screen Saver Available

But, they are still popular mainly because they are fun.

To use a screen saver, click on Screen Saver tab in the Display Properties dialog box. Click on the drop-down list box just below the Screen Saver prompt.

Select one: A preview appears in the top half of the window

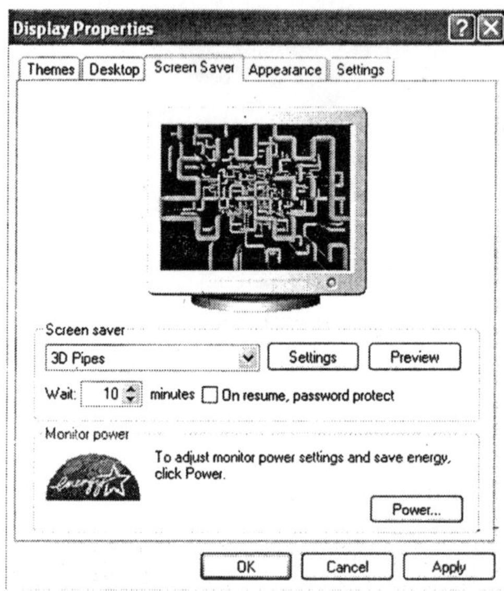

Fig. Preview of 3D Pipes Screen Saver

We can specify, in the Wait text box, the number of minutes the computer should wait before displaying the screen saver. According to the Figure, Windows will wait for 1 minute before displaying the screen saver.

We can protect our PC by giving Password to the screen saver. Now, whenever our computer is idle for some time, Windows will automatically activate our screen saver. To remove the screen saver, just move the mouse or press any key on the keyboard.

The Control Panel

The Control Panel allows we to install and manage the different hardware components attached to our computer. We can open the Control Panel window by clicking on the Start button, and then Control Panel.

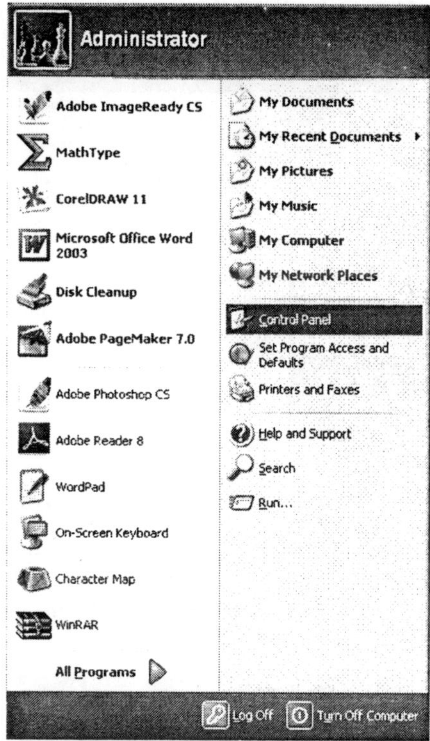

Fig. Opening Control Panel

We can also access Control Panel from My Computer window. Double-click on My Computer icon on the desktop and select Control Panel from the icons displayed in the My Computer window.

The Control Panel window opens in front of we. Winows XP Proffessional provides completely a new look to the Control Panel.

It provides two views to Control Panel. The default view is Category View and the other one is Classic View. Classic View is similar to the one available in Windows 98. Both views are shown in Figure, Whatever be the view all the Control Panel applets work in the same manner (applet is a small programme).

Many dialog boxes have new names, new tabs and new

functionality. If we are in Category View we can click on Switch to Classic View.

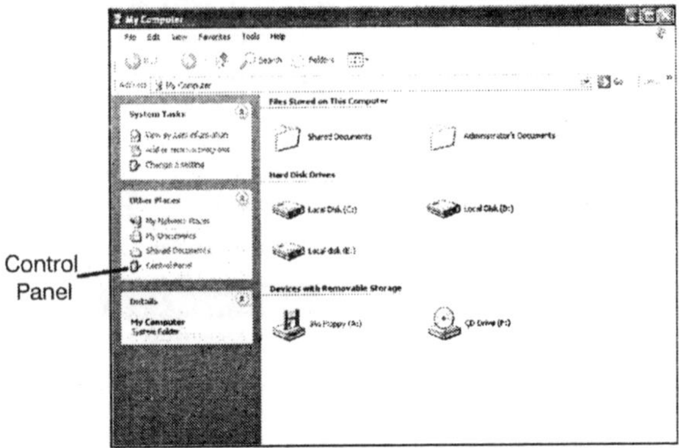

Fig. My Computer Window

This will take us to the Classic View. When we are in Classic View, we will be shown Switch to Category View. If we click on Switch to Category View, we will be taken to Category View. Category View Figure and Classic View Figure of the Control Panel are shown below.

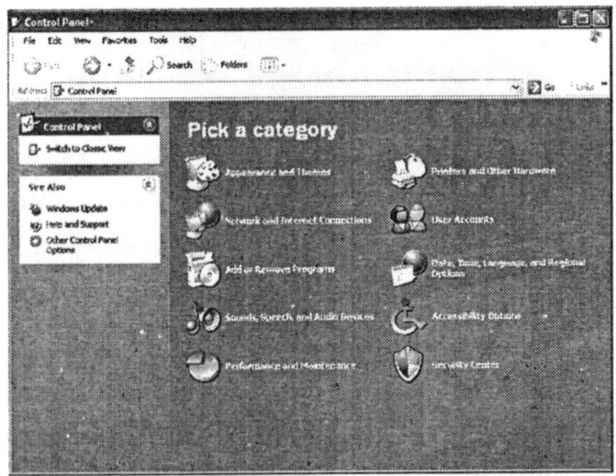

Fig. Category View

As we can see, the Control Panel window displays several icons. Using these icons, we can modify the system and hardware settings of our computer. Listed below are a few of these icons and their description.

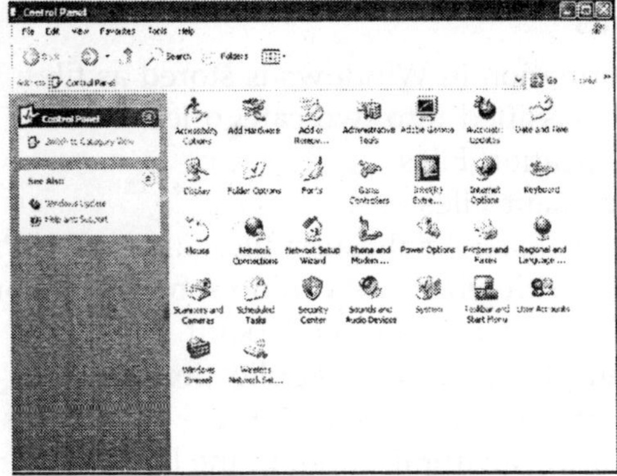

Fig. Classic View

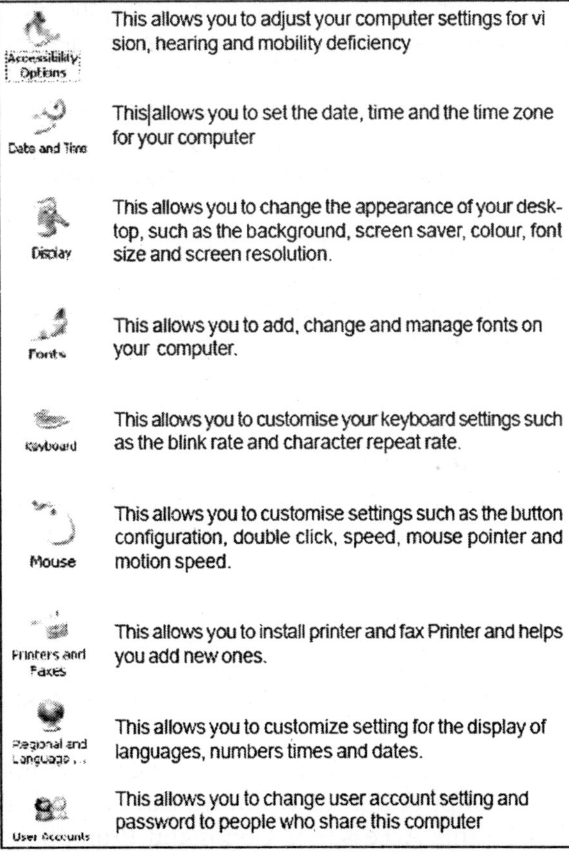

Accessibility Options	This allows you to adjust your computer settings for vi sion, hearing and mobility deficiency
Date and Time	This allows you to set the date, time and the time zone for your computer
Display	This allows you to change the appearance of your desk-top, such as the background, screen saver, colour, font size and screen resolution.
Fonts	This allows you to add, change and manage fonts on your computer.
Keyboard	This allows you to customise your keyboard settings such as the blink rate and character repeat rate.
Mouse	This allows you to customise settings such as the button configuration, double click, speed, mouse pointer and motion speed.
Printers and Faxes	This allows you to install printer and fax Printer and helps you add new ones.
Regional and Language ...	This allows you to customize setting for the display of languages, numbers times and dates.
User Accounts	This allows you to change user account setting and password to people who share this computer

Applications

All information in Windows is stored as files. These files are broadly classified into two categories:

- Application Files
- Document Files

Application Files: Application files (also called Programme files) are files with which we can do something. For example, files that allow us to draw and paint, enter and save text, calculate and play games are application files.

Document Files: Document files are files that are created by the user using an application. In the last Chapter we learnt how to start an application. We can start an application by clicking on its icon on the desktop or by using the Start menu. When we do this, the application appears on the screen in a window.

At the same time, a button representing the application also appears on the taskbar. This button stays on the taskbar as long as the application is active and disappears only when we close the application.

We are going to learn about some of the commonly used applications of Windows XP.

We will also learn how to start multiple applications, how to switch between them and how to transfer data between them.

USING APPLICATIONS IN WINDOWS

Several useful applications come as part of Windows. Using them, we can perform a wide variety of tasks. Discussed below are some of the commonly used ones

MS-DOS

Before the introduction of Windows, MS-DOS was one of the very popular operating systems among PC users. Hundreds of DOS-based applications were available in the market.

To start such programs or to use any DOS Command, the Command Prompt option of windows can be used. Perform Start All Programs Accessories Command Prompt.

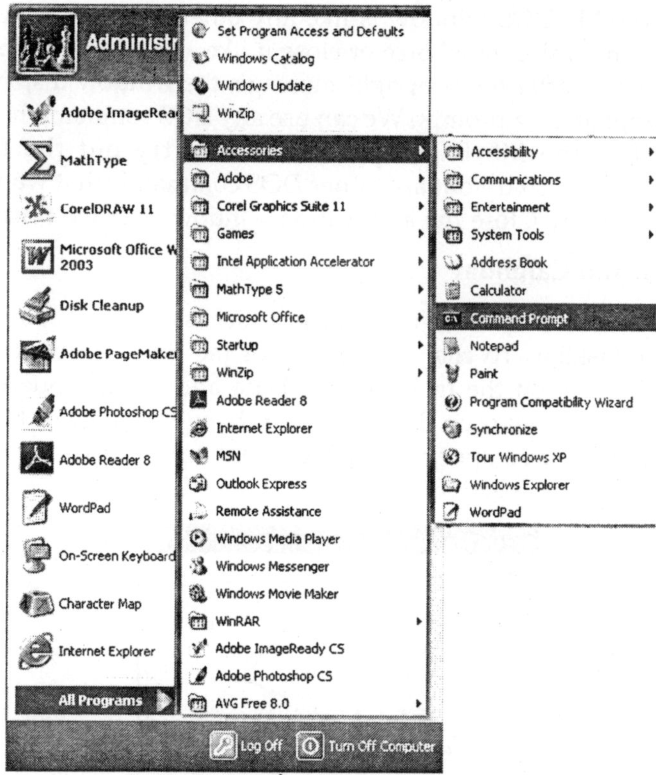

Fig. Getting MS-DOS Window

A window as shown in Figure appears on the screen.

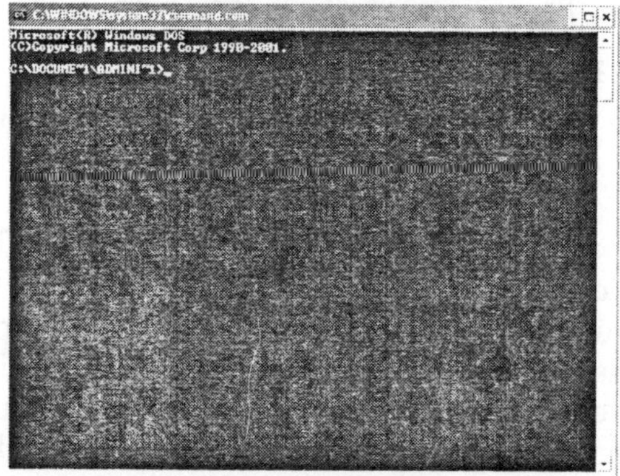

Fig. MS-DOS Window

The MS-DOS window is like any other window; we can move, minimize, maximize or close it like any other window. Notice that after the copyright message, the window displays the familiar C:\> prompt. We can use any DOS command here.

Start the MS DOS application and try out the Dir command. Also try out any other DOS commands that we are familiar with. Close the application window after we finish.

Clock and Calendar

Windows has an in-built clock, which is usually displayed on the taskbar. To change the date or the time, double-click on the clock on the taskbar. The Date and Time Properties dialog box appears on the screen. To change the date or time, we should have special privilege. Only administrator can undertake these activities.

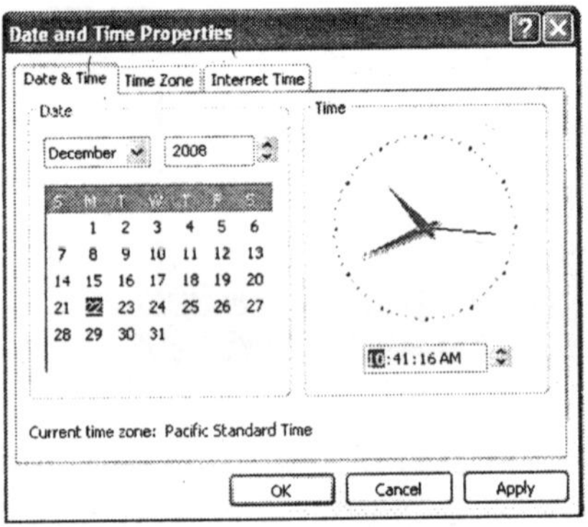

Fig. Date and Time Properties Dialog Box

On the left half of the dialog box, the current month's calendar is displayed. To view the calendar for some other month, click on the month and drop down list box and year spinner box and select the month and year we want. To change the time, click on the digital clock seen on the right. Highlight the hour, minute or second by dragging the pointer over it.

Increase or decrease the highlighted value by clicking on the up and down arrows in the box. Note that the time in the analog clock also changes correspondingly. Analog clock is the ordinary clock with hour hand minutes hand and second hand.

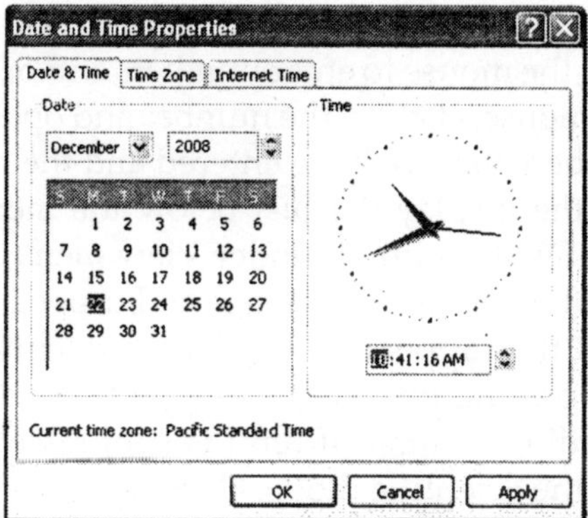

Fig. Clock Showing a Different Time

Click on OK after we finish.

Calculator

The Calculator is a useful application that comes with Windows. It can be used to perform mathematical and scientific calculations. To start the Calculator, execute the following action. Start All Programs Accessories Calculator.

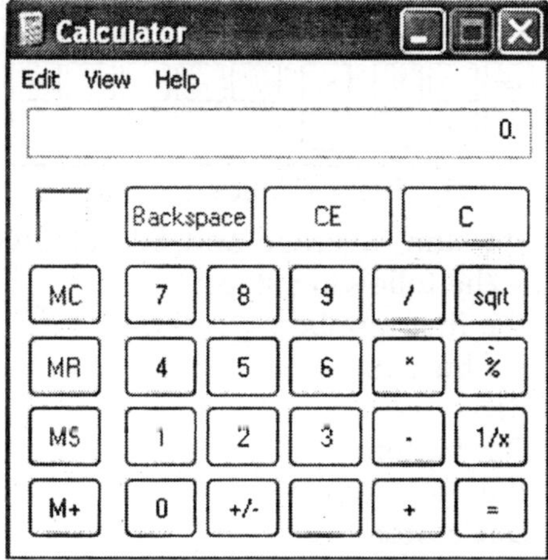

Fig. The Calculator

The Calculator can be used in one of the two modes - Standard mode or Scientific mode. Figure displays the Calculator in the Standard mode. As we can see, this calculator is very similar to an ordinary calculator. We can use the keyboard and the mouse to enter numbers and operators. If we are using the mouse, click on the number and operator buttons.

The numbers that we have entered and the results will be displayed in the display bar just below the menu bar. If we have selected Digit grouping under View menu, the numbers are separated by comma following the European convention. The numbers that appear to the left of decimal places are separated by comma for every three digits starting from the right. The leading comma (if any) is suppressed. To use the Calculator in the Scientific mode, click on the View menu and select Scientific. Figure shows the Calculator in the Scientific mode, with statistics box.

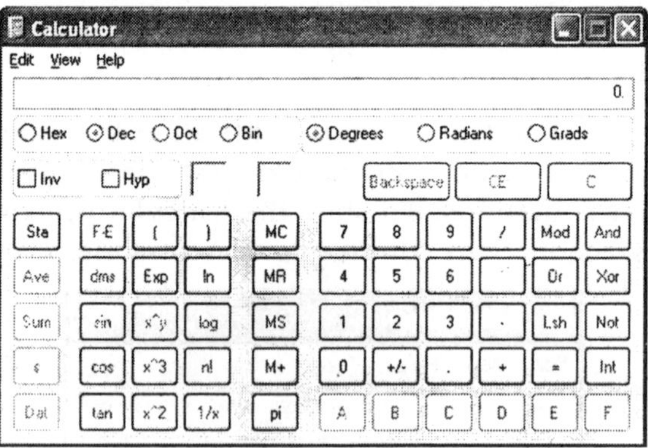

Fig. The scientific calculator

To calculate sum, average and S.D of given numbers execute the following steps:

- Enter the first number.
- Click Sta button.
- Click RET
- Click Dat button.
- Enter the next number.
- Click Dat button.
- Repeat step 5 and step 6 until we exhaust all the numbers.
- Click the s button.
- The Standard Deviation of the entered numbers is displayed.

- Click Sum we will be shown sum of the numbers entered.
- Click Ave we will be shown average of the numbers entered.

Note: If we click Start button, we will see Statistics Box. The entered numbers are in Statistics Box. If we click the LOAD button of Statistics Box, the highlighted number in the display area of the Statistics Box will be loaded into the display area of calculator display area. If we click CD button of Statistics Box, the highlighted number in the display area of Statistics Box will be deleted from the list of numbers. If we click the CAD button of Statistics Box, all the entered numbers are deleted.

Paint

Paint is an application that lets us draw and colour pictures. To start Paint, click on Start All Programs Accessories Paint.

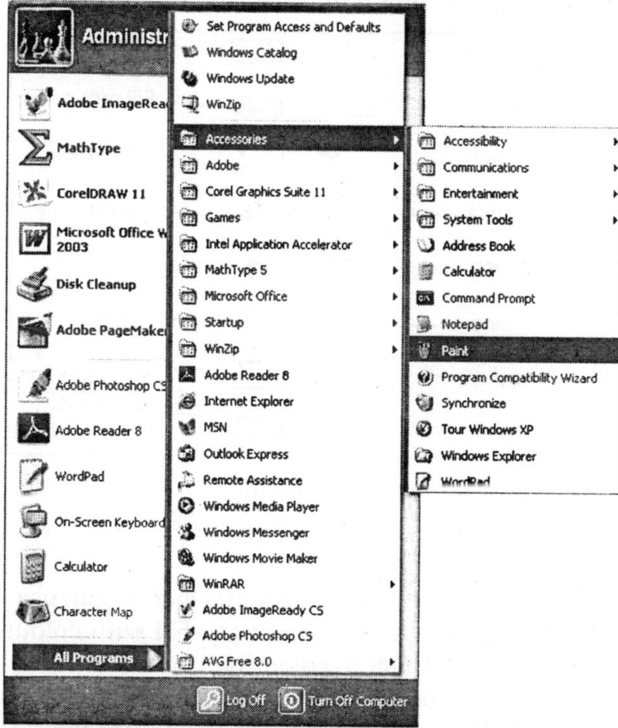

Fig. The Paint Window Appears on the Screen.

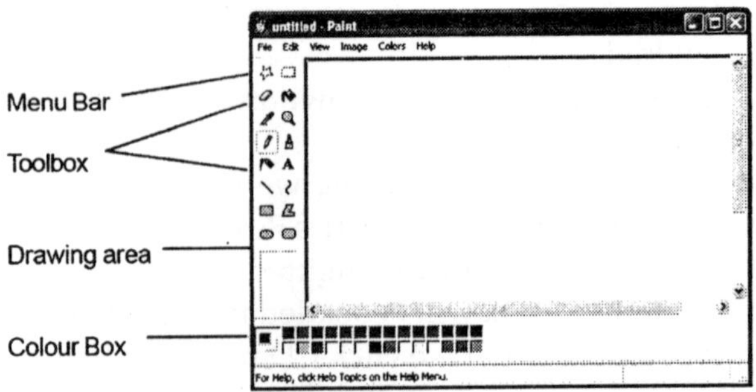

Fig. Paint Window

Just like any other window, the Paint window also has a title bar with sizing buttons, a menu bar and a status bar. In addition, it has a Toolbar and a Colour Box. The Toolbar has various tools that we can use to draw and colour. Figure shows the Toolbar with the different tools.

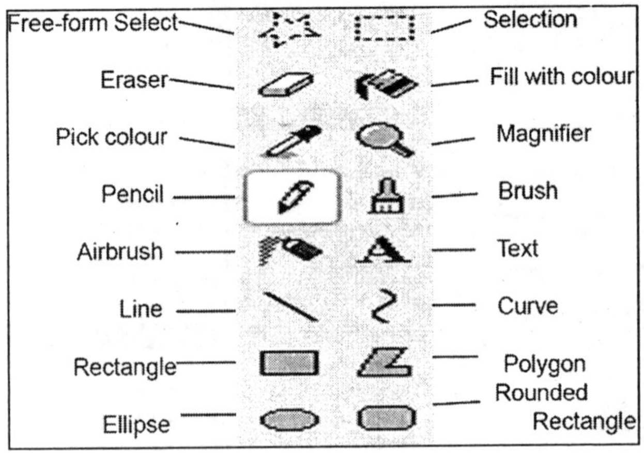

Fig. The Toolbar

Then, move the mouse to the drawing area and click and drag to draw the figure we want.

The Colour Box contains the colours that we can use. Click on the colour of our choice and use the Fill with colour tool, the Airbrush or the Brush to colour our pictures.

To use any of the tools in the toolbar, first click on the tool to select it. For example, click on the ellipse tool.

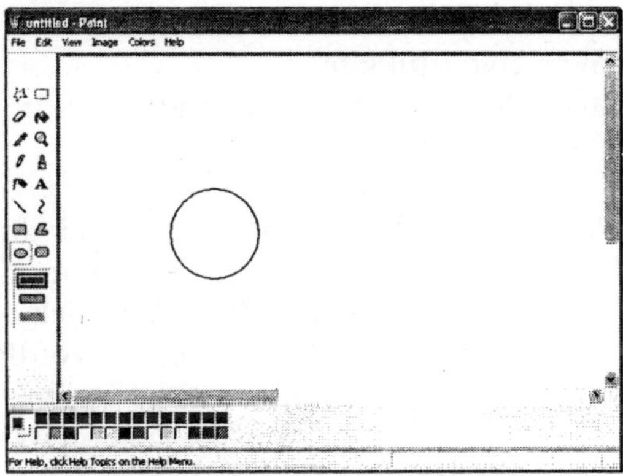

Fig. Click and Drag the Mouse to Draw

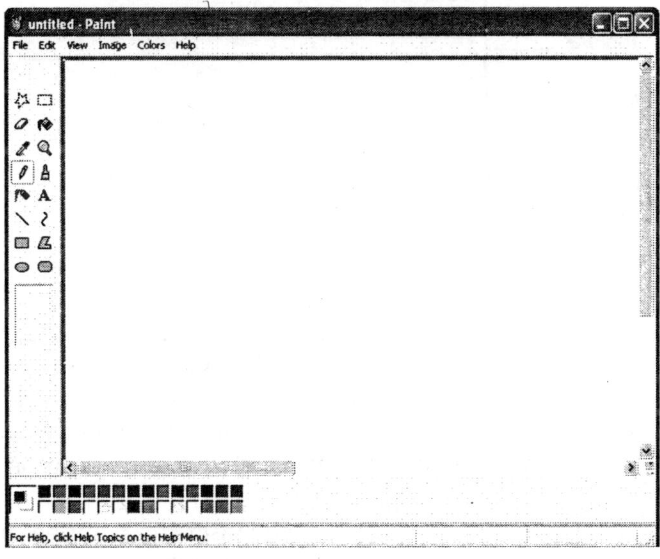

Fig. The Circle Tool is Selected.

We can close Paint by clicking on the Close button on the title bar or clicking on the File menu and selecting Exit (or Alt+F4 keys).

Do-it-Now Exercises

- Open the Paint application and draw a colourful bunch of balloons.

- Draw a simple house and colour it.
- Draw a colourful kite.
- Draw a flower of our choice and colour it.

WordPad

WordPad is a simple word processor that comes along with Windows. A Word processor is a programme that allows us to type and store text. To start WordPad, click on.

Start → All Programs → Accessories → WordPad.

The WardPad window appears on the screen.

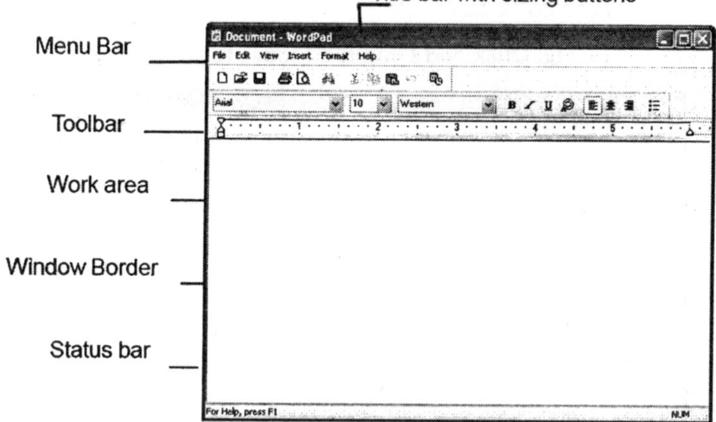

As we have already learnt, the WordPad window has a title bar, menu bar, toolbar, work area and a status bar. A small vertical blinking line appears at the top left corner of the work area. This is the Cursor. It indicates our current position on the screen.

Some users refer the cursor as the insertion point because it shows, on the screen, where the next text we type will be inserted. Use the keyboard to type in the text. Note that as we type in the text, the cursor moves. When we reach the end of a line, WordPad automatically moves the cursor to the beginning of the next line. This feature is called Word wrap. The Enter key on the keyboard is used to start a new paragraph to enter short line or a blank line. Figure shows the WordPad window with some sample text.

We do not have to press the Enter key when we reach the

right margin Do not think that the appearance in the screen will be the appearance of the output. If we want to set the margin that can be done with Page Setup of the File menu. We can use the following key or key combinations for editing the text.

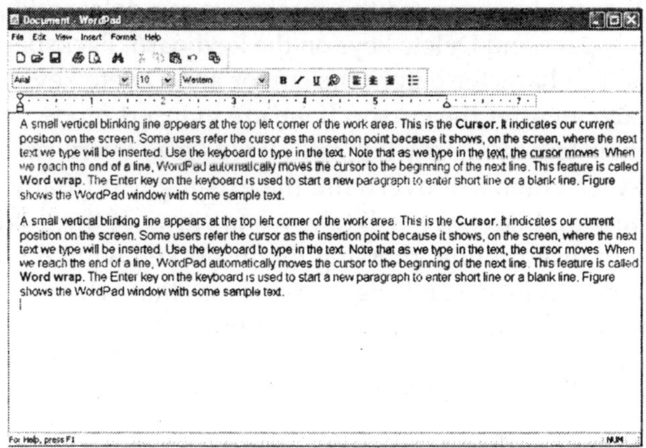

Fig. WordPad window with some text

Some useful Editing keys are given below.

Keys for Moving the Cursor through Text

Key	Where It Moves the Cursor
→	One character to the right
←	One character to the left
↑	Up one line
↓	Down one line
Home	Beginning of the line
End	End of line
Ctrl + Home	Top of document
Ctrl + End	End of document
Page Up (PgUp)	Up a page (or screen)
Page Down (PgDn)	Down a page (or screen)
Ctrl + →	One word to the left
Ctrl + ←	One word to the right
Ctrl + ↑	Up one paragraph
Ctrl + ↓	Down one paragraph
Ctrl + Page Up (PgUp)	To top of previous page
Ctrl + Page Down (PgDn)	To top of next page

After we have finished typing in the text, we can correct it, add or delete text. To do so, first move the cursor to the place where we want to edit, using the arrow keys on the keyboard. We can also use the mouse to move the cursor. To do so, place the mouse pointer at the place and click.

Once we have moved the cursor, we can delete text using the Backspace and Delete keys on the keyboard. Backspace key deletes the character before the cursor and Delete key deletes the character after the cursor. If we are in insert mode, we can insert new text by simply typing it. If we are in overwrite mode the text we enter will overwrite the existing text (if any).

Pressing Insert key will take we to either of the modes. If we are in insert mode, pressing the Insert key will take we to the overwrite mode and vice versa. Note that when we type in new text, the existing text moves to the right, if we are in Insert mode. To close WordPad, click on the Close button on the title bar or select Exit from the File menu.

WORKING WITH MULTIPLE APPLICATIONS

When we are using multiple applications, it will be very time consuming if we have to close one application before starting the next one. Moreover, transferring information from another application is very difficult if not impossible.

For example, in MS-DOS, a file created using a word processor cannot contain a graph created using a spreadsheet programme. Windows overcomes this problem by allowing the user to work on multiple applications at the same time. In Windows, a WordPad file can contain data or a graph created using Excel, a picture created using Paint and so on.

Starting Multiple Applications

Starting multiple applications is very simple. First start one application. The application appears on the screen in a window. At the same time, a button with the name of the application appears on the taskbar. Now, start the second application. Several things happen -

- The window of the second application appears on the screen overlapping the first window,

- The button of the second application appears on the taskbar,
- The title bar of the first application and its button on the taskbar become dim.

We can start more applications in the same way. Figure will help we understand this better.

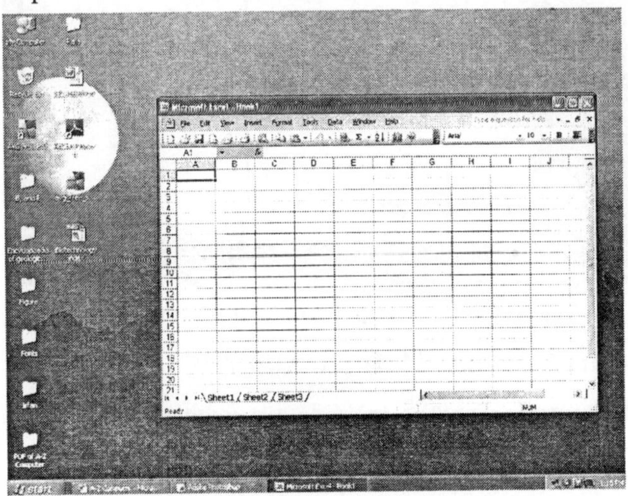

Fig. Desktop with Excel Application.

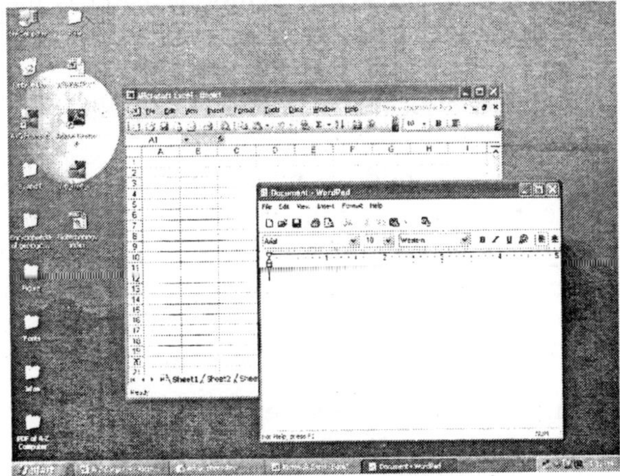

Fig. Desktop as it Appears after Word is also started. Note the Dimmed title bar and Button of the Excel Application.

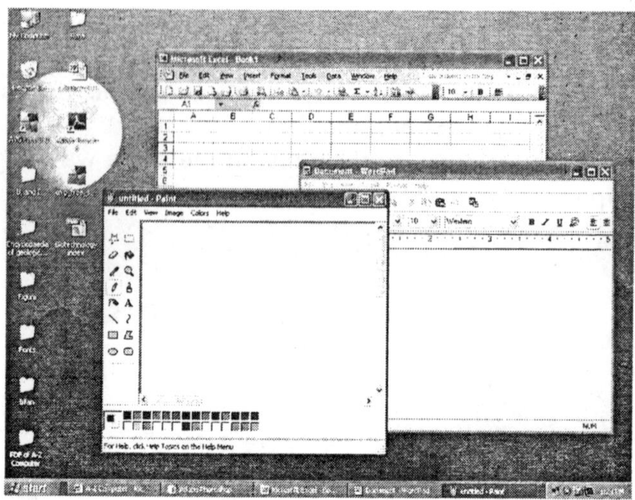

Fig. Desktop with 3 Application Windows

Switching Between Multiple Applications

The buttons on the taskbar are used to switch between the different applications. Remember that every time we start an application, its button appears on the taskbar. The button of the application we are currently using is highlighted and its window is called the Active Window. Paint is the active window. To switch to another application, click on any part of that application's window that is visible. If no part of the window is visible, click the button of the application on the taskbar.

The application window is moved in front of all the other windows and its button is highlighted. Figure shows WordPad as the active window. Windows Explorer (Which we are going to learn shortly) enables us to create only one button per application. If we click on the button, it will show us a list, from which we can select any one of them.

Transferring Information Between Different Applcations

Windows allows we to transfer data between the different applications we are running simultaneously. To do this,

Windows uses a temporary storage location called the Clipboard.

We can use the clipboard to store any kind of data. We can store text, pictures, numbers, group of files and so on.

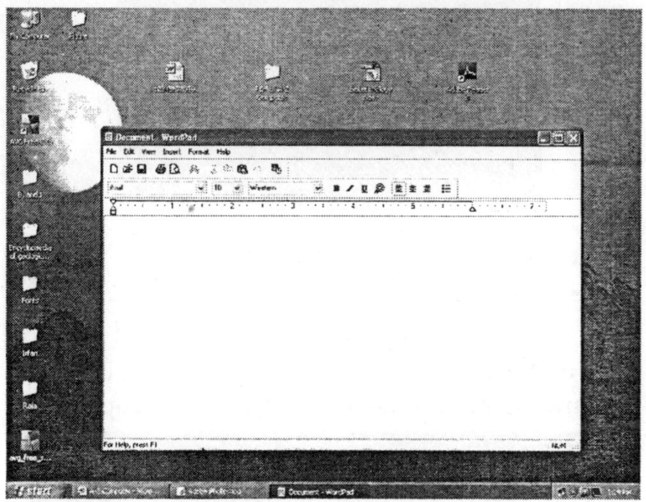

Fig. WordPad window is the Active Window

The information to be transferred is first copied from the source application to the Clipboard and from there to the destination application.

Windows also gives the option of either copying or moving data. The difference between copying and moving data is that moving removes the data from the source location and places them in the destination location. Copying leaves the source data untouched and makes a new copy in the destination location.

Let us understand this better with an example. Suppose, we have drawn a picture in Paint and want to include it in a document created using WordPad. To do so, first start both the applications.

We may recall that windows allows multiple applications to be started at the same time. However, we have to switch between the Applications by activating the application of our choice.

Fig. Desktop with Paint and WordPad

Click on the Paint window to make it active. Use the Select tool to mark the picture we want to move or copy.

Fig. Paint with the Picture Selected

Click on the Edit menu and select Copy or press(Ctrl+C). (If we want to move the picture select Cut or press (Ctrl+X)

Click on the WordPad window to make it active. In the WordPad window, click on the Edit menu and select Paste (Ctrl+V). Note: Moving and copying will be dealt elaborately later.

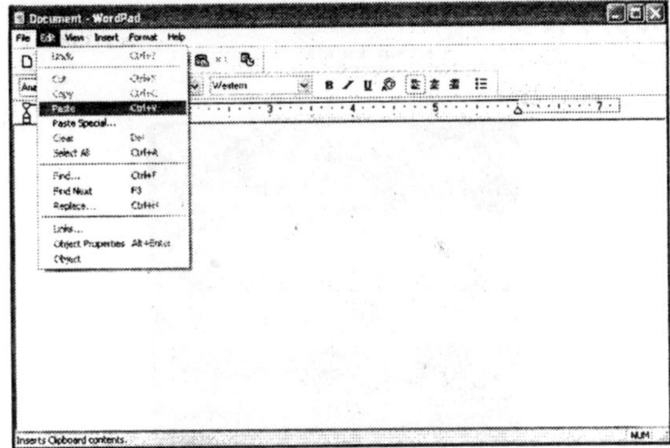

Fig. Select Edit, Copy

Fig. Click on Edit; Paste in the WordPad

The desktop will look as shown in Figure. Note that the picture in the Paint window remains untouched.

In the same manner, we can transfer data between any two Windows based applications.

There is, however, one important point that we should remember while using the clipboard. At any time, the Clipboard can hold only one set of data. When we copy or move a file or folder to the Clipboard, it overwrites whatever was stored there earlier. In addition to clipboard, windows XP provides with Clip Book.

Fig. WordPad after Pasting the Picture.

Without any effort on our part, now, we can store 24 different items in the Clip Book and we can paste them one by one. For more information, click Start and click Run on the Start menu, enter clipbrd.exe in the text box and press enter.

In the ensuing Clip Book Viewer, click Help and then click contents. After going through the help we can do whatever we like with Clip Book.

Chapter 8

Windows Explorer

FILES

We have learnt earlier that we can store a lot of information in our computer. Most computers in the market today have hard disks with capacities of several gigabytes. But how is all this information stored internally? And more importantly, how do we find what we need from all the information that is stored? Let us answer these questions one by one. All information in computers is stored in Files. Every file has a unique name that helps we to identify it. A file name is made up of two components:

- Main Component
- Extension

Main Component

The first part of the file name is the main component. This part precedes the dot and is also called the primary name. This is the name given to the file by the user. The dot (or full stop) separates the main component from the extension. The main component can contain alphabets, numbers, spaces and other characters like @, $, !, {, (,), [,]. However, there are a few characters that a file name cannot contain. They are:\,/,*, ?, ", <, >. Comma and full stop are not included in the set.

Extension

This is the second part of the file name. That is, the part that succeeds the decimal point is called the extension or the secondary name. The extension is used to identify the type of the file and is normally up to three to four characters long. When a file is created using an application, the extension is automatically added to the file's main component by the application itself. Some examples of file extensions are.DOC,.BAS,.XLS and.java.

The file name, including the extension, can be a maximum of 255 characters long. Though we can assign any fancy name to our file, it is always better to use a name that reminds we something about the contents of the file.

The aim of naming a file is to retrieve the contents easily. If we assign a fancy name to a file then we may probably not be able to associate the contents with the name of the file. For example, we have written a letter to our friend Ashok. We can call this file AAA or A8124343, but Ashok-letter would be a better choice. This concept is often refered to as the nameing convention.

What is the main use of the (file) extension? When we click on a document icon, this action not only opens the document but also an application, with which it was created. But, how does the application know that its services are required? File extension is the key to solve the problem.

The extension of the file name simply announces the format in which the data in the file is stored. Based on this, suitable application opens the file.

Normally the file extension is hidden. If we like, we can make it visible. But, it is a good practice to leave it hidden or else we may try to rename it. Renaming the extension, may lead to dangerous consequences and we may not be able to open the document. It is to be noted that MS-DOS, another operating system, follows a different set of rules for assigning a name to a file. The main component of files created or used on DOS-based computers can have a maximum of eight characters and cannot contain spaces. The extension should not exceed more than three characters in DOS.

Data Organization

In a computer having a 40 GB hard disk or an 80 GB hard disk, we can store several thousand files. But in these cases, finding one file will be very difficult. We will have to go through all the file names one by one till we locate the file that we need. This is like looking for a book in a library in which the books have not been arranged in any order. Many people never bother to store their files properly.

Windows XP (and DOS) overcomes this problem by using Folders (DOS calls them Directories). A folder is nothing but a collection of related files or subfolders. Let us understand this with an example. Consider an organization. Its office will have hundreds of papers relating to products, customers, suppliers, personnel, finance and accounts, and so on.

Normally, these papers are filed into different folders and stored in a filing cabinet. Labels on the folders and the cabinets make it easier to find what we need. So, when a person wants some information about a supplier named Shah and Co., he has to look only in the cabinet marked suppliers and search for the folder marked Shah and Co. In the same way, Windows XP allows we to organize the files on our disk by grouping them into folders.

WINDOWS EXPLORER

Windows Explorer is a programme that helps we to manage our files and folders. To start Windows Explorer, click on. Like any other window, the Explorer window also contains a title bar, a menu bar and a toolbar. But unlike the other windows, the Explorer window is selfless. It never shows its own name in the title bar; instead, it shows the name of the current folder whose contents are visible in the right pane (Main Pane).

The only time that it shows its name is when related files are grouped in the taskbar. If we open up to four folders, separate buttons are created on the Task Bar, but if we open the fifth folder or any application, folders are grouped and only one button is created whose name becomes Windows Explorer. We can see the number of folders preceding the name Windows Explorer.

Start → All → Programs → Accessories → Windows Explorer.

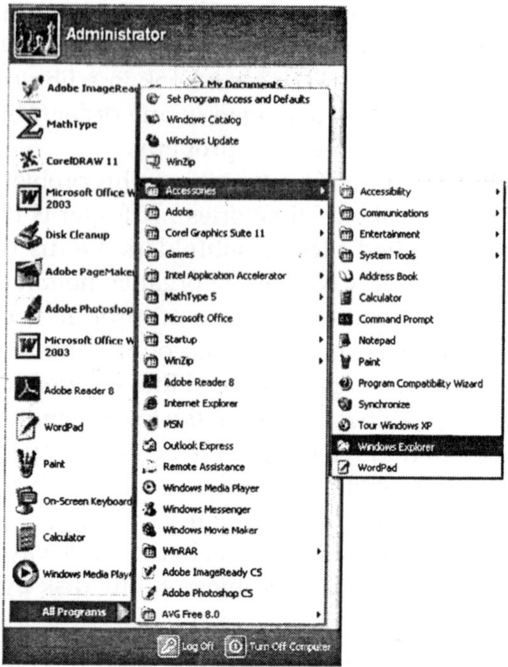

We can also start Windows Explorer by right clicking on the Start button and then selecting Explore from the short cut menu.

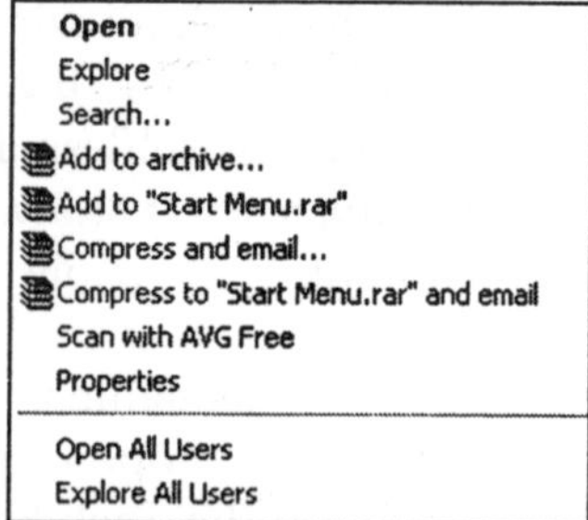

Fig. An Alternate way of Starting Windows Explorer

The Explorer window opens on the screen as shown in Figure. Again a single button is created for each application programme. This action not only preserves the space in the task bar but also if we right click on it, it will allow we to use Close Group.

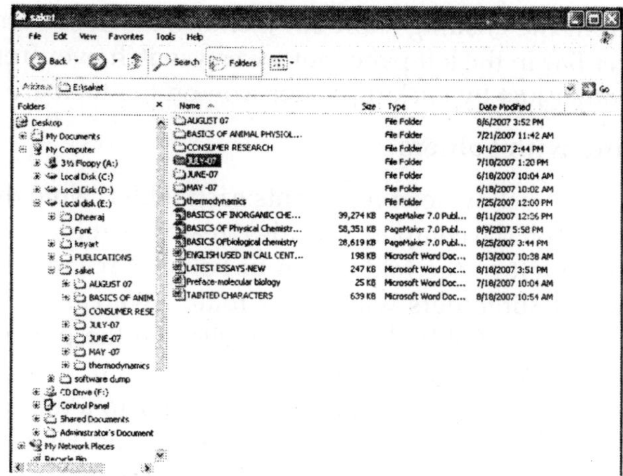

Fig. Windows Explorer Window in Folder Bar

This will close all the folders at one stroke. Even the audio, video files are treated as folders under this context. If we want to open/ close one of the grouped folders, we can left click the button.

This action displays all the folders within the button. We can either open the folder or close it. If the number of buttons exceeds four then normally a single button is created for each application.

Suppose we want to open five Word applications, five separate buttons will not be created in the task bar, only one button is created in the task bar.

Below the toolbar is the display area. As we can see, this area is divided into two panes.

The left pane displays either the Explorer Bar or the Folder Bar and the right pane always displays the contents of the currently selected folder in the left pane.

If we click the Search button from the toolbar, the left pane neither shows Explorer Bar nor Folder Bar, instead it shows the Search companion.

If we just double click a folder, we will see an Explorer Bar in the left pane. If we right click on the same folder and select explore from the ensuing shortcut menu, we will see the Folder Bar in the left pane. We right click a folder and choose open from the ensuing short cut menu, we will see only the Explorer Bar in the left pane. But we can switch over from one to the other just by clicking folder icon on the toolbar.

Working with Folders

A small yellow icon represents each folder. Note that the disk drives on the computer are also treated as folders. A plus sign to the left of the folder icon in Folder Bar indicates the presence of subfolders within this folder. We can see + or - sign only in the Folder Bar. We can click on the plus sign to display a list of the subfolders.

When we do this, the plus sign changes to a minus sign. Clicking on the minus sign will hide the details. Figure show the folder representing the hard disk C: in the expanded and collapsed forms.

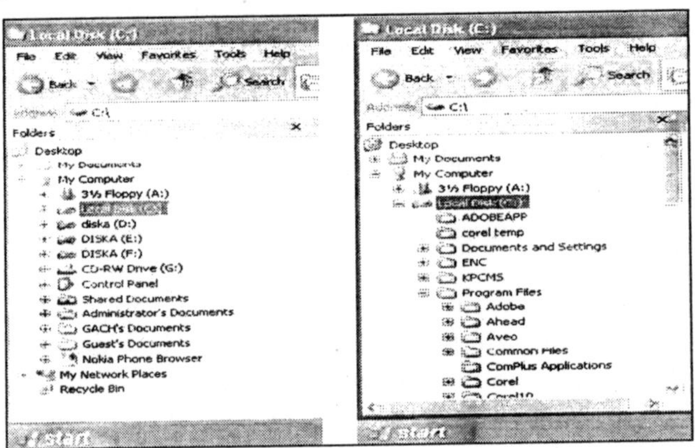

Fig. (a) Folder Bar **Fig.** (b) Folder Bar Expanded

If there is no plus sign to the left of a folder icon, it means that the folder does not have any subfolder. Scroll bars in this part of the window allow we to browse through the list of folders.

To see the contents of a folder we have to select the folder. To do so, just click the folder. The yellow file icon next to the folder changes to look like an open folder.

The selected folder is highlighted and its contents are displayed in the right pane of the Explorer window. In Figure the Windows folder has been selected in the left pane and its contents are displayed in the right pane.

The Explorer Bar

Old habits die hard!. What we have seen is the only facility available in Windows 98. But Windows XP provides additional facility in the name of Explorer Bar. The Explorer Bar with its sophisticated, more useful tools lets we navigate (travel) and to work with icons contained within the current folder. This bar is divided into three categories. They are:-

- File and Folder Task
- Other Places
- Details

File and Folder Tasks: As the name suggests File and Folder tasks allows us to work on files and folders, for example, by clicking Make a new folder under File and Folder Tasks, we can create a new folder. Share this Folder option shares the chosen files among the group users. It provides web facilities also. File and Folder Tasks is context sensitive (depends on what folder we choose). Whatever we find here is not visible in the Folder Bar. Other Places: If we want to switch over to other folders, we can select options in other places. Details: Details provides some detail about the open folder.

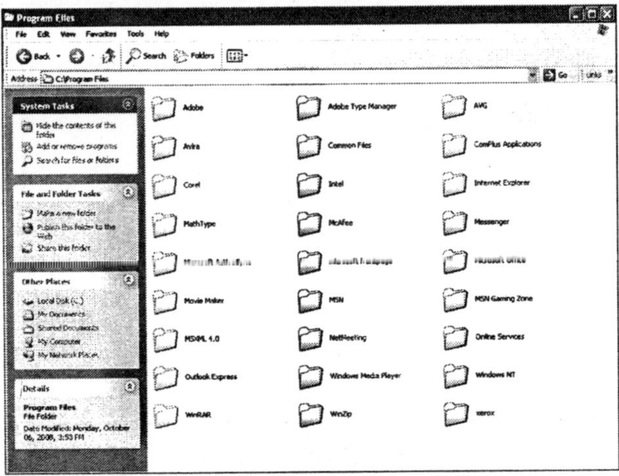

Fig. Windows Explorer Window in Explorer Bar

We can expand or collapse any of the categories by clicking any where in the caption (including Show/ Hide button two down/ up arrows). We can also navigate to any folder by means of the Address bar. Click the down arrow situated in the right most area of the Address text box. From the drop down list box we can navigate to any folder from our current position.

Changing the View

Windows Explorer allows us to change the way in which information is displayed in the right pane. We can display the list of files and folders using any of the following views. We click view in the menu bar or click view button in the explorer's toolbar. The view affects only how the information is displayed not what is displayed. Icons work in the same manner, whatever be the view. For example Double-clicking an Icon in any view will open it.

The Icons View: The Icons View shows each file or folder's icon and its name. This view will not provide any more detail.

The Tiles View: In this view, the icons are a little bigger. In addition to icon and its name, this view provides some more additional information for some icons.

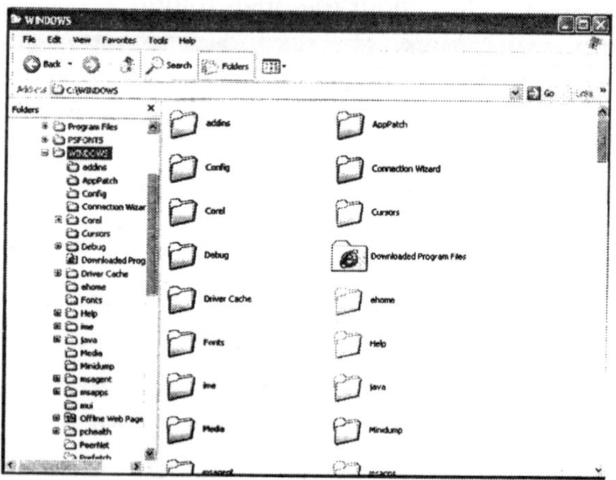

Fig. Icons with Tiles View

The Thumbnails View: The Thumbnails View works well

in folders that contain pictures. Documents that contain pictures are not shown as icons but they are displayed as minimized pictures.

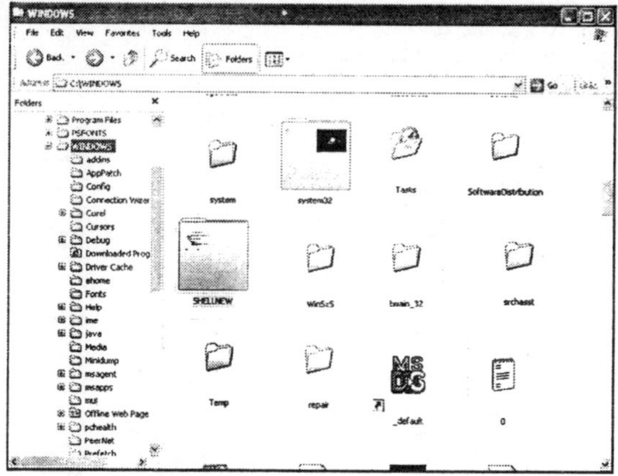

Fig. Thumbnails View

The Filmstrip View: This view is available only in folders that contain pictures such as My Pictures Folder.

Thumbnails View: When we click or point to a picture, an enlarged copy of the picture appears in preview area.

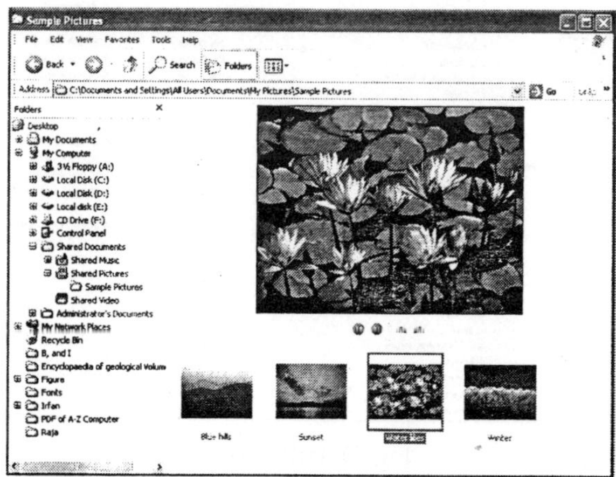

List View: This view retains the small icons but displays the files and folders one below the other in columns.

Details: This view displays details like file size, type, last modified date and time along with file names and small icons. If we cannot find all the information, use the scroll bar available in this view.

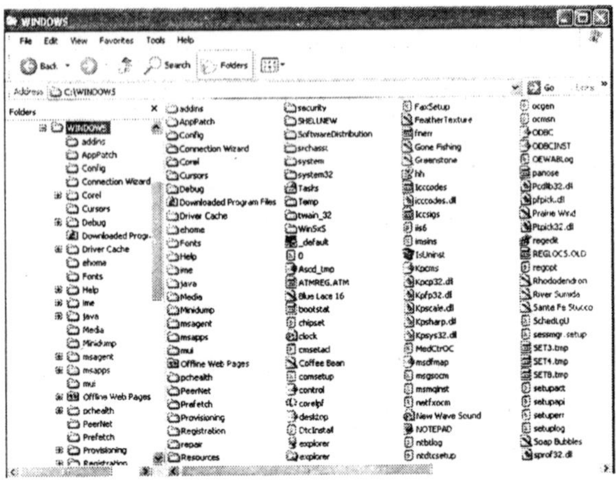

Fig. List View

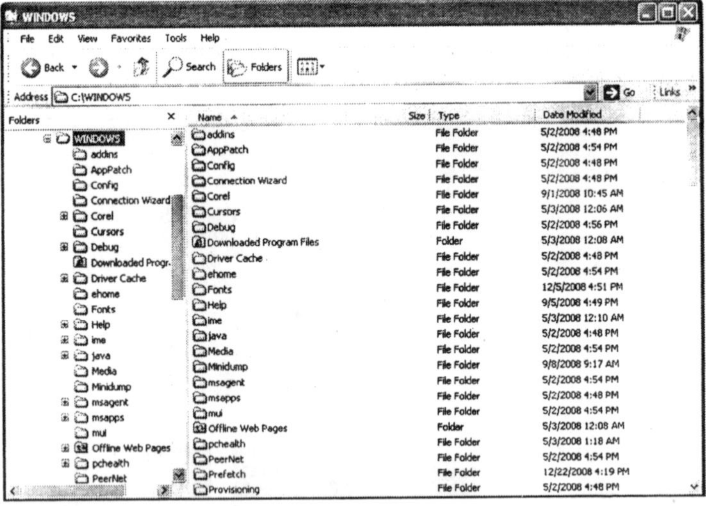

Fig. Details View

Note: All the View figures have Folders Bar in the left pane. We can have Explorer Bar in the left pane also. We may wonder why we need several views. Views will help we in finding a forgotten file. We may forget the name of a file, but we may remember, the date of creation or the extension of that file. Then sort, the contents of a folder that we expect our file will be, by date or file type (extension), in Windows Explorer. We can see whether the file is there or not at a glance. Note: A better way to search a file is by means Search option.

Creating a New Folder

Often, we may want to create a new folder to store some of our files. Creating new folders using Windows Explorer is very easy. Already we have seen a method to create a folder by simply clicking Make a New Folder under File and Folder Task in the Explorer Bar.

It will create a new folder in the right pane. We can enter the name that we have chosen for the folder in the highlighted box and then press ENTER key. First, select the folder under which we want to create the new folder. Then, right click anywhere in the empty space in the right pane of the Explorer window. Click on New from the menu shortcut.

Select Folder from the submenu that appears. We can also obtain the same result from the menu bar by Clicking File New Folder.

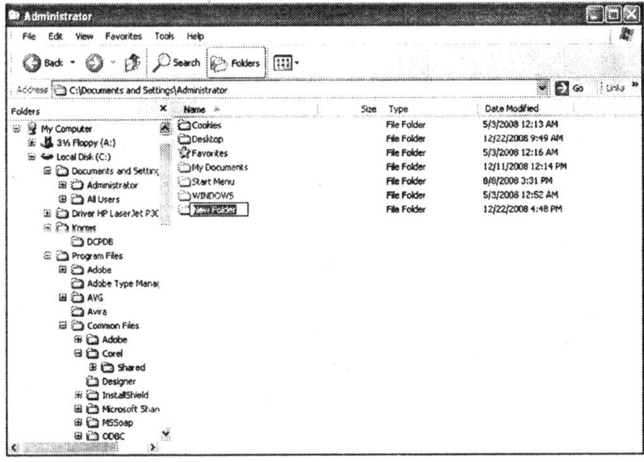

Fig. Explorer Bar to Create new Folder

In the folders bar also we can right click on the empty space on the right pane. Click New in the ensuing shortcut menu then click the Folder in the submenu.

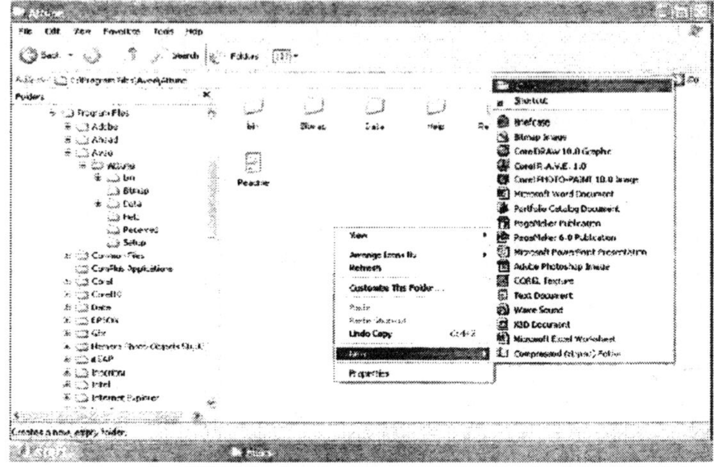

Fig. Click on New and Select Folder

A new folder with the temporary name "New Folder" is created as in figure.

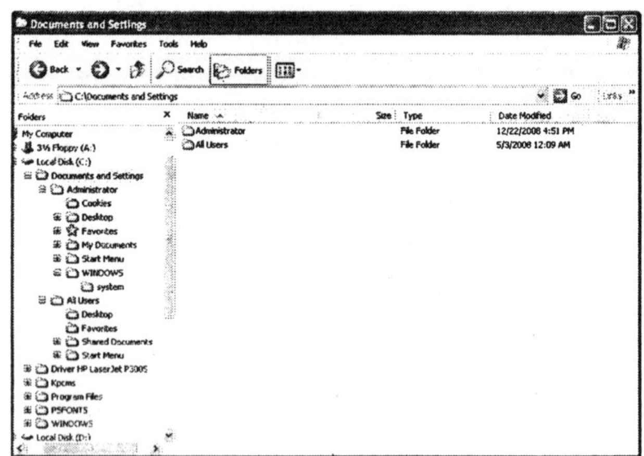

Fig. New Folder is Created

Simply type the name we want to give this new folder and press enter. Here Test is the chosen name and My

Documents is the chosen folder, under which test folder is created.

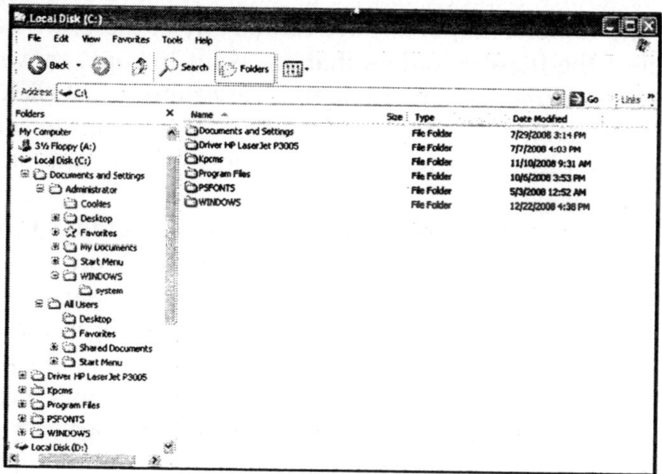

Fig. A new folder called TEST is created under My Documents.

Moving and Copying Files and Folders

Once the files are selected, we can move or copy them using Cut, Copy and Paste in three different ways.

- Click on the Edit menu and make appropriate choice.
- Right click on any one of the selected folders or files, in the ensuing short cut menu and make suitable selection.
- We can use the keyboard combinations Ctrl+X (Ctrl+x) to cut,

Ctrl+C (Ctrl+c) to copy and Ctrl+V (Ctrl+v) to paste.

The difference between copying and moving files is that moving removes the files or folders from the source location and places them in the destination location. Copying leaves the source files or folders untouched and makes a copy in the destination location.

The Windows Explorer copies or moves files using the Windows XP Clipboard. A clipboard is a temporary storage area where files or folders are stored before being copied to the new location. Let us understand copying and moving files with an example.

Selecting Files and Folders

Windows Explorer allows us to copy, move and delete files and folders. But, before we can do any of these, we have to select the files or folders that we want to copy, move or delete. Selecting one file or folder is very simple. Just click on the file or folder and it gets highlighted. If we want to select more than one file or folder, we can do so in any one of the following ways:

- If the files or folders to be selected appear consecutively on the screen, then, click on the first file or folder. Using the scroll bars (if necessary), point the mouse pointer to the last file or folder in the list, hold the Shift key down and click. Figure shows a list of six consecutive files, which have been selected.

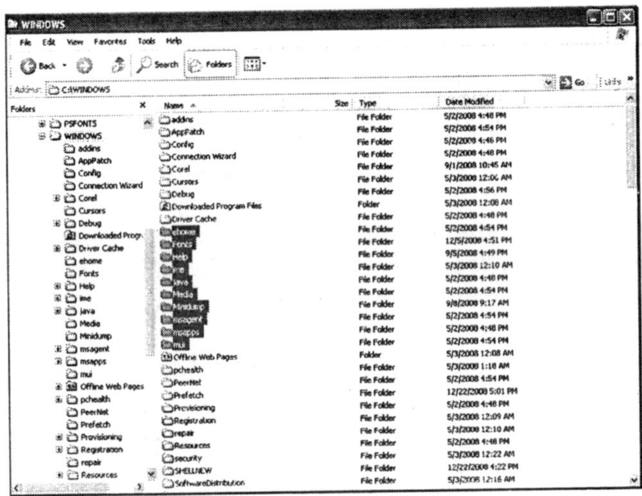

Fig. Six Consecutive Files Selected

- If the files or folders to be selected are not displayed consecutively, then, click on the first file, move the mouse pointer to the second file to be selected and click while holding the Ctrl key down. Repeat the procedure for each of the other files to be selected. Figure shows five selected files that are not displayed next to each other.

  If we select a file wrongly, in order to deselect it from

the group, press Ctrl and click on the file. Above selection can also be made with Explorer Bar in the left pane.

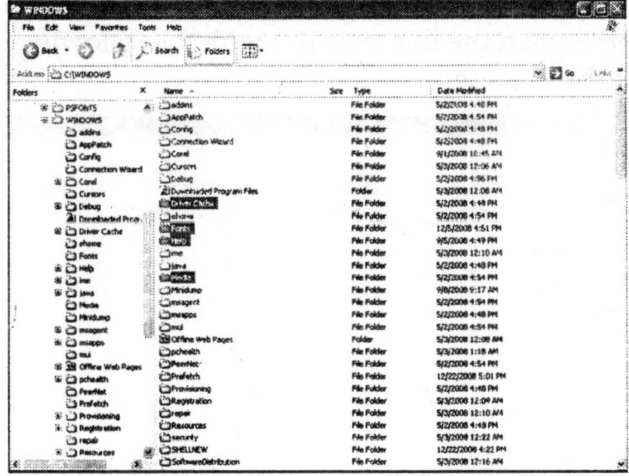

Fig. Five Non-consecutive files Selected

Moving Files and Folders

We are going to see how to move the files or folders by using Folder Bar. Explorer Bar may be used to move the files with ease.

But Folder bar is considered first. If the left pane of Explorer Window is not in Folder Bar then click Folders button on the toolbar. Now we are in Folder Bar. If the Folders button in the toolbar is highlighted, we are in Folders Bar, otherwise we are in Explorer Bar.

Consider the folder My Documents. It has 17 files and folders. Suppose we want to move the files Student, Raj, kumar and Exam from My documents to the folder Test. Select the files as explained above.

Then, Cut the items by using anyone of the three methods explained above. Next, click on the folder or disk drive to which we want to move these files. In this example, click on the folder Test.

Now, Paste the items by using anyone of the three methods explained above. Figure shows the folder Test after the files have been pasted. Remember that they have been removed from the folder My Documents. Now let us see how to move files and folders with Explorer Bar.

We can move or copy selected files easily in the Explorer Bar. If we are not in Explorer Bar, click the Folder in the toolbar. We will be shown the Explorer Bar with the following options under File and Folder Tasks.

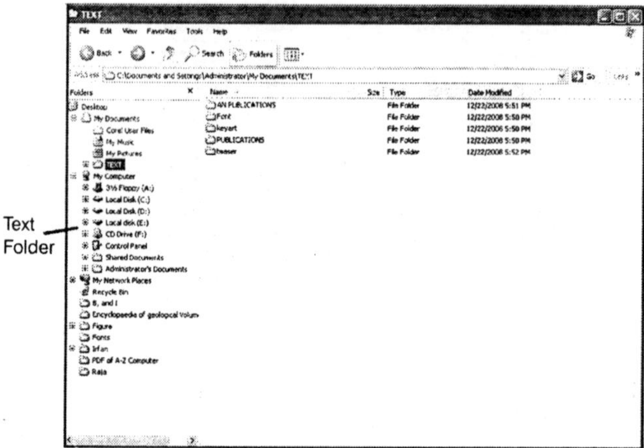

Fig. The Test Folder

- Move the selected items
- Copy the selected items
- Publish the selected items on the Web
- E-mail the selected items
- Delete the selected items

Let us suppose we want to move the selected items. To do so we click on Move the selected items. We will be provided with Move Items list box; we can browse and select the desired destination. We can even create a new folder by clicking Make New Folder button found at the bottom of the Move Items list box. Click Move button adjacent to Make New Folder button to store the selected items in the newly created folder. That is all; we have successfully moved the selected items under TEST. If we want to move a single item, clicking on the item will show us 6 options one among them is Move this folder under File and Folder Tasks. Follow the same procedure for moving group items.

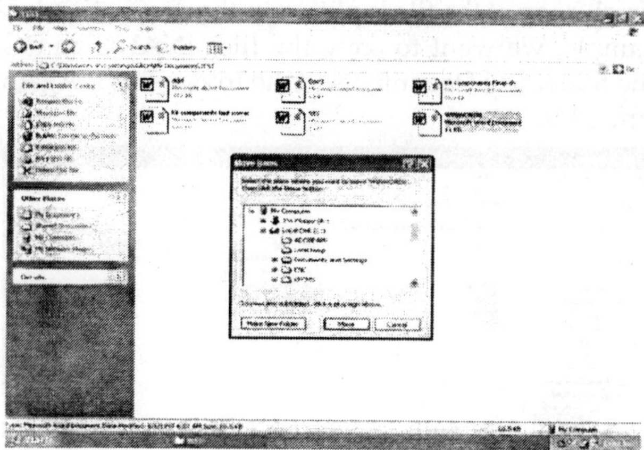

Fig. Moving Files and Folders with Explorer Bar We can also move selected items with Edit menu also.

From the menu bar, click Edit→Move To Folder as in figure.

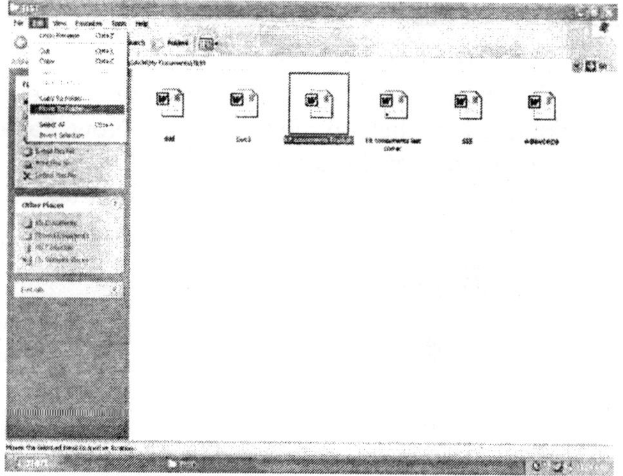

Fig. Moving through Edit submenu

We will be taken into Move Items drop down list box. Then follow the steps explained in the previous paragraph.

Copying Files and Folders

When we copy a file, the original file is left untouched

and a fresh copy of the file is placed in the destination location. For example, we want to copy the files INAUG and GACN from the folder My Documents to the folder TEST. Again, first select the files.

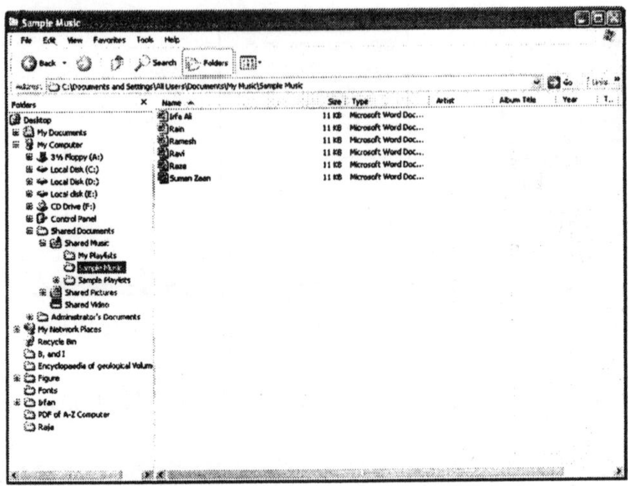

Fig. Files Selected for Copying

Then, Copy the items by using anyone of the three methods explained in Click on the folder Test. Now, Paste the items by using anyone of the three methods.

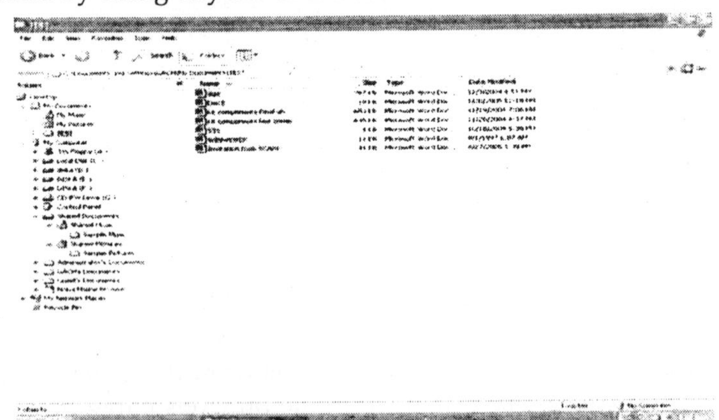

Fig. The Test Folder after Copying

When we want to copy files or folders to a disk in A or B

drive, we can use the Send To option in the pop up menu, which appears when we right click on the file or folder. For example, we want to copy the files Kumar and Raj, from the folder My Documents, to a floppy in drive A. To do so, first select the file and then, right-click on the selected files. A shortcut menu as shown in Figure appears.

- Click on Send To and 3 ½ Floppy [A]
- Click on 3 ½ Floppy [A] in the left pane to check that the files have been copied.

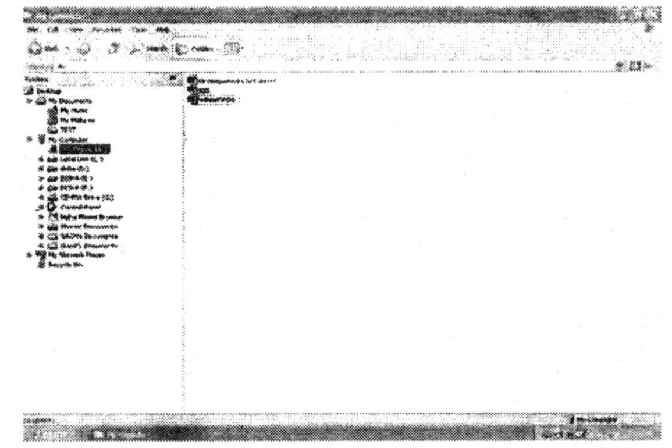

Fig. Contents of Floppy Disk in Drive A: after Copying

Let us see how to copy the files or folders by using Explorer Bar. We can copy selected files easily in the Explorer Bar. If we are not in Explorer Bar, click the Folders in the toolbar. We will be shown the Explorer Bar with Five options under File and Folder Tasks, if we select more than one item. Already we have seen the options under Moving and Copying Files and Folders.

Let us suppose we want to Copy the selected items we click on Copy the selected items, we will be provided Copy Items drop down list box, we can browse and select the desired destination. As already stated, we can even create a new folder by clicking Make New Folder tab found at the bottom of the Copy Items drop down list box.

Click Copy button adjacent to Make New Folder button to store the selected items in the newly created folder. That is all; we have successfully copied the selected items to the desired location. If we want to copy a single item, clicking on the item will show us Copy this folder under File and Folder Tasks. Follow the same procedure for copying group items.

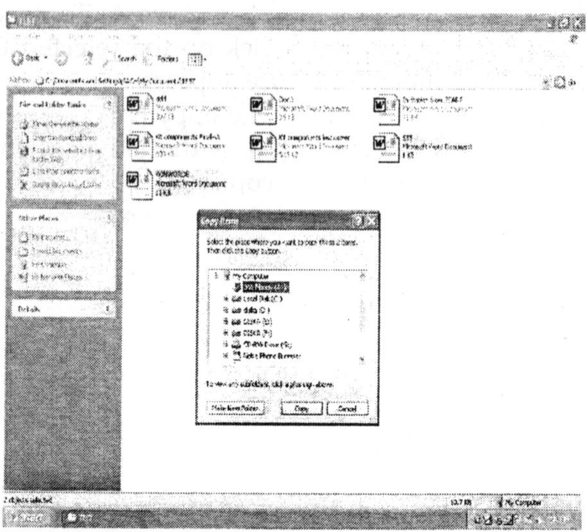

Fig. Copying Files to 3 ½ Floppy [A] with Explorer Bar We can also copy the selected items with Edit menu also.

From the menu bar, click Edit Copy To Folder...

We will be taken into Copy Items drop down list box. Then follow the steps explained in the previous paragraph. If we want to copy the selected files from the Explorer Bar to 3 ½ Floppy [A], if we have not inserted the Floppy into the Floppy drive, do it so now.

We just click the option Copy the selected items under File and Folder Tasks. Choose 3 ½ Floppy [A] from Copy Items drop down list box, under My Computer.

Click 3 ½ Floppy [A] then click the copy tab at the bottom of Copy Items drop down list box. That is all we have copied the selected items into the Floppy disk. If we want to copy only a single file we follow the same procedure.

Note: Remember that the clipboard can hold only one set of items at a time. When we copy or move a file or folder to the clipboard, it overwrites whatever was stored there earlier.

If we need to store the items we place in the clipboard permanently, we should make use of clip Book. The clip Book has 127 pages and we can store an item in each page.

The clip Book gets items through the clipboard. We can transfer item from the clipboard to Clip Book. The items stored in clip Book can be shared with the users through the Internet. For using clip Book, click Start Run. In the Run textbox,enter clipboard viewer and click OK. We will be taken to clip Book Viewer. Click Help Contents. In the ensuing help click Related Topics at the end of the help and click Save the contents of the Clipboard to the local clip Book. Follow the instruction in the ensuing Help.

Copying Files to CDs

Coping files to a CD is often referred to as burning the CD, because a laser actually burns the information on to the disk. If we write files on CD we should have CD burner installed, of course we should have blank disks. There are two types of CD burners and two types of blank CDs in the market. CD-R, CD-RW are the two types of CD burners. There are CD-R, CD-RW disks also.

CD-R burner is used to burn data to blank CD-R disk. We can make use of the resultant disks in any computer that has CD drive in it. If it is an audio CD we can use it in any standard stereo.

CD-RW burner is used to burn data to either a blank CD-R or CD-RW disk. The resulting disk can be used only in computers that have a CD drive. The CD-RW disk can be used as an ordinary floppy. We can add or delete files from it. But CD-R can be written only once.

General Method for Copying to CD

Insert a suitable blank CD into the suitable drive and wait for a few seconds. In the ensuing dialog box click, open writable CD folder using Windows Explorer and click OK. Here CD-RW Drive is used.

- If dialog box does not appear on the screen within a few seconds of inserting the blank disk, open our My

Computer folder. Then right -click the drive's icon and choose Open, then follow the previous step.

- Go to the source folders.
- Select items we want to copy to the CD. Right click any selected item and choose Send to à CD -RW Drive.
- Each item to be copied will appear as a temporary file, with black arrows pointing downwards as shown in figure.
- Check whether all files that we want to copy are there and verify that the data capacity of the combined files is less than the capacity of the disk. Then click write these files to the CD under CD Writing Tasks in the Explorer bar of the CD's folder Window.
- In the first page of CD writing wizard, we can enter a new name for CD. It is just like a label to the floppy disk. Delete the date that appears.
- Wait until the wizard burns the data to the CD. Then click Finish button on the last page of the CD Burning Wizard. That is all.

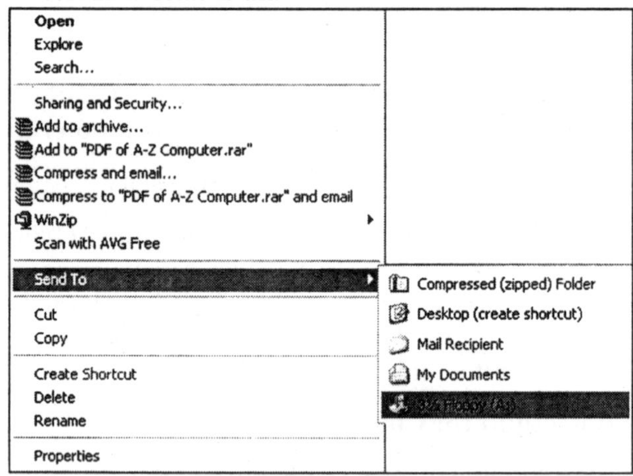

Fig. Selecting CD-RW Drive

When we click Send To, if we have CD-RW drive we will be shown CD-RW Drive otherwise the last option will be there. In Figure we can see CD Writing Tasks, this category will appear only in the computers which have CD-drive.

Fig. Files ready to be written to the CD

Renaming Files and Folders

Normally we Rename only one file or folder. In this case, we can Rename the file in any one of the following ways.

- Click the file or folder. When we are in Explorer Bar, we can choose Rename this folder from File and Folder Tasks. The name of the selected file MANI gets highlighted. Now, type the new name (SHIVA) and press Enter. The new name of the file SHIVA appears in the window. Figure shows the renaming process.

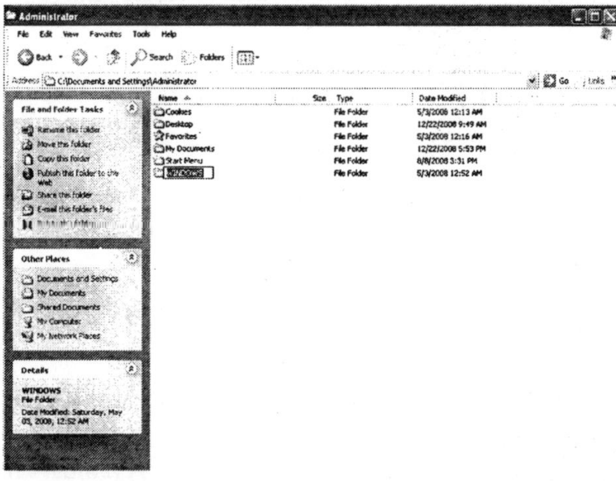

We can follow the following methods when we are either in Explorer Bar or folder Bar.

- To rename a file or folder, right click on the file or folder. Select Rename from the shortcut list, which pops up on the screen. Now change the name as given above.
- From the menu bar, click File Rename and rename the file as explained in method 1.

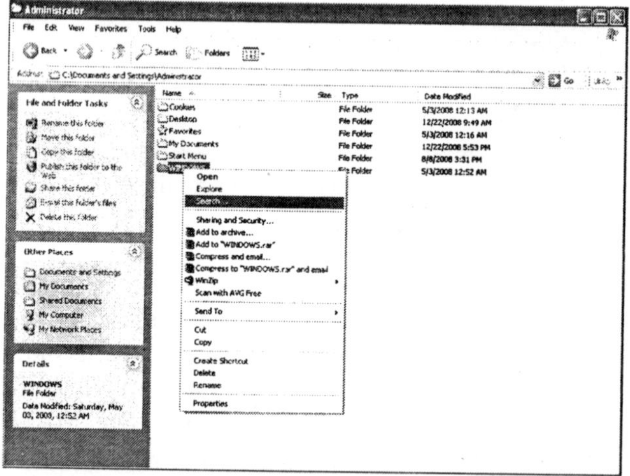

Fig. Single file Renaming option with Folders Bar

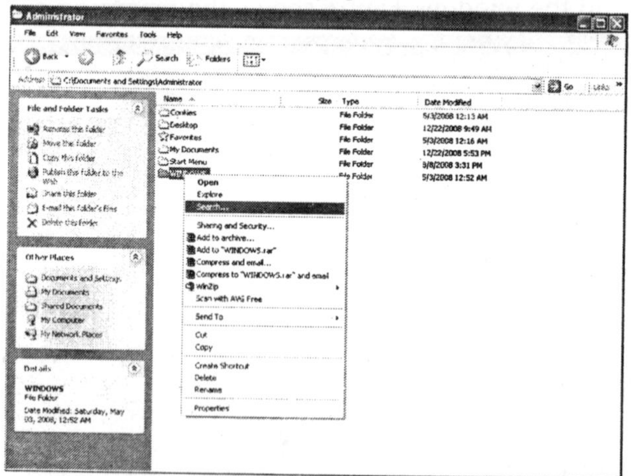

Fig. The file MANI has been renamed as SHIVA (Folders Bar)

If we want to Rename a group of files or folders, there is no special help from Explorer Bar. In fact, Explorer Bar misleads us. When we select files or folders to Rename, Explorer Bar will not show anything about renaming the group of files or folders. But we can follow method 2 and method 3 explained in the previous page.

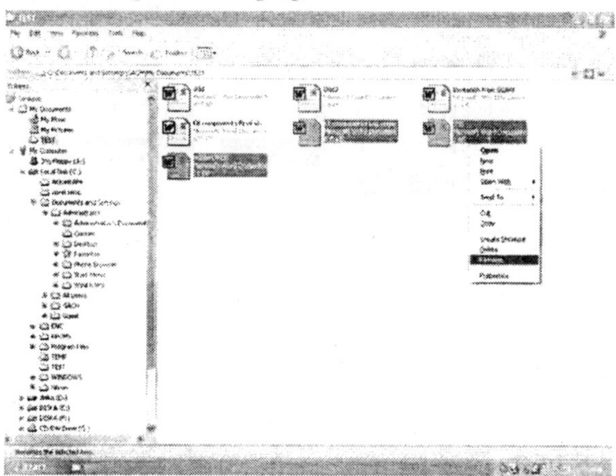

Fig. Renaming Group of Files

If we use the rightclick method the file or folder that we have chosen to right-click, will get the name that we have chosen.

Fig. Group of Files Renaming process

For example, we have selected kumar.doc, student.doc, exam.xls and raj.xls. If we have chosen the name "rajan" to rename the group of files or folder, the item that gets focus is named as rajan, the other file are named as rajan (1), rajan (2) and rajan (3). If we follow the menu method, we will have the same result.

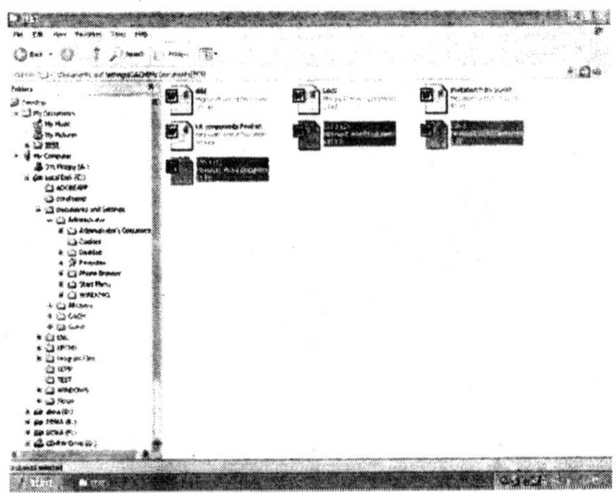

Fig. Group of Files Renamed

Deleting Files and Folders

Windows Explorer uses a special folder called the Recycle Bin to hold deleted files.

The Recycle Bin is like the garbage can in our house that we empty once it is full. In the same way, we can empty the recycle bin when we want. Using the recycle bin gives we a chance to get back files that we have deleted by mistake. To delete files, first select them. Then right click on the files and the shortcut menu appears.

Select Delete from the shortcut menu and the files will get deleted. (In reality, they are moved to the Recycle Bin). We can drag the selected file/ files to the Recycle Bin or to its Explorer Windows When we are in Explorer Bar, we can delete selected files by just clicking Delete the selected items from File and Folder Tasks.

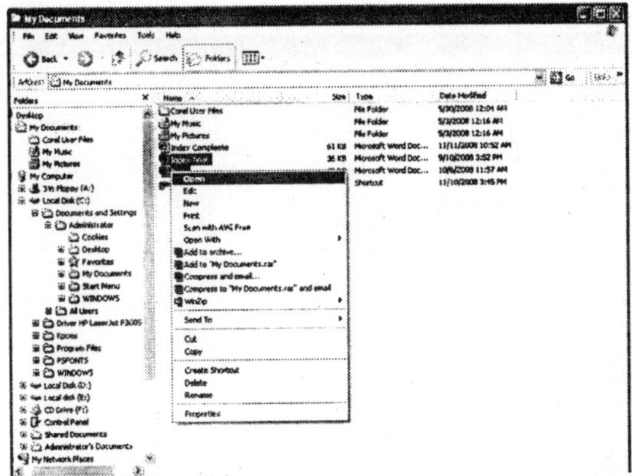

Fig. The shortcut menu with the Delete option

The Recycle Bin folder is available on the Desktop and can be used like any other folder.

Double-click on the icon to open it and check if the deleted files are present. If we do not want to send the deleted items to the Recycle Bin, Shift + Delete key combination will achieve our goal. If we delete some items from floppy or from CD-RW, the contents will be deleted for ever. The contents will not go to the Recycle Bin.

To empty the Recycle Bin, click on the File menu and choose Empty Recycle Bin. If we double click the Recycle Bin, it will open in the Explorer Bar. We can see the Explorer bar in the left pane. Contents of the Recycle Bin are shown in the right pane. Under the Recycle Bin Tasks we are shown two alternatives. If we want to restore some item, we select them. Then click the Restore, all the selected items are sent to their former destinations.

If we click Empty Recycle Bin, even if we select a few items, all the items whether they are selected or not will be eliminated from our computer's storage.

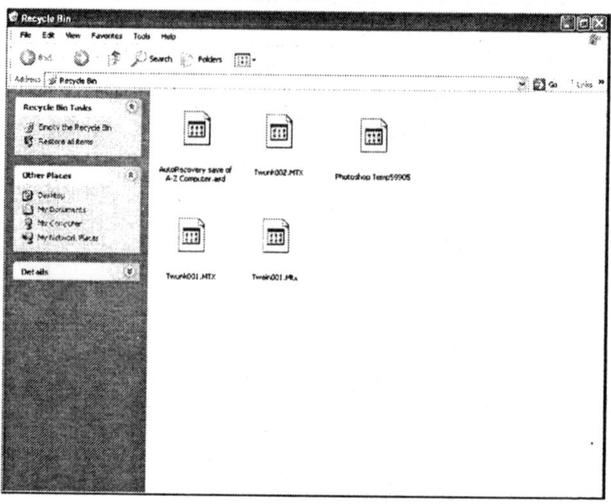

Fig. The Recycle Bin

First we select those items, which we want to recover from the right pane, and click Restore all items. We can then click Empty the Recycle Bin. Remember that once the Recycle Bin has been emptied, we cannot get back the deleted files.

To empty the Recycle Bin, click on the File menu and choose Empty Recycle Bin. If we double click the Recycle Bin, it will open in the Explorer Bar. We can see the Explorer bar in the left pane. Contents of the Recycle Bin are shown in the right pane. Under the Recycle Bin Tasks we are shown two alternatives.

If we want to restore some item, we select them. Then click the Restore, all the selected items are sent to their former destinations. If we click Empty Recycle Bin, even if we select a few items, all the items whether they are selected or not will be eliminated from our computer's storage. First we select those items, which we want to recover from the right pane, and click Restore all items. We can then click Empty the Recycle Bin. Remember that once the Recycle Bin has been emptied, we cannot get back the deleted files.

Deleting Files and Folders from CD-RW disk

We already know that a CD-R disk cannot beg modified

and CD-RW can be used as a floppy. If we want to delete the contents of CD- RW disk, we have to follow the following steps. First we should open the disk, next we should delete the contents.

- Insert CD-RW disk into our CD-RW drive. Then one of the three possibilities will happen.
  - The Windows XP Professional may provide we with a dialogue box asking we what we want to do. Choose open folder to view files using Windows Explorer. Go to step 2.
  - A programme opens and starts playing the CD, close the programme and then choose open folder to view files using Windows Explorer. Go to step 2.
  - If nothing happens, open our My Computer folder, right-click the icon for the CD-RW drive and choose open folder to view files using Windows Explorer. Go to step 2.
- In the ensuing Explorer Window, click Erase and follow the instructions on the screen.

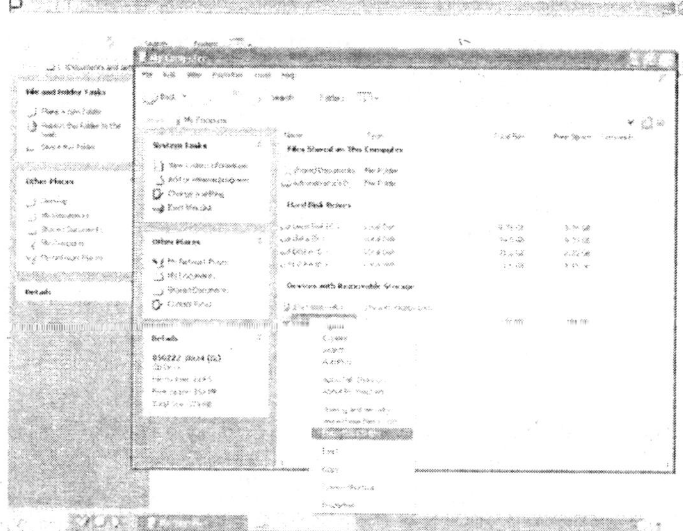

Fig. Using Erase 101

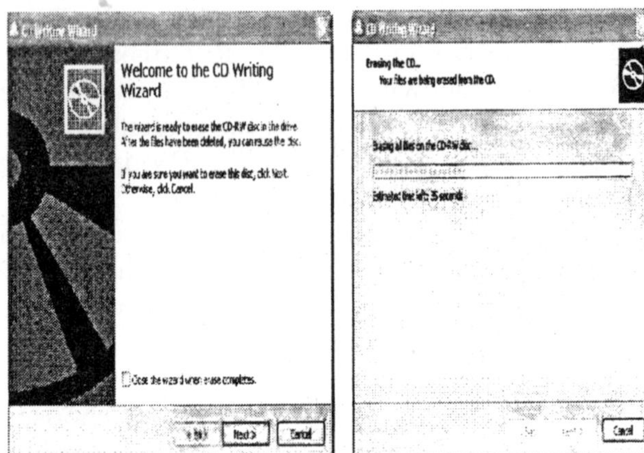

Fig. (a) Using Erase-1 (b) Using Erase-2

Creating Shortcuts

Among the many applications available on our computer, there will be a few that we use frequently. For example, we enjoy painting and frequently use Paint.

To start Paint, we should click on Start All Programs Accessories Paint.

It would be more convenient if we could start Paint directly from the desktop.

Windows XP allows we to create such shortcuts for frequently used applications. When we create a shortcut, Windows XP creates a link which points to the physical location of the programme. Windows XP allows we to create two kinds of shortcuts.

- Keyboard shortcuts
- Desktop shortcuts

Keyboard Shortcuts

We can create a keyboard shortcut for any programme by using the Properties dialog box of that application. Let us understand this better with an example.

Suppose we want to create a keyboard shortcut for Paint. To do so, first click on Start All Programs Accessories Paint and right click on it then select Properties.

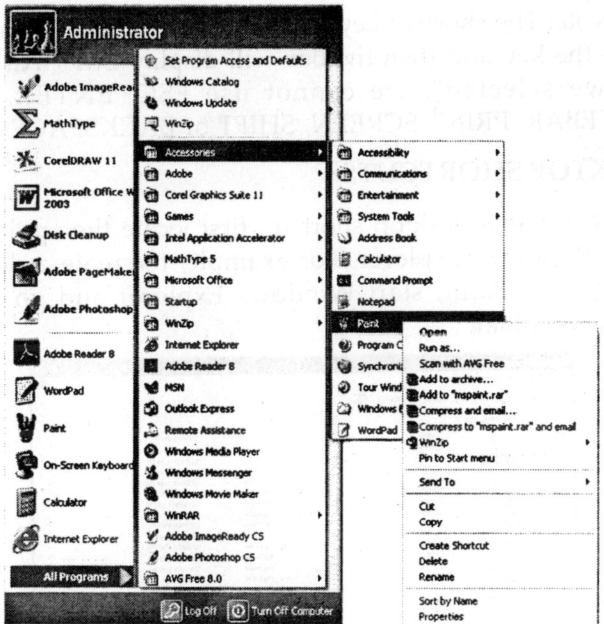

The Properties dialog box opens on the screen. Click the Shortcut tab.

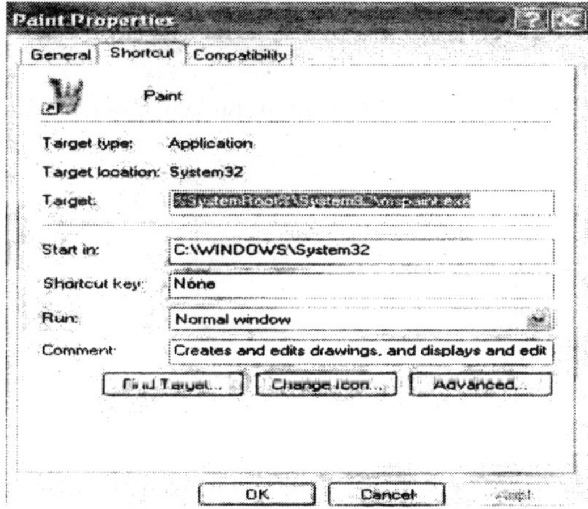

Fig. Paint Properties Dialog Box

In shortcut key text box type a letter of our choice, say P and click on OK. Now to start Paint, press Ctrl + Alt + P together.

Note: The shortcut key box will display " None " until we select the key and then the box will display Ctrl + Alt + "the key we selected", we cannot use ESC, ENTER, TAB, SPACEBAR, PRINT SCREEN, SHIFT or BACKSPACE keys.

DESKTOP SHORTCUTS

To create a desktop shortcut, first locate the application using Windows Explorer. For example, to create a desktop shortcut for Paint, start Windows Explorer and go to the Windows folder.

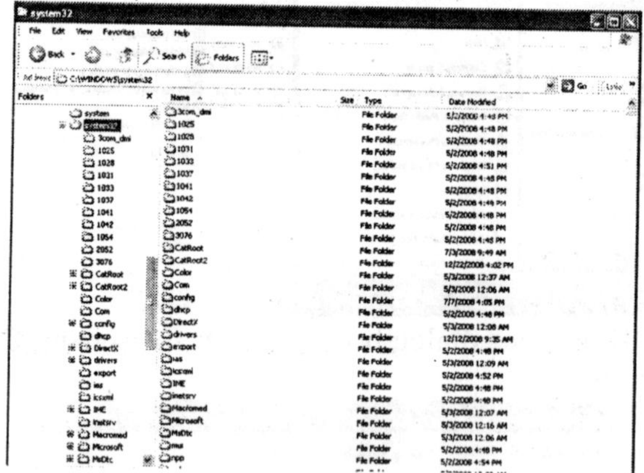

Fig. Paint Application file in the Windows Folder

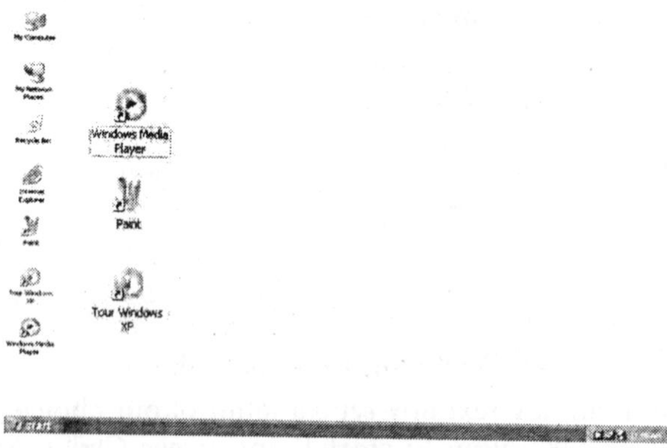

Fig. Desktop with the Shortcut to Paint icon

Right click on the application file and select Create Shortcut from the menu.

A new file called Shortcut to.... is created. Restore the Explorer window so that we can see a part of the desktop. Drag and drop the shortcut file. Now our desktop will look as shown in the figure below.

Note: The small arrow to the left of the icon indicates that the icon is a shortcut. We can start Paint by clicking on the shortcut icon.

Search

If we ask a novice computer user where his/her files are, the most probable answer will be "in the computer". This is just like saying my book is somewhere in the world. Even the experienced users sometimes lose their files; no matter how well they organize their files into folders on their hard drives. The computer will not eat the files.

So the items must be in the computer, unless we deliberately removed them. The Search facility of Windows XP allows we to find the so-called lost item. Suppose we want to find a lost file. We cannot find something out of nothing. So we should know something about the file that are being searched for.

We may inform the Search, all or part of the file name, approximate date (or with in a week, month etc.) on which the file is saved or modified or downloaded.

If we search for a document containing text we should provide a word or phrase that appears in the document. We click Start → Search (or we open any Explorer windows click search button in the toolbar or click View → Explorer Bar → Search). The left pane of the Explorer windows becomes Search Companion. In the right pane we can see To start our search, follow the instructions in the left pane.

In the left pane we can see what do we want to search for the first choice is Pictures, Music, or video. The meaning is self-explanatory. We select this under appropriate conditions. The next choice is "Documents (Word processing, spread sheet, etc.)". Select this, under appropriate conditions. The next choice is All files and folders (remote). If we want to search in All files and Folders, select this.

If we want Computers or People choice, we should have the Internet connection. Here we are going to find a lost file, so we have clicked All files and folders. We have shown the dialogue box expecting we to furnish the information about All or part of the file name.

We can make use of the wild card entries such as ?,*. The ? Stands for a single letter and * stands for zero or more letters. For example, if we know the document to be searched starts with "pur" and it is a picture document then we should enter a pur* in the text box.

In the next text box we are expected to provide a word or phrase that appears in the file. We enter.jpg there. In look in: drop down list box we browse through it to select appropriate entries. Here click Local Hard Drives (c::d:;e:;f:), we click it.

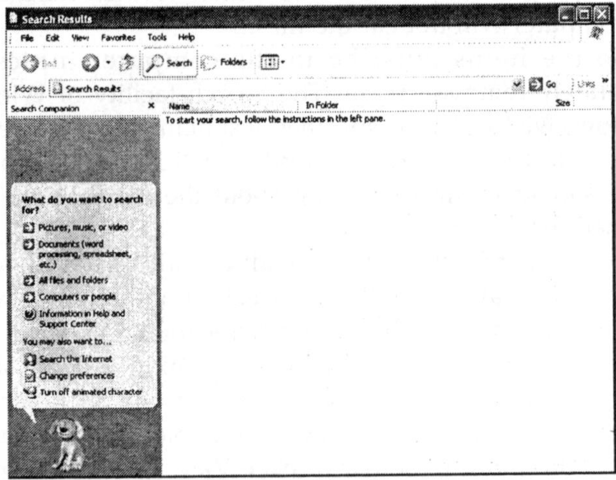

Fig. Search options

To answer the query when was it modified, if the required file is modified within the last week click on appropriate radio button. If we do not remember any thing about the period of modification, copying or downloading, leave the default selection as such. Click what size is it. It will display five options. We have to specify whether the size of the file is small, medium, large and another options is specify size.

If we do not remember the size, leave the default selection as such. We do not disturb more-advanced options. Then click Search. Then in the ensuing dialog box click Yes, finished searching or else we follow the instructions given on the screen or click Back button to repeat the Search. The result is shown below. Even though, All Files and Folders is chosen for the Search, to introduce we many options, the natural option for this Search is Pictures, Music, or video.

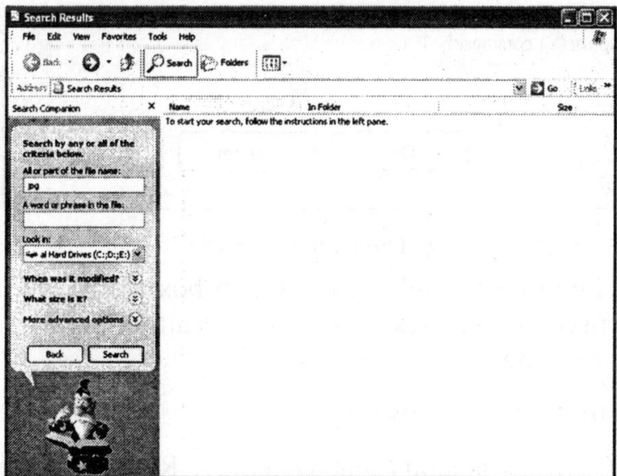

Fig. Expanded Search Options

The Run Command

The Run command on the Start menu offers an alternate method to start applications or open data files. There is one advantage in using the Run command. When we use the Run command to open a data file, say a word processing document or a paint picture, it automatically starts the corresponding application also. The Run command is most often used to install new software or games from a CD or a floppy disk.

The disadvantage of using the Run command is that we should enter the complete file name along with the Path. Path is the location of the file. Path names always start with the drive followed by folder names and end with the file name. The drive, folder names and file name are all separated by\ (backslash). For example, c:\My Documents\Project

Report.doc refers to the document file named Project Report in the folder My Documents in the C: drive.

To use the Run command, click on the Start button and select Run. Type the file name in the Open box.

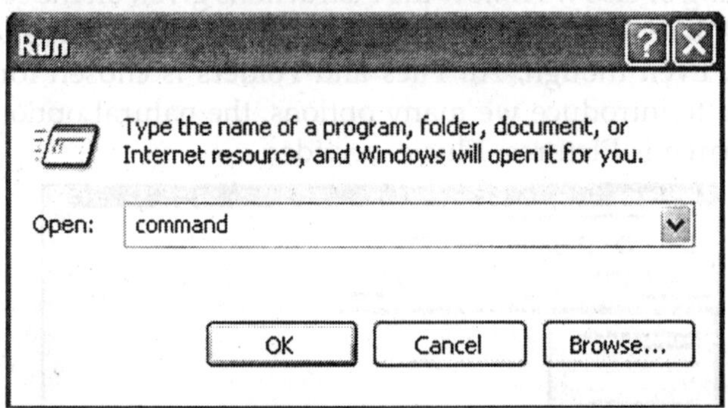

Fig. The Run command

The inverted triangle in the Open box displays a list of recently used pathnames. The Browse button lets we search for a file or folder.

What is new in Windows XP

- *Easier Installation and Updating*: Roughly speaking, installation means the addition of programme files and folders to our hard disk. Windows XP includes several features designed to make it easier to install and to keep up-to-date, the programme files and folders
- *Effective Multi-user Capabilities*: Windows XP keeps each user's files separate so that no user can see another users files unless they have been shared deliberately. It lets multiple users Log on at the same time. End users run their applications.
- *Redesigned Start menu*: Windows XP provides a redesigned start menu that is easier and quicker to use. The start menu appears as a panel containing two columns. The lower part of the left column automatically reconfigures itself to show our most used applications. The Start Menu can also be

customized to the show Classic Start Menu (similar to the start menu of Windows 98).

- *Taskbar Changes and Enhancements*: These improvements are designed to help beginners. Experienced user may switch back to how it was in the earlier versions of Windows, if they like.

Taskbar locking: By default, Windows XP Professional locks the Taskbar. This prevents taking the taskbar to an inaccessible area.

Taskbar scrolling: Taskbar locking prevents flexibility. If the taskbar is of a fixed size, buttons for the running applications must become very small and useless when 10 or more applications run. To tackle the situation Windows XP provides a scroll bar on the taskbar when required.

Taskbar Button Grouping: Windows XP provides only one button per application when there is not enough space to accommodate buttons on the Taskbar. This too prevents minimizing the size of buttons displayed on the taskbar. It shows the name of the current active window along with the number of windows and a drop-down arrow. If we click the button, it will show us the list of Windows by title, we can select any one of them.

- *Notification area*: The status area (system tray) is known as notification area. Notification area shows a few icons of the programs which are automatically executed at start up.
- *Better Audio and Video Features*: Windows XP includes a set of new features and improvements for audio and video.
- *CD Burning*: Windows XP provides built-in CD burning capabilities, which reduce the effort taken by the user while writing something into the CD.
- *Search Companion*: Windows XP includes Search Companion, an enhanced search feature to search for finding information both on our PC and in the World Wide Web.
- *Enhanced Autoplay Feature*: If we insert a CD and if it starts playing the music from it or installing any

software it contains, immediately, this facility is called Autoplay. This feature is enhanced considerably in Windows XP.

- *More Games*: Windows XP includes more games than the previous versions of Windows. This may be a welcome move for young people
- *Remote Desktop Connection*: This improved feature lets us use our computer to access a remote computer with less effort.
- *A more Useful Winkey*: One or two winkeys may be provided in modern keyboards. Normally the key is situated between Ctrl and Alt keys. This key possesses the Windows logo. Windows XP includes more functionality for the Winkey. We are provided table with the uses of Winkey.

WLNKEY COMBLNATLONS

Winkey: Combination What it does

Winkey: Toggles the display of the Start menu

Winkey+ B: Moves the focus to the notification area

Winkey+ box: Break Displays the System Properties dialog

Winkey+ : D Displays the Desktop

Winkey+ : E Opens an Explorer window showing My Computer

Winkey+F: Opens a Search Results window and activates Search Companion

Winkey+Ctrl+F: Opens a Search Results window, activates Search Companion, and starts a Search for Computer

Winkey+F1: Opens a Help and Support Centre window

Winkey+L: Locks the computer

Winkey+M: Issues a Minimize All Windows command

Winkey+Shift+M: Issues an Undo Minimize All command

Winkey+R: Displays the Run dialog box

Winkey+Tab: Moves the focus to the next button in the Taskbar

Winkey+Shift+Tab: Moves the focus to the previous button in the Taskbar

Winkey+U: Displays Utility Manager

- *Improvement for Portable Computers*: Windows XP includes several improvements for portable computers (such as Note book computers).
- *More Help*: Windows XP delivers more Help-and more different types of Help-than any other version of Windows. We have already seen some help topics of interest.
- *Network Connectivity*: Windows XP provides various improvements in network connectivity.
- Multiple Monitor Support-For Both Desktop and Laptop.

Windows XP Professional also introduces a new technology called Dual View, which offers excellent opportunities to multiple monitor support especially to laptops.

The above characteristics can apply to both Windows XP Professional and Windows XP Home.

The following Characteristics strictly belong to Windows XP Professional

- *Backup and Automated System Recovery* (ASR): Windows XP Professional includes a Backup utility and an ASR feature that can be activated from boot up to restore a damaged system.
- *Offline Files*: Offline files allows we to store copies of files located on network drives on our local drive so that we can work with them when our computer is no longer connected to the network.
- *Remote Desktop*: Remote Desktop allows we to access the Desktop of the computer connected remotely as if we are accessing the Desktop of our own computer. If we need to connect to our computer remotely via Remote Desktop Connection, we need Windows XP Professional rather than Windows Home. So far, we have seen features that caught our eyes. Now, we are going to see the facilities hidden in Windows XPProfessional.
- *Protected Memory Management*: Windows XP offers fully protected memory management. With this

facility, Windows XP can handle memory errors effortlessly.

- *System File Protection*: Windows XP offers a feature called System File Protection that protects our system files from inadvertent mistakes on our part.
- *System Restore*: Windows XP provides a System Restore feature. This is more effective than System Restore feature found in Windows Me. We can use System Restore to rollback the changes to an earlier point at which the system was working properly..
- *Device Driver Rollback*: Windows XP tracks the drivers we install and lets we roll back the installation of the driver. In other words, we can revert to the driver we were using before.
- *Compatibility with Windows 9 x Applications*: Windows XP runs all applications that would run on Windows 9x, Windows NT and Windows 2000.

GUARDING AGAINST VIRUSES

The literal meaning of virus is poison. Virus enters into the living things and passes its code to the cells of the host. The host cell forgets to undertake its own work, it becomes the industry for producing viruses. Computer virus is a mischievous programme designed to damage the Software, Hardware and/ or data.

The technique of the biological virus is employed by the computer virus also. It enters our computer as innocuous software and multiplies many times. In that process, it takes the lion's share of the memory normally, erasing our own useful programs.

Though virus started from the Bell Laboratory in the name of core wars, it showed its ugly head to the world by the handiwork of a self taught Software Engineer. But still the method of creating viruses was kept as a secret. One of the eminent computer professionals, while receiving a prestigious award, revealed the secret of creating viruses to the audience. The entire computer world was shell-shocked.

This opened the Pandora box. From then on, the computer

world is cursed with many viruses. Most of them are created by the students to just show their intelligence to the world, thus causing a loss of millions of dollars. The virus designers mainly attack windows OS. Viruses come in three basic flavours. They are File infectors, Boot sector viruses and Trojan horse viruses

File infectors attach themselves to executable files and spread among other files when we run the programme.

- Boot sector viruses replace the hard disk's master boot record (or the boot sector on a floppy disk) with their own twisted version of the bootstrap code. This lets them load themselves into memory whenever we boot our system (the famous "Michelangelo" virus is one of these boot sector beasts).
- Trojan horse viruses, which appear to be legitimate programs at first glance but when loaded, proceed to viciously damage our data:
- Viruses are, by now, an unpleasant fact of computing life, and we just have to learn to live with the threat. But somehow in the beginning, the Microsoft chose to ignore this ugly threat, but now Microsoft deals with this crime more seriously in Windows XP. There are vendors who provide antiviral vaccines that will protect we from the hazards of this threat. Antivirus is a programme to safeguard our system from the virus programs. There are many such antiviruses, which make the life of the programmers somewhat easy.
- *Here are two tips to keep our system virus-free*: The main source of the viruses is the floppy disk. So, one should be very careful about the floppies.
- Now-a-days, the Internet is the major source of producing viruses. One should be very careful while downloading files from the Internet. Keep our virus utility's virus library up-to-date. By some accounts, more than 100 new virus strains are released each month, and they just get nastier and nastier. Regular updates will help us keep up-to-date.

The Economical Explorer Keyboard

If we want to have alternative methods for the mouse click, here is the table.

Alt+Enter: Display the properties sheet for the selected objects.

Alt+F4: Closes Explorer (actually closes the active window).

Alt+left arrow: Take us back to a previously displayed folder.

Alt+right arrow: Take us forward to a previously displayed folder.

Backspace: Take we to the parent folder of the current folder.

Ctrl+A: Selects all the objects in the current folder.

Ctrl+C: Copies the selected object to the Clipboard

Ctrl+V: Pastes the most recently cut or copied objects from the Clip

Ctrl+X: Cuts the selected objects to the Clipboard.

Ctrl+Z: Reverses the most recent action.

Delete: Sends the currently selected objects to the Recycle Bin.

F2: It helps to rename the selected object.

F3: Displays the Find dialog box with the current folder as the default.

F4: Opens the Address toolbar's drop-down list.

F5: Refreshes the Explorer window. This is handy if we have made changes to a folder via the command line or a DOS programme and we want to update the Explorer window to display the changes.

F6: Cycles the highlight among the All Folders list, the Contents list, and the Address toolbar.

Shift + Delete: Delete the currently selected objects without sending them to the Recycle Bin.

Shift+F10: Displays the context menu for the selected objects.

Tab: Cycles the highlight among the All Folders list, the contents list, and the `address toolbar. F6 does the same thing.

Chapter 9

Spreadsheet

The personal computer (PC) first appeared in 1975. But, initially, the PCs were of interest primarily to the electronics hobbyists. Later in 1977 when more usable PCs started appearing, it attracted a wider population. The PCs became more popular when Dan Bricklin and Bon Frankston invented VisiCalc for Apple II in 1979. VisiCalc, "The visible calculator" was the first electronic spreadsheet.

This attracted accountants, book keepers, managers and all those who created budget, analysed statistics or collected numerical research data. This powerful computational tool could save time, help avoid endless and brain-numbing arithmetic, and eliminate mathematical errors. It was acknowledged by many that the invention of the spreadsheet, more than any other event, launched the personal computer revolution.

ELECTRONIC SPREADSHEET

An electronic spreadsheet is a worksheet used in a computer to create and quickly perform "What if" analysis of interrelated columnar data in workspaces. Spreadsheets are made up of rows and columns as shown in figure. The intersection of rows and columns creates cells. The cells are addressed in terms of the row and column labels.

Any data, like numbers, text or formulae can be typed into a cell. The power of the spreadsheet lies in the fact that the cells can contain formulae, which perform certain mathematical operations on the data in other cells and display the results in a new cell

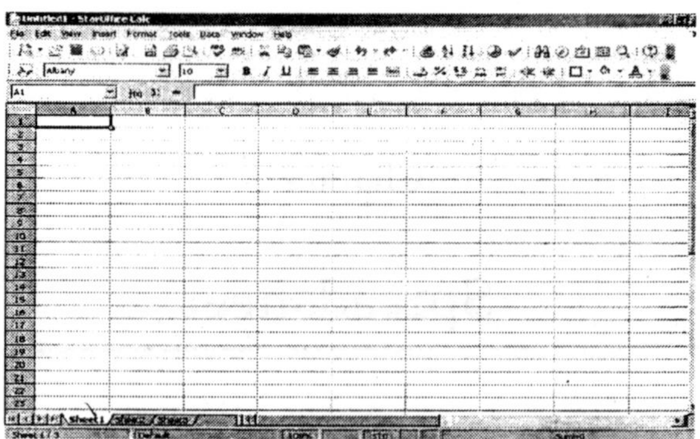

Fig. Empty Spreadsheet

In a spreadsheet, the rows are numbered from 1 to some length (upto 32,000 in the case of StarOffice Calc) and the columns designated with the letters A through Z, AA through AZ, and so on, as provided by different spreadsheet packages.

The following simple example illustrates how to use spreadsheets: Consider an example of storing a number 150 in a cell and another number 16 in another cell. Add these two numbers electronically and store the result in a new cell. For this purpose, let us use the cells A3 and A4 for storing the numbers 150 and 16 respectively and the cell B4 for storing the sum of these two numbers.

To enter the value 150 in a cell A3, position the cursor in the cell A3, click the mouse to select it and type 150. Now, we will find the number 150 appearing in cell A3. Similarly, enter the number 16 in cell A4.

Let us now add the values in the cells A3 and A4 and store the result in B4. To perform this operation, select the cell B4 by taking the cursor to B4 and clicking the same. Type the formula as = A3 + A4 or use the sum function as = sum (A3:A4). The formula appears in the input line of the Formula bar (below the menu bars). Press the Enter key.

A spreadsheet is like a grid of cells with a programmable calculator attached to each cell. The computer can perform calculations at a blinding speed. It does not matter how many numbers and formulae we put in a spreadsheet, the computer can recalculate every formula every time we change any number. For instance, change the number in the cell A4 in the above example. The spreadsheet recalculates the sum automatically and shows the result in the Cell B4.

B4 f(x) Σ = =A3+A4

	A	B	C	D
1				
2				
3	150			
4	16	166		
5				
6				

Fig. Recalculations in a Spreadsheet

B4 f(x) Σ = =A3+A4

	A	B	C	D
1				
2				
3	150			
4	76	226		
5				
6				

Fig. Calculations in a Spreadsheet

Electronic spreadsheets can also be used for presenting the worksheet data in an impressive manner such as bar-charts, pie-charts, line graphs, three-dimensional charts and other visual forms. The terms 'spreadsheet' and 'worksheet' mean one and the same. But now, over time, the term 'spreadsheet' has come to refer specifically to the software packages, while 'worksheet' refers to the files that we create with spreadsheet software.

Spreadsheet applications

There are numerous applications possible using electronic spreadsheets. A few of the common applications are given below:

- Payment of bills
- Income tax calculations
- Invoices or bills
- Account Statements
- Inventory Control

- Cost-Benefits Analysis
- Financial Accounting
- Tender Evaluation
- Result analysis of students

Advantages of using Electronic spreadsheets

The electronic spreadsheet offers several advantages over the manual one. The following are some of the main advantages of electronic spreadsheets:

- Calculations are automated through the built-in mathematical, financial and statistical functions.
- Accurate results to any desired level of decimal points are Possible
- Worksheets can be quite big in size
- Any part of the worksheet can be viewed or edited.
- Worksheet can be saved and retrieved later.
- Any part or whole of an existing worksheet can be merged with any existing or new worksheet.
- Any part or whole of the worksheet can be printed in a desired format.
- Worksheet data can be viewed in the form of graphs or charts
- The worksheet information can be transferred to any database or word processing software.

Popular Spreadsheet Software

Commercial electronic spreadsheet packages are in use since late 1970s. VisiCalc (Visible Calculator) was the first commercial spreadsheet package developed for microcomputers in 1979. It contained 63 columns (A, B,..............BK) and 254 rows. VisiCalc was essentially a financial analysis programme.

After seeing the power the success of VisiCalc, Several companies tried to develop spreadsheet packages. Lotus Development Corporation introduced Lotus 1-2-3 in 1982. This package became very popular because of its ability to combine database management and graphics features with its spreadsheet.

The other popular spreadsheet programs are 'Excel from Microsoft Corporation 'Quattro Pro from Borland International, 'Improve' from Lotus Corporation and 'Star Office Calc' from Sun Microsystems.

Working with Star Office Calc

StarOffice Calc is a powerful spreadsheet programme included in Star Office. It offers all the functions needed for business use, including various financial and statistical functions, Star Office Calc database functions and much more.

Creating a worksheet is a process that involves several steps like organizing the data, entering the data, creating formulae, editing the worksheet, formatting values, labels, and cells, adding charts if required, analysing the data and printing the worksheet. Let us learn how to create a worksheet using Star Office Calc.

Creating First Worksheet

To work with Star Office Calc, open Star Office and click on the File option in the main menu bar. Then click on New? ?Spreadsheet. A new spreadsheet opens up as shown in figure. At the top of the window is the Menu bar. To use a menu, point to it with the mouse cursor and press the left mouse button.

The menu will open displaying a list of options and we can select any option by clicking on it. Below the Menu bar is the Main toolbar. Below the Main toolbar are the Function bar and the Object bar. These bars have shortcut icons for frequently done tasks.

Below these bars is the Formula bar. This bar is used to display the current cell and its contents. It also has a few more shortcut icons. Below the formula bar are the column headings of the worksheet. Next to it are the row headings. The data area is in the middle of the window. At the extreme bottom are the Status Bars and Scroll bars.

Before we can create our first worksheet, we have to first collect the data that we want to include in the worksheet. Suppose we want to create a worksheet containing the details of marks obtained by students. To do this, we can collect details such as 'Reg.No.', 'Name of the student' and 'Marks' of different subjects, obtained by each student.

Then we can enter the data into the worksheet. Once the data has been entered into the worksheet, we can perform various calculations on this data and calculate things like 'Total marks' of all the subjects and 'Average marks'. We can then, format the data in the worksheet to make it look attractive. We can also draw a graph using this data.

Entering Data in the Worksheet

After deciding and collecting the data to be entered in the worksheet, we are now ready to actually enter the data. The active cell in which we want to type the data is identified by the cell pointer which is a rectangular box covering that cell. To begin with, the cell pointer is always in cell A1. We can change the position of the cell pointer by clicking the mouse on the concerned cell or by using the arrow keys on the keyboard.

The Tab, Home, End, PgUp and PgDown keys on the keyboard also allow we to move around the worksheet. After selecting the cell, enter the data. If the data entered is a number, the programme recognizes that as a number and allows we to perform calculations on it. If the data entered is a word, the programme recognizes it as a label and does not permit we to perform calculations on it.

Star Office Calc also allows we to enter dates and time in the worksheet. This is very useful because we can also perform various calculations using them. For example, we can find the difference between two dates, add a number to a date and find the new date and so on.

We will learn more about this later. We can enter dates in the worksheet just like we enter numbers and labels. Place the cursor in the cell where we want to enter the date and type it in as MM/DD/YY. We can enter the time in the worksheet by typing it as HH:MM:SS. Listed below are the steps to create the worksheet for the student marks. Note that the cursor is in Cell A1 to begin with.

Fig. Blank Screen

- In cell A1, type the title as 'Student Mark Details of 9th Standard'. Press the down arrow key to move to cell A2.
- In Cell A2, type the heading 'Reg.No'. Press the right arrow key to move to cell B2.
- In cell B2, type 'Name'. Move to cell C2.
- In cell C2, type the subject name as 'English'
- In cell D2, type 'Tamil'
- In cell E2, type 'Maths'
- In cell F2, type 'Science'
- In cell G2, type 'Total'
- In cell H2, type 'Average'

The worksheet thus created is shown in figure.

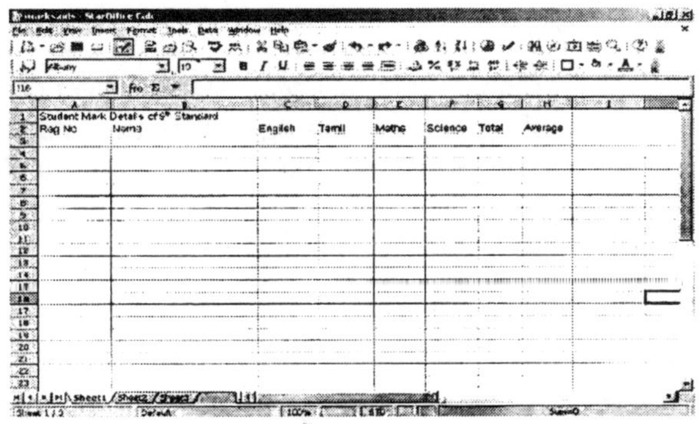

Fig. The Student Marks Worksheet

Saving the Worksheet

To save the worksheet created, go to the File menu and

select the Save or the Save As option. A screen appears as shown in figure.

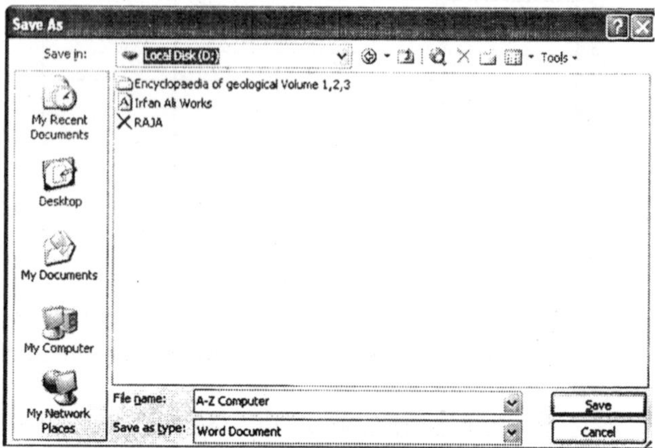

Fig. Save As Dialog Box

Type in a file name and click on Save. For example, to save the student marks, type the name Marks in the File name box and click on the Save button. We can also click on the Save icon on the Standard toolbar.

Closing the worksheet

In order to close the worksheet, go to File menu and select the Close option.

Opening a Worksheet

To open a worksheet that has been saved, select the Open option from the file menu. A dialog box with a list of files appears on the screen. Select the file that we want by clicking on it and then click on Open. We can also click the Open icon on the Standard toolbar to open an existing file.

Quitting from StarOffice

The Exit option under the File menu can be used to quit from StarOffice.

Learn by Solving

Create the Marks worksheet created above with the following data:

Reg No.	*Name*	*English*	*Tamil*	*Maths*	*Science*
1000	Kumar A.	87	85	74	86
1001	Aravindan J.	63	86	62	94
1002	Govindan S.	63	76	73	75
1003	Velmurugan T.	75	72	63	85
1004	Thamizharasi G.	75	46	52	64

After we complete the data entry the worksheet will look be as shown below.

F7 f(x) Σ = 64

	A	B	C	D	E	F	G	H
1	Student Mark Details of 9th Standard							
2	Reg No	Name	English	Tamil	Maths	Science	Total	Average
3	1000	Kumar A	87	85	74	86		
4	1001	Aravindan J	63	86	62	94		
5	1002	Muthu S	63	76	73	75		
6	1003	Vijay V	75	72	63	85		
7	1004	Swetha A	75	46	52	64		
8								
9								

Fig. Worksheet of the Student Database

Note that in cells B6 and B7, the complete name is not displayed.

This is because the width of Column B is not enough; Star Office Calc indicates this with small red triangles, we will learn how to increase the column width. Save the worksheet as Marks

Editing the Data in the Worksheet

To edit the data present in a worksheet, first open the worksheet by clicking on File open. Next, move the cursor to the cell, which we want to edit. Note that the contents of the cell are displayed on the formula bar also. We can edit the contents in the following two ways:

- Type in the new data. The new data will simply overwrite the old contents of the cell.
- Click on the formula bar with the mouse, press the F2 function key or simply double-click on the cell. A vertical cursor appears on the formula bar. Move the cursor to the left using the left arrow key or the backspace key and edit the data.

Creating Formulae

After entering data in the worksheet we can perform calculations on the data in the worksheet.

This is done using formulae. In order to create formulae, we first need to know the syntax that describes the format of specifying a formula.

The syntax of formula begins with an equal sign followed by a combination of values, operators and cell references. The various operators available for calculations, in StarOffice Calc are given below:

Arithmetic Operators

These operators return numerical results

Operator	*Name*	*Example*
+(plus)	Addition	1+1
–(minus)	Substraction	2–1
–(Minus)	Negation	–5
*(asterisk)	Multiplication	2*2
/(Slash)	Division	9/3
% (Percent)	Percent	15%
∧(Caret)	Exponentiation	3∧2

Comparative Operators

These operators return either true or false.

Operator	*Name*	*Example*
=	Equal	A1 = B1
>	Greater than	A1 > B1
<	Less than	A1< B1
> =	Greater than or equal to	A1 >= B1
< =	Less than or equal to	A1 <= B1
< >	Inequality	A1 <> B1

Text Operators

The operator combines sections of text to the entire text.

Operator	*Name*	*Example*
&(And)	Textoperator:	
	And	"Star" & "Office" yields StarOffice"

Reference Operators

These operators combine areas.

Operator	*Name*	*Example*
:(Colon)	Range	A1:C108
!(Exclamation point)	Intersection	SUM(A1:B6!B5:C12)

When arithmetic operators are used in formulae, StarOffice Calc calculates the results using the rules of precedence followed in Mathematics. The order is as follows:

- Exponentiation (∧)
- Negation (–)
- Multiplication and Division (*,/)
- Addition and Subtraction (+,–)

Here is an example to illustrate how to create formulae:

- Place the cell pointer in the cell where we want to enter the formula. In the Marks worksheet example, place the cursor in cell G3. o Type the formula as =C3+D3+E3+F3 and press the Enter key.

The total mark of the student Kumar A. appears in the Cell G3. The marks worksheet with the total thus calculated is shown in figure.

G3 f(x) Σ = =C3+D3+E3+F3

	A	B	C	D	E	F	G	H	I
1	Student Mark Details of 9th Standard								
2	Reg No	Name	English	Tamil	Maths	Science	Total	Average	
3	1000	Kumar A	87	85	74	86	332		
4	1001	Aravindan J	63	86	62	94			
5	1002	Muthu S	63	76	73	75			
6	1003	Vijay V	75	72	63	85			
7	1004	Swetha A	75	46	52	64			
8									

Fig. The Worksheet of the Student Database with Total

Fill Command

We have learnt how to create and use formulae to calculate. But, in the above example, we have calculated only one total. To calculate the other totals, we can type the corresponding formulae in the cells G4, G5, G6 and G7. There is an easier way of entering these formulae.

We can type the formula in cell G3 and then copy it to the remaining cells. This can be done using the Copy and Paste icons on the standard toolbar. Recall that we learnt how to use these icons in StarOffice Writer. We can also use the Automatic Fill feature of StarOffice Calc. AutoFill automatically generates a data series based on a defined pattern.

- On a sheet, click in cell, and type a number.
- Drag the fill handle in the bottom right corner of the cell across the cells that we want to fill, and release the mouse button. The cells are filled with ascending numbers. To copy the contents of a cell, click on the cell. Click and drag the mouse to highlight all the cells where we want to copy the contents.

Now, select Edit → Fill → Down (or Left). The content of first cell will be copied in all the highlighted cells.

Note: A continuous group of cells in a worksheet is called a Range. A range is referred to by the range address. A range address is the address of the first cell in the range, followed by a colon, followed by the address of the last cell in the range. For example, the cells, G1, G2, G3, G4 and G5 can be called G1:G5.

The cells A1, B1, C1, D1, E1 and F1 can be called A1:F1 and the cells A4, A5, A6, B4, B5 and B6 can be referred to as A4:B6.

G7 =C7+D7+E7+F7

	A	B	C	D	E	F	G	H
1	Student Mark Details of 9th Standard							
2	Reg No	Name	English	Tamil	Maths	Science	Total	Average
3	1000	Kumar A	87	85	74	86	332	
4	1001	Aravindan J	63	86	62	94	305	
5	1002	Govindan S	63	76	73	75	287	
6	1003	Velmurugan	75	72	63	85	295	
7	1004	Thamizharasi	75	46	52	64	237	
8								
9								
10								
11								

Fig. The Contents of cell G3 has been Copied to G4:G7

For example, to copy the contents of cell G3 in the cells

G4, G5, G6 and G7, highlight the cells G3 to G7 (also referred to as G3:G7).Click on Edit → Fill → Down. The contents of the cell G3 will be copied to all the other cells, as shown in figure.

We can also use the Fill command to generate a series of data directly from the values of the selected cells. First, select the cells of the worksheet that we want to fill. Choose the command Edit →Fill →Series. Select the type of series from the options that appear as shown in figure.

For example, if we want to enter numbers in the cells of a column in an increasing order with a difference of 3 between subsequent cell values, we will have to just enter only the initial value in the first cell of the column and specify the direction, type and increment. In this case, select Direction as Down, Type as Linear and Increment as 3. Then by clicking the OK button the values in the subsequent cells of the column will be automatically generated.

As another example, select the range A1:D6 in the worksheet.

Click on Edit → Fill → Series. Choose

2 as your Start value

2 as your Increment

Growth as the Type, and Down as the Direction. Now, click on OK and we will find the worksheet filled as shown in figure.

	A	B	C	D	E
1	2	4	8	16	
2	4	8	16	32	
3	8	16	32	64	
4	16	32	64	128	
5	32	64	128	256	
6	64	128	256	512	
7					

Fig. Result for Fill Command

As we can see in the dialog box, we can also automatically fill in series of dates and times. For example, to list all Sundays in a given period, say March to May 2005, proceed as follows:

- Enter the date as 3/5/05 into a cell
- Select this cell and adequate number of cells

depending upon the stop value (in this case, 13 cells since the period is March - May 2005).

- Select the command Edit→ Fill→Series
- In the dialog box, select Day as the Date Unit and enter the Increment as 7. Click OK.

The Sundays of March, April and May 2005 automatically appear in the selected cell as shown in figure.

	A	B	C	D
1	Dates of Sundays in March, April and May 2005			
2				
3		03/06/2005		
4		03/13/2005		
5		03/20/2005		
6		03/27/2005		
7		04/03/2005		
8		04/10/2005		
9		04/17/2005		
10		04/24/2005		
11		05/01/2005		
12		05/08/2005		
13		05/15/2005		
14		05/22/2005		
15		05/29/2005		
16				
17				

Fig. Auto Filling Date and Month

Cell Referencing

In the Marks worksheet example, we typed the formula = C3+D3+E3+F3 in cell G3 and then copied it to the cells G4:G7. Click on the cell G4. Note that the formula in this cell is =C4+D4+E4+F4. This is because spreadsheets refer the cell addresses in a formula not as absolutes but in a relative way. For example, consider the formula in cell G3. Star Clac reads this formula as

- Add the value in the cell 4 columns to the left of current cell
- With the contents of the cell 3 columns to the left of current cell
- With the contents of the cell 2 columns to the left of the current cell
- With the contents of the cell 1 column to the left of the current cell.

So, when this formula is copied to the cell G4, it does not read as = C3+D3+E3+F3 but as

- Add the value in the cell 4 columns to the left of current cell
- with the contents of the cell 3 columns to the left of current cell
- with the contents of the cell 2 columns to the left of current cell
- with the contents of the cell 1 columns to the left of current cell

That is, = C4+D4+E4+F4.

This type of cell referencing is called Relative cell addressing. Relative cell addressing is the default type of cell addressing used by Star Office Calc. Relative cell addressing is also the reason why formulae are automatically recalculated every time the contents of the cells used in the formulae change.

The other type of referencing used in spreadsheets is Absolute cell addressing. A cell address can be made absolute by using the $ (dollar) sign in front of row and column names. For example, the C4 becomes absolute when we enter it as C4.

Absolute cell addresses do not change when copied.

Using Functions

Star Office Calc has a wide variety of functions that allow we to perform several frequently done calculations. Functions are predefined formulae that are available in Star Office Calc. These functions are available in Star Office Calc in the pull down menu of Function Wizard window as shown in figure. The functions available are divided into different categories. The categories are listed in the category pull down menu.

To select a function, go to Insert menu and Select the Function option. The Function Wizard dialog box appears. A list of all functions is displayed in the Function box when All is selected in the Category box. If a category is selected (e.g. Mathematical) the functions related to that category alone will be displayed in the function box.

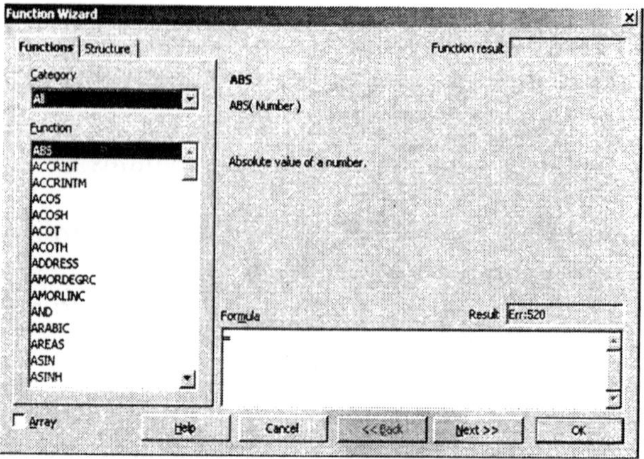

Fig. Function Wizard Window

To select a function:

- Select the category in the Category box.
- Scroll down the list to find the function we want. Click once on the function name to see a short description of that function on the right side of the window. Double - click on it to insert it into the worksheet.

The Function Wizard shortcut icon on the formula bar can also be used to select and insert functions.

For example, to insert the SQRT function (a function to find the square root of a number), place the cursor in the cell where we want to insert the function and click on the Function Wizard icon.

Select Mathematical from Category. Select the SQRT function from the list of functions, which appears by double clicking on it. The Function Wizard displays a brief description of the function and prompts we to enter the number or the cell address on which the function should work. Enter the number 64.

One of the most commonly used function is the Sum function. This function calculates the sum of a given set of numbers. To use this function, we can either click on the Function Wizard icon or then select SUM or we can just click on the Sum icon on the formula bar. Star Office Calc suggests a range of cells for which sum is to be calculated. Press Enter to accept this suggested range or press the Backspace key and type in the range that we want. For example, in the Marks worksheet, to calculate the total marks in cell G3, follow the steps given below.

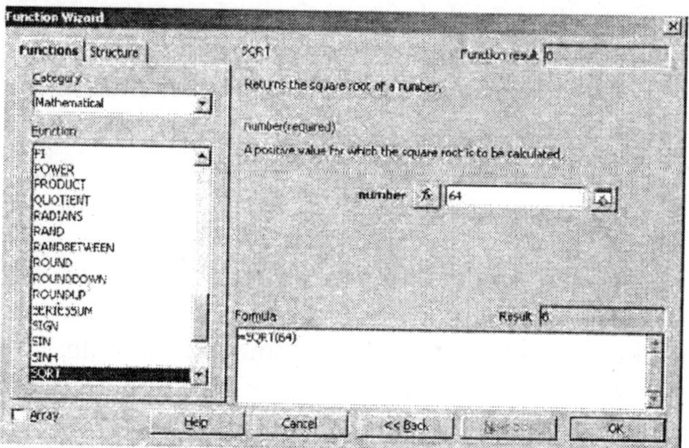

Fig. The Function Wizard Prompts we to Enter a Number or a Cell Address

When we click on OK, the result is displayed in the cell in the worksheet.

- Click on the cell G3 to place the cursor there.
- Click on the Sum icon on the function bar. = SUM (C3: F3) appears in the cell.
- Press Enter to accept the suggested range.

The result, that is, 332 is displayed in the cell G3.

Learn by solving

- Open the worksheet Marks.
- Use a formula to calculate the total in cell G3.
- Use the Fill command to copy the formula to the cell G4:G7.
- Close the worksheet without saving.
- Open the worksheet again and use the Sum function to calculate the total in cell G3.
- Use the Fill command to copy the formula to the cells G4:G7.
- Save the worksheet.

- Enter a formula in cell H3 to calculate the average marks.
- Use the Fill command to copy the formula to the cells H4:H7.
- Close the worksheet without saving.
- Open the worksheet again and use the AVERAGE function to calculate the average in cell H3.
- Use the Fill command to copy the formula to the cells H4:H7.
- Save and close the worksheet.

Date Arithmetic

Manual date calculations can be tricky because we have to keep track of the number of days in a month. In spreadsheets, date calculations become very simple. Here we can add a number to a date and arrive at a new date, find the difference between two dates and use a wide variety of function and formats to get what we want.

For example, enter a date 03/04/05 in a cell, say A2. Remember that while entering dates the month always comes first. Suppose we want to calculate the date 79 days after this date. To do so, enter the formula, = A2 + 79, in another cell, say A4. The date 05/22/05 appears in the cell.

Now, suppose we want to calculate the difference between two dates, 05/10/05 and 12/8/70. To do so, enter the two dates in two different cells. In a third cell enter the formula = first cell - second cell. The result will be displayed as 12572.

Formatting the Worksheet

In the earlier Chapters, we learnt the various formatting options of Star Office Writer. We can use several of those options in Star Office Calc also. In addition, Star Office Calc provides us with several formatting options for formatting numbers. It is important to remember that by formatting the contents of a cell, only the display changes; the contents remain unchanged.

Before formatting the cells in a worksheet, we have to select the cells that we wish to format. We already know how to select one cell. Just click on the cell and it will be selected. To select a group of cells (a range), click on the first cell in the range and click and drag to the last cell in the range.

To select a complete row or a column, click on the respective row number or column name. To select more than one row or column, click on the first row number or column name and click and drag till all the rows and columns we want are selected. Listed below are some of the formatting options available in Star Office Caic.

B This is the **Bold** icon and is used to display data in bold. To use this icon, highlight the cells and click on the icon.

I This icon is used to display the data in italics.

U This is used to underline the data in highlighted cells.

This is the Change Font icon. This icon displays list of fonts that can be used. Select the font by clicking on it.

This icon is used to change the font size of the data. To do so, select the data and click on this icon.

This is the Font Colour icon. This can be used to change the font colour.

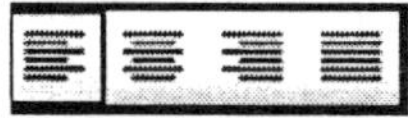

These are the Align Left, Align Centre, Align Right and Justify icons. They are used to align the contents of cells.

This is the Number Format: Currency icon. Clicking on this will display the contents of the selected cells in currency format, that is with a $ in front and with two decimal digits.

This is the Number Format: Percent icon. Clicking on this icon will display the current contents in percentage format. Note that it multiplies the contents of the cell by 100 and displays the result with 2 decimals.

This is the Number Format: Standard icon. Clicking on this icon will display the contents of the selected cells in default format. These are the Number Format: Add Decimal and Number Format: Delete Decimal icons. They are used to increase or decrease the number of decimal digits that are to be displayed in the selected cells.

The Format menu can also be used to format cells. To do so, select the cells we want to format and click on Format_ Cells. The Format Cells dialog box appears as shown in figure.

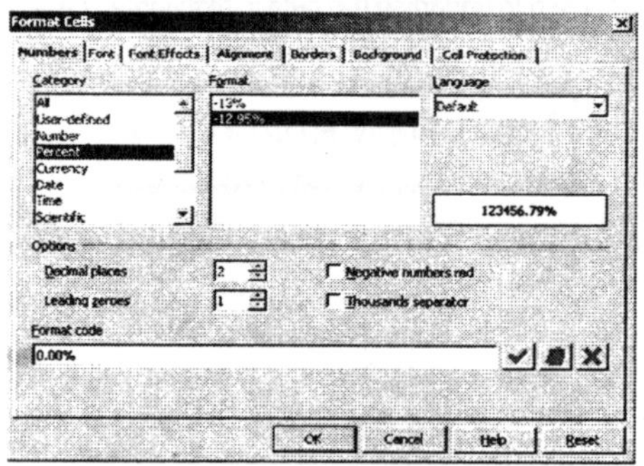

Fig. Format Cells Dialog Box

Tabs at the top of the dialog box can be used to choose the type of cell attribute we want to use. For example, the Numbers tab can be used for changing the format of numbers and the Alignment tab can be used to change the alignment of data in cells. Clicking on a tab will display all the formatting options available along with a preview of how the data will look if that format is used.

AutoFormat Sheet

The AutoFormat Sheet facility of StarOffice Calc helps to format the worksheet with different predefined styles and colours. For example, let us format the market worksheet as detailed below:

- In the Marks worksheet, select the cell from A1 to H7.
- Click on the AutoFormat option on the Format menu.

The AutoFormat dialog box appears, as shown in figure, displaying various predefined format styles. A preview for each style is also displayed in the box.

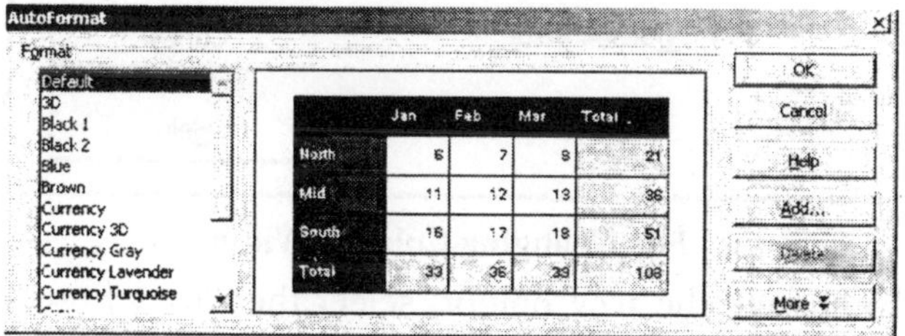

Fig. AutoFormat Dialog Box

- Select the Default format. The formatted worksheet is shown below.

	A	B	C	D	E	F	G	H
1	Student Mark Details of 9th Standard							
2	Reg No	Name	English	Tamil	Maths	Science	Total	Average
3	1000	Kumar A	87	85	74	86	332	83
4	1001	Aravindan J	63	86	62	94	305	76.25
5	1002	Govindan S	63	76	73	75	287	71.75
6	1003	Velmurugan	75	72	63	85	295	73.75
7	1004	Thamizharasi	75	46	52	64	237	59.25
8								
9								

Fig. Auto Formatted Worksheet

Changing Column Width and Row Height

Often while entering data into a worksheet we will realise that the width of the column is not enough. Star Office Calc. allows we to change the width of a column and the height of a row. To change the column width, select the column whose width we want to change.

Click on Format → Column → Width and type the new column width in the dialog box, which appears as shown in figure. Click on OK.

We can also change the column width in another way. Point to the line separating the column whose width we want to change from the next column. The mouse pointer becomes a double -. headed arrow. Click and drag this pointer to the left to decrease the width and to the right to increase the width.

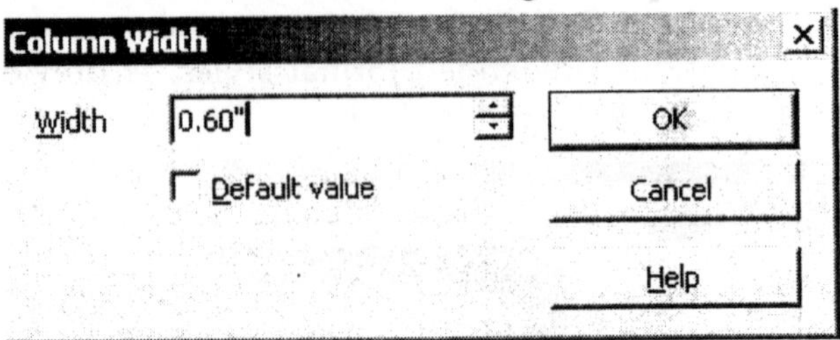

Fig. Changing Column Width

To change the row height, select the row whose height we want to change. Right click on the selected row and select Height from the menu that appears. Type the new height and click on OK.

Fig. Changing Row Height

We can also change the row height of a particular row by clicking and dragging the line separating that row from the next.

Learn by solving

Format the Marks worksheet as follows,

- Format all heading in Bold.
- Change the font, size and colour of the headings.
- Change the format of the average column to display 2 decimal digits.
- Using AutoFormat change the style and colors of the worksheet.
- Change the row width and column width wherever necessary.

Inserting Cells, Rows and Columns

Often after creating a worksheet, we find the need to insert a row or column in the worksheet. For example, we may want to add another subject to the Marks worksheet. Star Office Calc allows we to insert one or more cells, rows and column. To insert an empty cell or an empty row or a column in a worksheet already created, follow the procedure given below:

- Click the Insert Cell from View → Toolbar menu. A floating toolbar with four icons appears. These icons are Insert Cells Down, Insert Cells Right, Insert Rows and Insert Columns icons.

- In order to insert an empty cell in a column and move the existing cells down, place the cursor in the cell where we want to insert the new cell and click on the Insert Cells Down icon. For example, in the Marks worksheet, to insert a cell in D4 and move the contents of the cell D4:D7 down, select D4 and click the icon. The output screen in shown in figure.

	A	B	C	D	E	F	G	H	I
1	Student Mark Details of 9th Standard								
2	Reg No	Name	English	Tamil	Maths'	Science	Total	Average	
3	1000	Kumar A	87	85	74	86	332	83	
4	1001	Aravindan J	63		62	94	305	76.25	
5	1002	Govindan S	63	86	73	75	287	71.75	
6	1003	Velmurugan	75	76	63	85	295	73.75	
7	1004	Thamizharasi	75	72	52	64	237	59.25	
8				46					
9									

Fig. Worksheet with cell inserted

- In order to shift the content of a cell to the right and to create an empty cell, select the cell and click the Insert Cells Right icon. For example, suppose that the data in the fifth row of the Marks worksheet has to be shifted from C5-F5 to D5-G5. To do so, select the cell C5 and click the icon. The output screen is shown in the figure below.

	A	B	C	D	E	F	G	H	I
1	Student Mark Details of 9th Standard								
2	Reg No	Name	English	Tamil	Maths	Science	Total	Average	
3	1000	Kumar A	87	85	74	86	332	83	
4	1001	Aravindan J	63	86	62	94	305	76.25	
5	1002	Govindan S		63	76	73	75	287	71.75
6	1003	Velmurugan	75	72	63	85	295	73.75	
7	1004	Thamizharasi	75	46	52	64	237	59.25	
8									
9									

In order to insert an empty row in a worksheet, select the row where we want to insert the new row and click the Insert Rows icon. For example, if we want to insert a new row between rows 4 and 5 in the Marks worksheet select the row 5 and click the icon. The output screen is shown below.

	A	B	C	D	E	F	G	H	I
1	Student Mark Details of 9th Standard								
2	Reg No	Name	English	Tamil	Maths		Science	Total	Average
3	1000	Kumar A	87	85	74		86	332	83
4	1001	Aravindan J	63	86	62		94	305	76.25
5									
6	1002	Govindan S	63	76	73		75	287	71.75
7	1003	Velmurugan	75	72	63		85	295	73.75
8	1004	Thamizharasi	75	46	52		64	237	59.25
9									

Fig. Worksheet with column inserted

Deleting Cells, Rows and Columns

The procedure for deleting a cell (s), row or a column is the same. Delete Contents specifies the contents to be deleted from a cell or cell range. Before deleting, we must first select the cell or range.

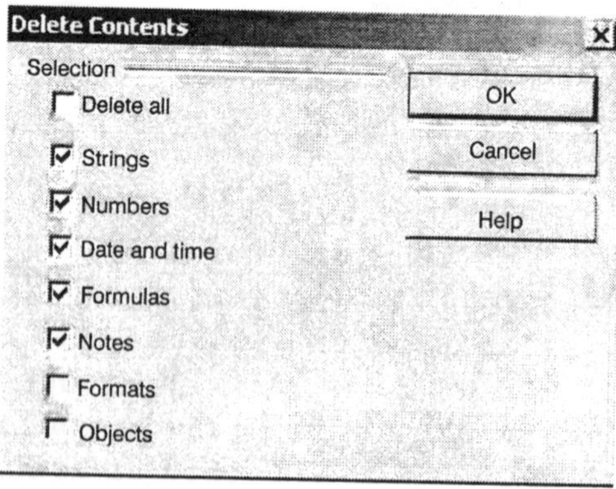

Contents are only deleted from the selected cells or active cell. Similarly, if several sheets are selected, only the active one will be affected. To access this command choose Edit Delete Contents.

Click on the Delete all check box and click OK. To delete all contents from the selected cell range, select Delete Cells from the same menu.

+A window appears as shown below. Select an option to specify how the sheets are displayed after deleting cells. Shift cells up fills the space produced by the deleted cells with the cells underneath it. Shift cells left fills the resulting space by the cells to the right of the deleted cells.

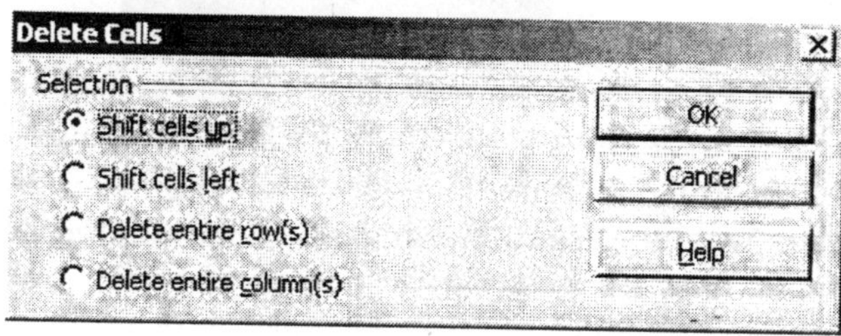

Fig. Deleting cells

If we want to delete an entire row or column, choose Edit Delete Cells. The Delete Cells dialog box will display Delete entire Row(s) or Delete entire Column(s). Clicking Ok will delete the row or column without prompting.

Inserting Pictures and Special characters

In the worksheet, Star Office Calc also provides for inserting pictures and special characters like á, â. For inserting a picture or a special character in a worksheet follow the procedure given below:

- Place the cell pointer in any cell, say B2.
- Choose Insert Picture From File.

The Insert Picture dialog box appears. In the File name combo box, we can type the path of the file that contains the picture or we can directly select the desired file from the gallery directory of Star Office. After selecting the picture file click Open. For example, select Apple file from the gallery directory and click Open. Now we will find a picture of an apple appearing in our worksheet as shown in figure.

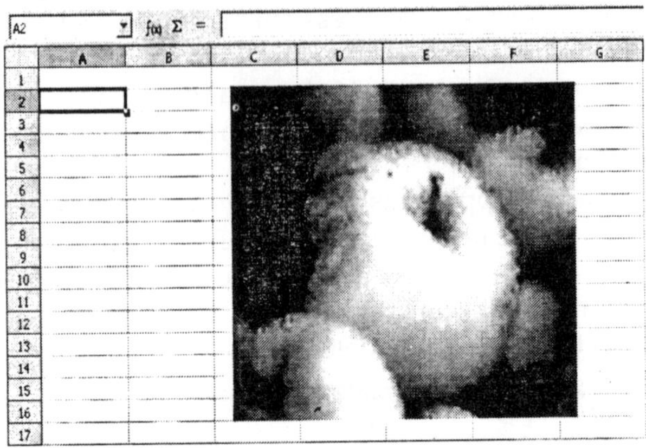

Fig. Worksheet with Apple Picture

For inserting special characters, click the Insert Special characters from the menu bar and select the desired special characters from the Special Character dialog box. For example, select ^{2} from the Special Character dialog box and click the OK button. The resultant output is shown in figure.

Fig. Worksheet with Special Character

Drawing in a Spreadsheet

Star Office Calc provides the facilities for drawing lines, circles, ellipse, square, rectangle, etc. within a worksheet. For this purpose, click the Show Draw Functions icon in the Standard toolbar. The Draw Functions bar appears as shown below:

Fig. Draw Functions Toolbar

We can select any tool from this toolbar according to our requirement, following the procedure given below: Click on a tool. For example, to draw an ellipse in the worksheet, click the Ellipse tool.

Keep the pointer (cursor) in the worksheet area at the desired location and drag it till we get the desired shape and size. The resultant screen is shown in the following figure.

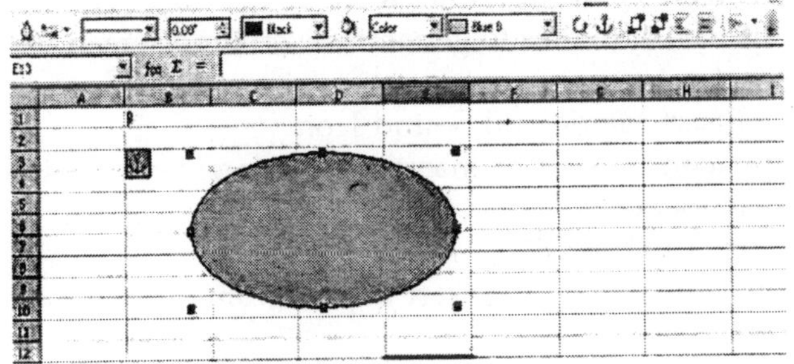

Fig. Worksheet with Ellipse drawn

Inserting Objects

Star Office Calc provides tools for inserting objects like charts, images from image editor, formula, etc. in a worksheet. For this purpose, click on the Insert Object from View Toolbar.

A floating toolbar appears with the following icons in the order listed below:

- Insert Chart Icon
- Insert Formula Icon
- Insert Floating Frame Icon
- Insert Movie and Sound Icon
- Insert OLE Object Icon
- Insert Applet Icon

It is to be noted that some of the icons are used in very advanced applications that are beyond the scope of this book.

- Insert Chart Icon

This icon is used for presenting the data in the worksheet in from of charts of different kinds such as Bar Chart, Pie Chart, Lines, XY plot, etc. More details on charting are given in a later section.

- Insert Formula Icon

This icon is used for inserting a formula in the worksheet for performing calculations.

- Insert Floating Frame Icon

This icon provides to generate a scrolling screen within a worksheet.

- Insert Movie and Sound Icon

This icon is used to insert sound or video files into the current worksheet.

- Insert OLE Object Icon

This icon is used to insert objects from other application into a worksheet.

- Insert Applet Icon

This icon is used to import Applets written in Java programming language into the worksheet.

Working With Charts

One of the most popular features of StarOffice Calc software is the ability to generate charts based on numeric data.

The purpose of chart is to visually present the data for easy understanding. To draw a chart, follow the procedure given below:

- Select the data we want to chart.
- Click on Insert ?Chart or click on the Insert Chart icon as discussed earlier.
- The cursor becomes a + sign with a small picture of the graph. Place this cursor where we want to insert the chart and click.

  The Autoformat Chart window appears as shown in figure.

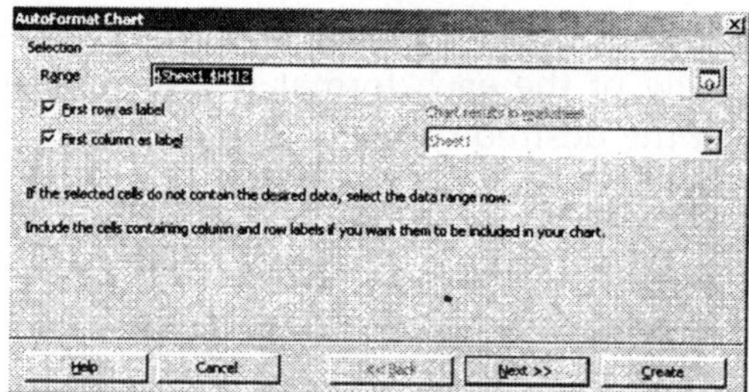

Fig. Auto format Chart Window

- It prompts we to enter the area in the worksheet to be charted. Enter the range as C3: F7 and click Next.

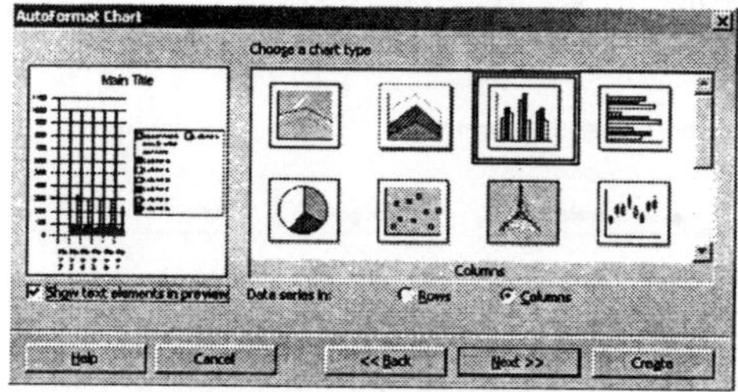

Fig. Types of Chart

- The next window, which appears as shown in figure displays the different types of charts that can be created along with a preview of each. Select the type of chart in which we want to present the data. The preview. Window shows the chart. Click on Next.

Note: Click the Show text elements in preview check box if it is not selected.

- For each type of the chart (say Pie, Bar, Column, etc.), there are different formats available.

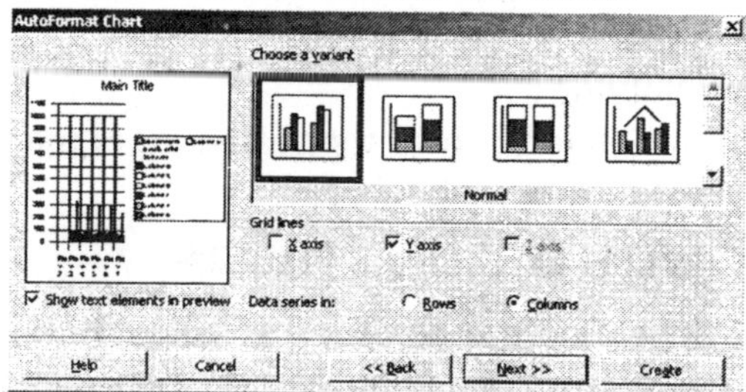

Fig. The Different Format of a Chart Type

These formats are displayed in the next window. a preview of the each format is also displayed. Here, select the desired format. Click on Next.

- In the next window, we have provisions to give a Title for the chart, Titles for X and Y axes and legends.

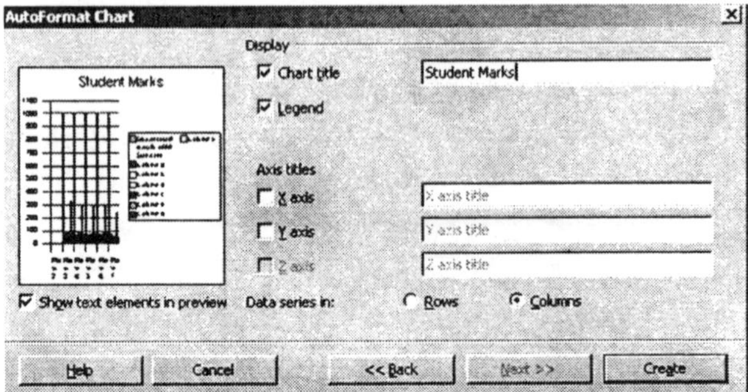

- Click on Create. Now, our worksheet will look as shown below.

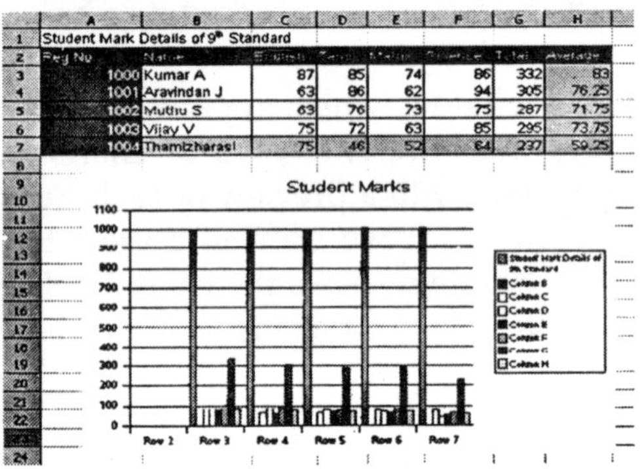

Fig. The Worksheet with the chart

Learn by Solving

Create a line chart to show the variations of mark secured by each student in different subjects.

WORKING WITH MULTIPLE SHEETS

In Star Office Calc, a spreadsheet contains multiple sheets. Each sheet has its own name and a list of sheets appears as tabs at the bottom of the window. To select a different sheet, click the tab with the sheet's name. The tab of the selected sheet appears in white.

Each sheet of a spreadsheet can be used entirely independently of the other sheets. We can also make them dependent on each other by referring to the data in another sheet or using the data from another sheet in calculations.

For example, we can enter data in Sheet 1 and Sheet 2 and can do the calculations in Sheet 2. We can calculate the sum of the numbers in the cell A1 of Sheet 1 and A1 of Sheet 2 and store the result in A3 of Sheet 2. To do this, type the 3-D formula as = SUM (Sheet 1.A1; Sheet 2.A1)

Here is another example. Let the cells B4 and C4 in Sheet 1 have numbers 87 and 54 respectively. Let the cells B4 and C4 in Sheet 2 have numbers 45 and 34 respectively.

	A	B	C	D
1				
2		87	54	
3				
4				
5				
6				
7				
8				

Fig. Worksheet with Values in Sheet 1

Now, let us add cell values B4 and C4 in the two sheets and store the total in cell D5 of Sheet 2. For this purpose, enter the 3D formula = SUM (Sheet 1. B4: C4; Sheet 2. B4:C4). In this formula, the: (colon) separating the cells of the same sheet adds up the values of B4 and C4 in that sheet and the; (Semi - colon) adds up the sums of B4 and C4 of Sheets 1 and 2.

D5 f(x) Σ = =SUM(Sheet1.B4:C4;Sheet2.B4:C4)

	A	B	C	D	E
1					
2					
3					
4		45	34		
5				220	
6					
7					

Fig. Worksheet with Values and Results in Sheet 2

Printing Worksheets

If we click the Print icon on the function bar (Standard toolbar), all the data in all the sheets of our document will be printed. We can also print a part of the worksheet. To do so, select the range to be printed and click on Format → Print Ranges → Edit and select the print range.

Now, if we click on the Print icon, only the selected range will be printed.

To remove the print range setting click on Format → Print Ranges → Delete.

The Print option under the File menu can be used to print the worksheet. The Print dialog box appears as shown in figure.

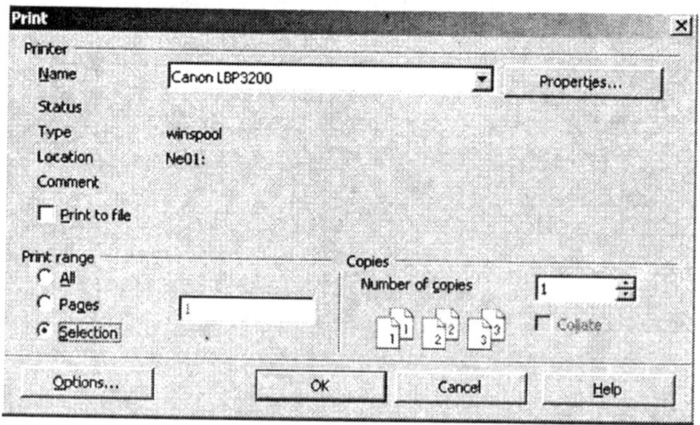

Fig. Print Dialog Box

In the Print dialog box, under Print range choose the option All to print all the sheets in the document. Select the option Pages to specify the pages, which are to be printed. The Selection option allows we to print only the selected area in a worksheet.

The Page View option on the File menu can be used to preview a worksheet before printing.

The above procedure will print the worksheet without grids. In order to print with the grids select the Page option from the Format menu. Click on the Sheet tab in the dialog box, which appears. Click the Grid check box to print the worksheet with gridlines.

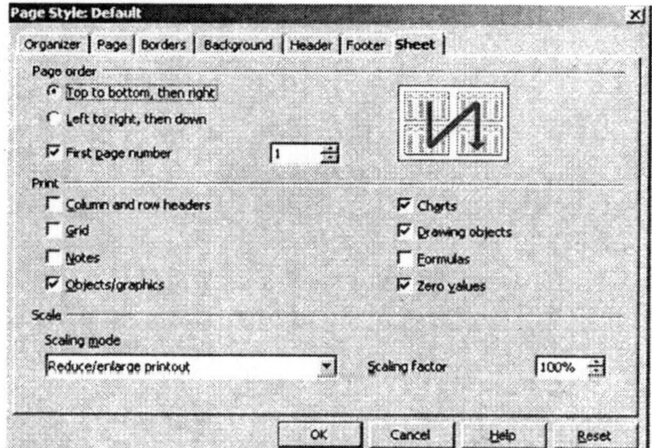

Fig. Page Styles Dialog Box

Database Functions in Star Office Calc

Spreadsheets in Star Office can be used to manage large amounts of data. We can sort this data, search for specific information, group information based on some criteria, calculate totals, and much more.

Chapter 10

Computer Virus

A computer virus is a computer programme that can copy itself and infect a computer without permission or knowledge of the user. The term "virus" is also commonly used, albeit erroneously, to refer to many different types of malware (a portmanteau of the words malicious and software) and adware (a portmanteau of the words advertisement and software) programs.

The original virus may modify the copies, or the copies may modify themselves, as occurs in a metamorphic virus. A virus can only spread from one computer to another when its host is taken to the uninfected computer, for instance by a user sending it over a network or the Internet, or by carrying it on a removable medium such as a floppy disk, CD, or USB drive. Meanwhile viruses can spread to other computers by infecting files on a network file system or a file system that is accessed by another computer.

Viruses are sometimes confused with computer worms and Trojan horses. A worm can spread itself to other computers without needing to be transferred as part of a host, and a Trojan horse is a file that appears harmless. Worms and Trojans may cause harm to either a computer system's hosted data, functional performance, or networking throughput, when executed. In general, a worm does not actually harm either the system's hardware or software, while at least in theory, a Trojan's payload may be capable of almost any type of harm if executed.

Some can't be seen when the programme is not running, but as soon as the infected code is run, the Trojan horse kicks in. That is why it is so hard for people to find viruses and other malware themselves and why they have to use spyware programs and registry processors.

Most personal computers are now connected to the Internet and to local area networks, facilitating the spread of malicious code. Today's viruses may also take advantage of network services such as the World Wide Web, e-mail, Instant Messaging and file sharing systems to spread, blurring the line between viruses and worms.

Furthermore, some sources use an alternative terminology in which a virus is any form of self-replicating malware.Some malware is programmed to damage the computer by damaging programs, deleting files, or reformatting the hard disk. Other malware programs are not designed to do any damage, but simply replicate themselves and perhaps make their presence known by presenting text, video, or audio messages.

Even these less sinister malware programs can create problems for the computer user. They typically take up computer memory used by legitimate programs. As a result, they often cause erratic behaviour and can result in system crashes. In addition, much malware is bug-ridden, and these bugs may lead to system crashes and data loss. Many CiD programs are programs that have been downloaded by the user and pop up every so often. This results in slowing down of the computer, but it is also very difficult to find and stop the problem.

COMPUTER VIRUS HISTORY

The first PC virus in the wild was a boot sector virus called (c)Brain, created in 1986 by the Farooq Alvi Brothers, operating out of Lahore, Pakistan. The brothers reportedly created the virus to deter pirated copies of software they had written. However, analysts have claimed that the Ashar virus, a variant of Brain, possibly predated it based on code within the virus.

Before computer networks became widespread, most viruses spread on removable media, particularly floppy disks. In the early days of the personal computer, many users regularly exchanged information and programs on floppies. Some viruses spread by infecting programs stored on these disks, while others installed themselves into the disk boot sector, ensuring that they would be run when the user booted the computer from the disk.

Traditional computer viruses emerged in the 1980s, driven by the spread of personal computers and the resultant increase in BBS and modem use, and software sharing. Bulletin board driven software sharing contributed directly to the spread of Trojan horse programs, and viruses were written to infect popularly traded software. Shareware and bootleg software were equally common vectors for viruses on BBS's. Within the "pirate scene" of hobbyists trading illicit copies of retail software, traders in a hurry to obtain the latest applications and games were easy targets for viruses.

Since the mid-1990s, macro viruses have become common. Most of these viruses are written in the scripting languages for Microsoft programs such as Word and Excel. These viruses spread in Microsoft Office by infecting documents and spreadsheets. Since Word and Excel were also available for Mac OS, most of these viruses were able to spread on Macintosh computers as well. Most of these viruses did not have the ability to send infected e-mail. Those viruses which did spread through e-mail took advantage of the Microsoft Outlook COM interface.

Macro viruses pose unique problems for detection software. For example, some versions of Microsoft Word allowed macros to replicate themselves with additional blank lines. The virus behaved identically but would be misidentified as a new virus. In another example, if two macro viruses simultaneously infect a document, the combination of the two, if also self-replicating, can appear as a "mating" of the two and would likely be detected as a virus unique from the "parents".

A virus may also send a web address link as an instant message to all the contacts on an infected machine. If the recipient, thinking the link is from a friend (a trusted source) follows the link to the website, the virus hosted at the site may be able to infect this new computer and continue propagating.

The newest species of the virus family is the cross-site scripting virus. The virus emerged from research and was academically demonstrated in 2005. This virus utilizes cross-site scripting vulnerabilities to propagate. Since 2005 there have been multiple instances of the cross-site scripting viruses in the wild, most notable sites affected have been MySpace and Yahoo.

INFECTION STRATEGIES

In order to replicate itself, a virus must be permitted to execute code and write to memory. For this reason, many viruses attach themselves to executable files that may be part of legitimate programs. If a user tries to start an infected programme, the virus' code may be executed first. Viruses can be divided into two types, on the basis of their behaviour when they are executed.

Nonresident viruses immediately search for other hosts that can be infected, infect these targets, and finally transfer control to the application programme they infected. Resident viruses do not search for hosts when they are started. Instead, a resident virus loads itself into memory on execution and transfers control to the host programme. The virus stays active in the background and infects new hosts when those files are accessed by other programs or the operating system itself.

Nonresident Viruses

Nonresident viruses can be thought of as consisting of a finder module and a replication module. The finder module is responsible for finding new files to infect. For each new executable file the finder module encounters, it calls the replication module to infect that file.

Resident Viruses

Resident viruses contain a replication module that is similar to the one that is employed by nonresident viruses. However, this module is not called by a finder module. Instead, the virus loads the replication module into memory when it is executed and ensures that this module is executed each time the operating system is called to perform a certain operation.

For example, the replication module can be called each time the operating system executes a file. In this case, the virus infects every suitable programme that is executed on the computer.

Resident viruses are sometimes subdivided into a category of fast infectors and a category of slow infectors. Fast infectors are designed to infect as many files as possible. For instance, a fast infector can infect every potential host file that is accessed.

This poses a special problem to anti-virus software, since a virus scanner will access every potential host file on a computer when it performs a system-wide scan. If the virus scanner fails to notice that such a virus is present in memory, the virus can "piggy-back" on the virus scanner and in this way infect all files that are scanned. Fast infectors rely on their fast infection rate to spread.

The disadvantage of this method is that infecting many files may make detection more likely, because the virus may slow down a computer or perform many suspicious actions that can be noticed by anti-virus software. Slow infectors, on the other hand, are designed to infect hosts infrequently. For instance, some slow infectors only infect files when they are copied.

Slow infectors are designed to avoid detection by limiting their actions: they are less likely to slow down a computer noticeably, and will at most infrequently trigger anti-virus software that detects suspicious behaviour by programs. The slow infector approach does not seem very successful, however.

Vectors and Hosts

Viruses have targeted various types of transmission media or hosts. This list is not exhaustive:

- Binary executable files (such as COM files and EXE files in MS-DOS, Portable Executable files in Microsoft Windows, and ELF files in Linux)

- Volume Boot Records of floppy disks and hard disk partitions
- The master boot record (MBR) of a hard disk
- General-purpose script files (such as batch files in MS-DOS and Microsoft Windows, VBScript files, and shell script files on Unix-like platforms).
- Application-specific script files (such as Telix-scripts)
- Documents that can contain macros (such as Microsoft Word documents, Microsoft Excel spreadsheets, AmiPro documents, and Microsoft Access database files)
- Cross-site scripting vulnerabilities in web applications
- Arbitrary computer files. An exploitable buffer overflow, format string, race condition or other exploitable bug in a programme which reads the file could be used to trigger the execution of code hidden within it. Most bugs of this type can be made more difficult to exploit in computer architectures with protection features such as an execute disable bit and/ or address space layout randomization.

PDFs, like HTML, may link to malicious code.

It is worth noting that some virus authors have written an.EXE extension on the end of.PNG (for example), hoping that users would stop at the trusted file type without noticing that the computer would start with the final type of file. (Many operating systems hide the extensions of known file types by default, so for example a filename ending in ".png.exe" would be shown ending in ".png".).

Methods to Avoid Detection

In order to avoid detection by users, some viruses employ different kinds of deception. Some old viruses, especially on the MS-DOS platform, make sure that the "last modified" date of a host file stays the same when the file is infected by the virus. This approach does not fool anti-virus software, however, especially that which maintains and dates Cyclic redundancy check on file changes. Some viruses can infect files without increasing their sizes or damaging the files. They accomplish this by overwriting unused areas of executable files. These are called cavity viruses.

For example the CIH virus, or Chernobyl Virus, infects Portable Executable files. Because those files had many empty gaps, the virus, which was 1 KB in length, did not add to the size of the file. Some viruses try to avoid detection by killing the tasks associated with antivirus software before it can detect them. As computers and operating systems grow larger and more complex, old hiding techniques need to be updated or replaced. Defending a computer against viruses may demand that a file system migrate towards detailed and explicit permission for every kind of file access.

Avoiding bait Files and other Undesirable Hosts

A virus needs to infect hosts in order to spread further. In some cases, it might be a bad idea to infect a host programme. For example, many anti-virus programs perform an integrity check of their own code. Infecting such programs will therefore increase the likelihood that the virus is detected.

For this reason, some viruses are programmed not to infect programs that are known to be part of anti-virus software. Another type of host that viruses sometimes avoid is bait files. Bait files (or goat files) are files that are specially created by anti-virus software, or by anti-virus professionals themselves, to be infected by a virus. These files can be created for various reasons, all of which are related to the detection of the virus:

- Anti-virus professionals can use bait files to take a sample of a virus (i.e. a copy of a programme file that is infected by the virus). It is more practical to store and exchange a small, infected bait file, than to exchange a large application programme that has been infected by the virus.
- Anti-virus professionals can use bait files to study the behaviour of a virus and evaluate detection methods. This is especially useful when the virus is polymorphic. In this case, the virus can be made to infect a large number of bait files. The infected files

can be used to test whether a virus scanner detects all versions of the virus.

- Some anti-virus software employs bait files that are accessed regularly. When these files are modified, the anti-virus software warns the user that a virus is probably active on the system.

Since bait files are used to detect the virus, or to make detection possible, a virus can benefit from not infecting them. Viruses typically do this by avoiding suspicious programs, such as small programme files or programs that contain certain patterns of 'garbage instructions'.

A related strategy to make baiting difficult is sparse infection. Sometimes, sparse infectors do not infect a host file that would be a suitable candidate for infection in other circumstances. For example, a virus can decide on a random basis whether to infect a file or not, or a virus can only infect host files on particular days of the week.

Stealth

Some viruses try to trick anti-virus software by intercepting its requests to the operating system. A virus can hide itself by intercepting the anti-virus software's request to read the file and passing the request to the virus, instead of the OS.

The virus can then return an uninfected version of the file to the anti-virus software, so that it seems that the file is "clean". Modern anti-virus software employs various techniques to counter stealth mechanisms of viruses. The only completely reliable method to avoid stealth is to boot from a medium that is known to be clean.

Self-modification

Most modern antivirus programs try to find virus-patterns inside ordinary programs by scanning them for so-called virus signatures. A signature is a characteristic byte-pattern that is part of a certain virus or family of viruses. If a virus scanner finds such a pattern in a file, it notifies the user that the file is infected.

The user can then delete, or (in some cases) "clean" or "heal" the infected file. Some viruses employ techniques that make detection by means of signatures difficult but probably not impossible. These viruses modify their code on each infection. That is, each infected file contains a different variant of the virus.

Encryption with a Variable key

A more advanced method is the use of simple encryption to encipher the virus. In this case, the virus consists of a small decrypting module and an encrypted copy of the virus code. If the virus is encrypted with a different key for each infected file, the only part of the virus that remains constant is the decrypting module, which would (for example) be appended to the end. In this case, a virus scanner cannot directly detect the virus using signatures, but it can still detect the decrypting module, which still makes indirect detection of the virus possible.

Since these would be symmetric keys, stored on the infected host, it is in fact entirely possible to decrypt the final virus, but that probably isn't required, since self-modifying code is such a rarity that it may be reason for virus scanners to at least flag the file as suspicious.

An old, but compact, encryption involves XORing each byte in a virus with a constant, so that the exclusive-or operation had only to be repeated for decryption. It is suspicious code that modifies itself, so the code to do the encryption/decryption may be part of the signature in many virus definitions.

Polymorphic Code

Polymorphic code was the first technique that posed a serious threat to virus scanners. Just like regular encrypted viruses, a polymorphic virus infects files with an encrypted copy of itself, which is decoded by a decryption module.

In the case of polymorphic viruses however, this decryption module is also modified on each infection. A well-written polymorphic virus therefore has no parts which remain identical between infections, making it very difficult to detect directly using signatures.

Anti-virus software can detect it by decrypting the viruses using an emulator, or by statistical pattern analysis of the encrypted virus body. To enable polymorphic code, the virus has to have a polymorphic engine (also called mutating engine or mutation engine) somewhere in its encrypted body. See Polymorphic code for technical detail on how such engines operate.

Some viruses employ polymorphic code in a way that constrains the mutation rate of the virus significantly. For example, a virus can be programmed to mutate only slightly over time, or it can be programmed to refrain from mutating when it infects a file on a computer that already contains copies of the virus.

The advantage of using such slow polymorphic code is that it makes it more difficult for anti-virus professionals to obtain representative samples of the virus, because bait files that are infected in one run will typically contain identical or similar samples of the virus. This will make it more likely that the detection by the virus scanner will be unreliable, and that some instances of the virus may be able to avoid detection.

Metamorphic Code

To avoid being detected by emulation, some viruses rewrite themselves completely each time they are to infect new executables. Viruses that use this technique are said to be metamorphic. To enable metamorphism, a metamorphic engine is needed. A metamorphic virus is usually very large and complex. For example, W32/Simile consisted of over 14000 lines of Assembly language code, 90 per cent of which is part of the metamorphic engine.

VULNERABILITY AND COUNTERMEASURES

The Vulnerability of Operating Systems to Viruses

Just as genetic diversity in a population decreases the chance of a single disease wiping out a population, the diversity of software systems on a network similarly limits the destructive potential of viruses. This became a particular concern in the 1990s, when Microsoft gained market dominance in desktop operating systems and office suites. The users of Microsoft software (especially networking software such as Microsoft Outlook and Internet Explorer) are especially vulnerable to the spread of viruses.

Microsoft software is targeted by virus writers due to their desktop dominance, and is often criticized for including many errors and holes for virus writers to exploit. Integrated and non-integrated Microsoft appications (such as Microsoft Office) and applications with scripting languages with access to the file system (for example Visual Basic Script (VBS), and applications with networking features) are also particularly vulnerable.

Although Windows is by far the most popular operating system for virus writers, some viruses also exist on other platforms. Any operating system that allows third-party programs to run can theoretically run viruses. Some operating systems are less secure than others. Unix-based OS's (and NTFS-aware applications on Windows NT based platforms) only allow their users to run executables within their protected space in their own directories.

An Internet based research revealed that there were cases when people willingly pressed a particular button to download a virus. A security firm F-Secure ran a half year advertising campaign on Google AdWords which said "Is your PC virus-free? Get it infected here!". The result was 409 clicks.

As of 2006, there are relatively few security exploits targeting Mac OS X (with a Unix-based file system and kernel). The number of viruses for the older Apple operating systems, known as Mac OS Classic, varies greatly from source to source, with Apple stating that there are only four known viruses, and independent sources stating there are as many as 63 viruses.

It is safe to say that Macs are less likely to be targeted because of low market share and thus a Mac-specific virus could only infect a small proportion of computers (making the effort less desirable). Virus vulnerability between Macs and

Windows is a chief selling point, one that Apple uses in their Get a Mac advertising. That said, Macs have also had security issues just as Microsoft Windows has, though none have ever been fully taken advantage of successfully in the wild.

Windows and Unix have similar scripting abilities, but while Unix natively blocks normal users from having access to make changes to the operating system environment, older copies of Windows such as Windows 95 and 98 do not. In 1997, when a virus for Linux was released - known as "Bliss" - leading antivirus vendors issued warnings that Unix-like systems could fall prey to viruses just like Windows. The Bliss virus may be considered characteristic of viruses - as opposed to worms-on Unix systems.

Bliss requires that the user run it explicitly (so it is a trojan), and it can only infect programs that the user has the access to modify. Unlike Windows users, most Unix users do not log in as an administrator user except to install or configure software; as a result, even if a user ran the virus, it could not harm their operating system. The Bliss virus never became widespread, and remains chiefly a research curiosity. Its creator later posted the source code to Usenet, allowing researchers to see how it worked.

The Role of Software Development

Because software is often designed with security features to prevent unauthorized use of system resources, many viruses must exploit software bugs in a system or application to spread. Software development strategies that produce large numbers of bugs will generally also produce potential exploits.

Anti-virus Software and other Preventive Measures

Many users install anti-virus software that can detect and eliminate known viruses after the computer downloads or runs the executable. There are two common methods that an anti-virus software application uses to detect viruses. The first, and by far the most common method of virus detection is using a list of virus signature definitions. This works by examining the content of the computer's memory (its RAM, and boot sectors) and the files stored on fixed or removable drives (hard drives, floppy drives), and comparing those files against a database of known virus "signatures".

The disadvantage of this detection method is that users are only protected from viruses that pre-date their last virus definition update.

The second method is to use a heuristic algorithm to find viruses based on common behaviors. This method has the ability to detect viruses that anti-virus security firms have yet to create a signature for.

Some anti-virus programs are able to scan opened files in addition to sent and received e-mails 'on the fly' in a similar manner. This practice is known as "on-access scanning." Anti-virus software does not change the underlying capability of host software to transmit viruses. Users must update their software regularly to patch security holes. Anti-virus software also needs to be regularly updated in order to prevent the latest threats.

One may also minimise the damage done by viruses by making regular backups of data (and the Operating Systems) on different media, that are either kept unconnected to the system (most of the time), read-only or not accessible for other reasons, such as using different file systems. This way, if data is lost through a virus, one can start again using the backup (which should preferably be recent).

If a backup session on optical media like CD and DVD is closed, it becomes read-only and can no longer be affected by a virus. Likewise, an Operating System on a bootable can be used to start the computer if the installed Operating Systems become unusable. Another method is to use different Operating Systems on different file systems.

A virus is not likely to affect both. Data backups can also be put on different file systems. For example, Linux requires specific software to write to NTFS partitions, so if one does not install such software and uses a separate installation of MS Windows to make the backups on an NTFS partition, the backup should remain safe from any Linux viruses.

Likewise, MS Windows can not read file systems like ext3,

so if one normally uses MS Windows, the backups can be made on an ext3 partition using a Linux installation.

Recovery Methods

Once a computer has been compromised by a virus, it is usually unsafe to continue using the same computer without completely reinstalling the operating system.

However, there are a number of recovery options that exist after a computer has a virus. These actions depend on severity of the type of Virus.

Virus Removal

One possibility on Windows Me, Windows XP and Windows Vista is a tool known as System Restore, which restores the registry and critical system files to a previous checkpoint. Often a virus will cause a system to hang, and a subsequent hard reboot will render a system restore point from the same day corrupt.

Restore points from previous days should work provided the virus is not designed to corrupt the restore files. Some viruses, however, disable system restore and other important tools such as Task Manager and Command Prompt. An example of a virus that does this is Cia Door.

Administrators have the option to disable such tools from limited users for various reasons. The virus modifies the registry to do the same, except, when the Administrator is controlling the computer, it blocks all users from accessing the tools. When an infected tool activates it gives the message "Task Manager has been disabled by our administrator.", even if the user trying to open the programme is the administrator. Users running a Microsoft operating system can go to Microsoft's website to run a free scan, if they have their 20-digit registration number.

Operating System Reinstallation

Reinstalling the operating system is another approach to virus removal. It involves simply reformatting the OS partition and installing the OS from its original media, or imaging the partition with a clean backup image (taken with Ghost or Acronis for example).

This method has the benefits of being simple to do, can be faster than running multiple anti-virus scans, and is guaranteed to remove any malware. Downsides include having to reinstall all other software as well as the operating system. User data can be backed up by booting off of a Live CD or putting the hard drive into another computer and booting from the other computer's operating system.

THE COMPUTER TROJAN HORSE

A computer trojan horse is a programme which appears to be something good, but actually conceals something bad. One way to spread a trojan horse is to hide it inside a distribution of normal software. In 2002, the send mail and Open SSH packages were both used to hide trojan horses. This was done by an attacker who broke into the distribution sites for these software packages and replaced the original distributions with his own packages. A more common method of spreading a trojan horse is to send it via e-mail.

The attacker will send the victim an e-mail with an attachment called something like "prettygirls.exe." When the victim opens the attachment to see the pretty girls, the trojan horse will infect his system. A similar technique for spreading trojan horses is to send files to unsuspecting users over chat systems like IRC, AIM, ICQ, MSN, or Yahoo Messenger.

The Trojan Horses Virus

Unlike viruses, trojan horses do not normally spread themselves. Trojan horses must be spread by other mechanisms. A trojan horse virus is a virus which spreads by fooling an unsuspecting user into executing it.An example of a trojan horse virus would be a virus which required a user to open an e-mail attachment in Microsoft Outlook to activate.

Once activated, the trojan horse virus would send copies of itself to people in the Microsoft Outlook address book.The trojan horse virus infects like a trojan horse, but spreads like a virus.

Effects of a Trojan Horse

The victim running the trojan horse will usually give the attacker some degree of control over the victim's machine. This control may allow the attacker to remotely access the victim's machine, or to run commands with all of the victim's privileges.

The trojan horse could make the victim's machine part of a Distributed Denial of Service (DDoS) network, where the victims machine is used to attack other victims. Alternatively, the trojan horse could just send data to the attacker. Data commonly targeted by trojan horses includes usernames and passwords, but a sophisticated trojan horse could also be programmed to look for items such as credit card numbers.

Protecting Against a Trojan Horse

Anti-virus programs detect known trojan horses. However, trojan horse programs are easier to create than viruses and many are created in small volumes. These trojan horse programs will not be detected by anti-virus software.The best defence against a trojan horse is to never run a programme that is sent to us. E-mail and chat systems are not safe methods of software distribution.

VIRUSE A SYSTEM ENEMY

A virus is a piece of programming code inserted into other programming to cause some unexpected and, for the victim, usually undesirable event. Viruses can be transmitted by down loading code from other sites, from email or internet, or by using an infected diskette. The source of the file we are downloading, or of a diskette we have received, is often unaware of the virus. This virus lies dormant until circumstances cause its code to be excused by the computer. Since, viruses are playful in intent and effect ("Happy Birthday, Ludwig") and some one can be quite harmful, erasing data or causing our hard disk to require reformatting.

There are two types' main categories of viruses:

- Micro Viruses
- Macro Viruses

MICRO VIRUSES

The File Inflectors and system boot infectors are belongs to categories of micro virus

File Infector Viruses

File infector viruses attach themselves to executable programs (i.e..COM,.EXE,.SYS, OVL, PRG), such as word processors, spreadsheet applications and computer games. When they have infected a programme, they propagate to infect other programs on the system and on other systems that use a shared infected programme.

The virus may also reside in the system's memory, so that each time a new programme is executed, the virus infects the programme.

Another method of file infector execution involves the virus modifying the manner in which the computer opens a file, rather than modifying the actual programme running the file. In this scenario, the virus executes first, and then the programme is run. Jerusalem and Cascade are two of the best-known file infector viruses.

Boot Sector Viruses

A boot sector virus infects the master boot record (MBR) of a hard drive or the boot sector of removable media, such as floppy diskettes. The boot sector is an area at the beginning of a drive or disk where information about its structure is stored. Boot sectors contain boot programs that are run at host startup to boot the operating system.

The MBR of a hard drive is a unique location on the disk where a computer's basic input/output system (BIOS) can locate and load the boot programme.

Removable media such as floppy disks need not be bootable to infect the system; if an infected disk is in the drive when the computer boots, the virus could be executed. Boot sector viruses are easily concealed, have a high rate of success, and can harm a computer to the point of complete inoperability. Symptoms of a boot sector virus infection include a computer that displays an error message during booting or cannot boot. Form, Michelangelo, and Stoned are examples of boot sector viruses.

Macro Viruses

Macro viruses are the most prevalent and successful type of virus. Macro viruses attach themselves to documents such as word processing files and spreadsheets. As the name implies, a macro virus uses an application's macro programming language to execute and propagate. Many popular software packages, such as Microsoft Office, use macro programming languages in their products to automate complex or repetitive tasks.

Attackers have taken advantage of macro programming capabilities to distribute malicious code. Macro viruses tend to spread quickly because users frequently share documents from applications with macro capabilities. Furthermore, when a macro virus infection occurs, the virus also infects the template that the programme uses to create and open files. Consequently, every document that is created or opened with the infected template is also infected. The Concept, Marker, and Melissa viruses are well-known examples of macro viruses.

Virus Hoaxes

As the name implies, virus hoaxes are false virus warnings. The phony viruses are usually described as being of devastating magnitude and requiring immediate action to adequately protect computer resources from infection. Despite the illegitimacy of their messages, virus hoaxes are just as prevalent in the digital world as actual viruses. Virus hoaxes are circulated by innocent end users who believe they are helping by distributing these warnings to the Internet community.

The hoaxes usually cause little damage, although some malicious virus hoaxes direct users to alter operating systems settings or delete files, which may cause security or operational problems. Virus hoaxes can be time consuming, as many of the hoax recipients may contact technical support

permit a review of data during processing. These holes also permit insertion of unauthorized logic. Trap doors exist because sometimes programmers insert code that allows them to bypass an operating system's integrity for the purpose of debugging programs during development of an application system and later during maintenance and system improvements.

Trapdoors typically are eliminated in the final editing of code, but sometimes they are forgotten or intentionally left for future access into the system.

Additionally, logic design flaws and programming errors in complex programs also may introduce trap doors into a system, such as incomplete parameter checking resulting in a system fault occurring when all parameters have not been checked fully for accuracy and consistency by the operating system.

IMPACT AND PROBLEM ANALYSIS

It is difficult to access impact of the viruses attacks described above, but in generic terms the following types of impact could occur:

Generic Problem

- Loss of income.
- Increase cost of recovery (correcting of information and reestablishing services)
- Increase cost of retrospectively securing systems
- Loss of information (critical data, proprietary information, contracts)
- Loss of Trade secrets
- Damage of reputation
- Legal and regulatory noncompliance
- Failure to meet contractual commitments
- Legal action by customers for loss of confidential data

Technical Problem

- Hungering of CPU time (System throughput became slowdown)

- Slowdown of Network throughput.
- Loss of Communication component.

File Infector Viruses

- File infector viruses attach themselves to executable programs (i.e..COM,.EXE,.SYS, OVL, PRG), such as word processors, spreadsheet applications and computer games.

There should be a detective & preventive action plan can be done through the Computer emergency response team (CERT). Various types of Antivirus Software (Mac fee, Norton) available in the modern sophisticated market, which would be implemented as per high level policy of the top management. Periodically should be scanned the hard disk & net work drive automatically.

Periodically updated the latest patches to keep clean & safe mode of the system perfectly.

To minimize the risk, preventive and detective action are the most well advanced action plan for the long term business activities of the every organization. Therefore, contingency plan is the most effective & efficient plan for safe guard of the organizational assets. The Anti-virus solution is the most preventive, detective and corrective control to safe guard of the valuable assets company.

Index